ALL IN DUE TIME

ALL IN DUE TIME

The Collected Essays and Broadcast Talks of

HUMPHRY HOUSE

Essay Index Reprint Series

BOOKS FOR LIBRARIES PRESS
FREEPORT, NEW YORK

First published 1955 by Rupert Hart-Davis.

Reprinted 1972 by arrangement with
Hart-Davis Mac Gibbon Limited.

Library of Congress Cataloging in Publication Data

House, Humphry, 1908-1955.
    All in due time.

    (Essay index reprint series)
    Reprint of the 1955 ed.
    1. English literature--19th century--Addresses,
essays, lectures. I. Title.
[PR453.H6 1972]   824'.9'12   72-8514
ISBN 0-8369-7318-6

TO
MADELINE
who became my wife just before
the first of these papers was published

CONTENTS

CONTENTS

PREFACE

Most of this book was collected and prepared for press by Humphry House early in 1949. The title, part-titles and arrangement were all of his choosing, and he added the following Preface:

This book is a collection of papers selected from miscellaneous work of the past fifteen years. During much of that time I have been teaching in one university or another; but these papers are not in any sense academic. Most of them were commercial in origin; and a number were written to make money in the intervals between one spell of teaching and the next. Yet among the many friends who have helped with their talk and criticisms my pupils have formed by far the largest group, and so I wish to thank them, both for what they have said and also for listening to some of these ideas in other forms.

Many of the papers are reprinted book-reviews or articles. I have to thank the editors of the *New Statesman & Nation*, *The Times Literary Supplement* and the *News Chronicle* for permission to use again what originally appeared in those periodicals.

Many more of the papers were originally given as broadcast talks; some of these were drafted first in a longer form (which is represented here) and then compressed for broadcasting; others have been expanded since; in most cases slight revisions have been made. Permission to use these talks again is not technically needed under the terms of the contracts: but thanks are most certainly due to the B.B.C. staff—especially to Miss Anna Kallin and Mr Basil Taylor for their extraordinarily patient analgesic methods as producers. The talk called *Man and Nature* was in fact almost a full collaboration with Mr Taylor.* Some of the talks have already

* [To these acknowledgments House would certainly have added the name of Mr P. H. Newby, who was associated with him in most of the later talks.]

appeared in the *Listener* and three have also been published in the Sylvan Press volume, *Ideas and Beliefs of the Victorians* (1949).

Many of the papers contain opinions that I should express differently now. The three papers on Hopkins are reprinted without alteration, though the earliest of them was published fifteen years ago. There is some apparent discrepancy in I and II, between the two discussions of Hopkins's influence on the poetry of this century. I have deliberately not revised the original words to smooth the differences over; but I should now explain the matter by saying that his influence was valuable in pointing the way to a far wider range of vocabulary and rhythm and helping to restore intelligence and energy to verse, but that it was on the whole deplorable in so far as it led to imitation of his highly individual idiom and habits of thought. Even though it is true that Hopkins seemed in my youth to be a contemporary and we enjoyed him in that spirit, he now appears an even more remarkable and in some ways more intelligible poet seen in his nineteenth-century context. I hope to make this clearer in another publication.

April 1949   HUMPHRY HOUSE

At the last moment the book was delayed so as to include a new essay, other work supervened, the book's title became steadily more apt, and eventually House decided to withhold the volume until such time as he had written enough new talks and essays to replace some of the less worthy papers in the original collection.

House died suddenly on 14 February 1955, aged forty-six, and as his literary executor I have endeavoured to arrange the final volume as he would have wished it. I have included most of the talks and essays of his last five years, at the expense of earlier pieces, and I believe that the result does present a conspectus of House's interests and scholarship in their depth, breadth and minuteness. Later I hope to be able to publish some kind of personal memoir of him.

I have been helped and guided everywhere by Mrs Madeline House, but the responsibility of final choice and arrangement is mine alone. The few additional footnotes which it seemed helpful to include have been enclosed within square brackets, to distinguish them from House's own notes.

My thanks are due to the Oxford University Press for permission to reprint the Introduction to *Oliver Twist*, and to Mr James Thornton for making the index.

It may interest readers to know that the new edition of Dickens's Letters, which House discusses on pp. 221–29, is to be carried through under the general editorship of Mr Graham Hough of Christ's College, Cambridge.

July 1955   RUPERT HART-DAVIS

PART ONE

POETS AND EVENTS

BIOGRAPHIA LITERARIA

It is odd that these two books should now be published within ten days of each other.* For over forty years James Dykes Campbell's short *Narrative* has been the best available life of Coleridge. E. H. Coleridge's full biography, for which he had collected so much material, was never written; a large box of his notes and drafts and other manuscripts was stolen from a railway goods-yard; he patiently set to work to build up his work again; but anxiety, age, and death overtook him. As editor he had done what nobody else then could have done. Not only the *Poems* and the *Letters*, but most of all *Anima Poetae*, which is perhaps the most entirely interesting collection of informal prose by any Englishman, are evidence of his devotion, and have been the basis of the work of all later editors and critics: even now, when so much has been added, they hold their own.† Perhaps, on top of age and worry, Ernest Hartley understood the intricacies of the huge mass of documents and of his grandfather's mind too well to dare the book before he died. Now an adequate biography of Coleridge needs tremendous abilities and about twenty years.

In one of his notebooks he points to his own biographer's chief problem. "Of all men I ever knew, Wordsworth himself not excepted, I have the faintest pleasure in things contingent and transitory. . . . I am not certain whether I should have seen with any emotion the mulberry-tree of Shakspere." But sometimes, he goes on, thoughts that places or objects were associated with great men would come on him "like a storm, and fill the place with something more than nature. But these are not contingent and transitory.

* *Samuel Taylor Coleridge* by E. K. Chambers (Oxford), and *The Life of S. T. Coleridge: The Early Years* by Lawrence Hanson (Allen & Unwin). Reviewed *New Statesman & Nation*, 7 Jan 1939.

† [For Humphry House's later opinion of the editing of *Anima Poetae*, see his *Coleridge*, 1953.]

... A Shakspere, a Milton, a Bruno, exist in the mind as pure *action*, defeated of all that is material and passive." And as a young man he scribbled: "The whale is followed by waves. I would glide down the rivulet of quiet life, a trout." There never was a more hopeless wish: he was already thrashing the sea when he made it. His life was full of events—meetings, quarrels, partings, journeys, debts—mostly documented several times over (though some mysteries were left for research): hundreds of things and places have Coleridge "associations". But through all this, for sixty-two years, moved the man as pure *action*, the Coleridge who sat in all the squalls of a poky servantless cottage calmly reading Spinoza. The biographer must relate the events to the mind so that they do not appear contingent and transitory, give the quality of the man as action.

Sir Edmund has not attempted it, and he wisely calls his dry, congested narrative a "biographical study". "Some intrepid scholar", he says, "will, no doubt, one day take up the task" of writing a full life; and pat comes Mr Hanson. But Sir Edmund is the better scholar: his range of material is wider, his ordering of it clearer, and on many points in the early years (e.g. the quarrel with Southey in 1794 which led to the abandonment of pantiso-cracy; and the dating of *Kubla Khan*) I think his conclusions more likely to be right. But his connected reference-book is for ordinary purposes unreadable, and for pleasure everyone will turn to Mr Hanson. His book is very attractive, particularly in the pictures faced by excellent quotations about their subjects. It covers the first twenty-eight years in 400 pages, and relies very largely on quotations: letters often run to two or three pages on end; there are seven and again five-and-a-half pages of continuous Hazlitt. Though Mr Hanson himself often writes very well, the book lives by its documents. For there is otherwise no unifying vigour in it, no conception of Coleridge that fills it with "something more than nature". Mind and events fall apart into separate chapters. Mr Potter has shown* how even more desperate dichotomy can help towards understanding Coleridge; but a biographer must try to put

* Stephen Potter, *Coleridge and S. T. C.* (Cape, 1935).

him together again. The great danger is focusing too much on his failures—in terms of the documents, relying too much on the letters, which are so often full of tortuous struggling, at the expense of the notebooks (*Anima Poetae* is only the "cream"), which record far better the life of his mind. It is easy to minimise the extent to which his life was a reading life (or "absorbing" would perhaps be a better word), and its chief events books. He once went to Durham to read, he said, Duns Scotus in the Cathedral Library. Sir Edmund hints that the real reason for going was to be near Sara Hutchinson. Even if that is true, it is as important that it was Duns Scotus and not somebody else who was used as a blind, as that it was Sara Hutchinson and not another woman. This is typical of a kind of situation that is continually cropping up. Above all, his biographer must not repeat the mistake of his friends and look on his metaphysics as just another form of dope.

In the letters and comments of all his friends (Mr Hanson gives an excellent portrait of Poole) the tone of regret and remonstrance is likely to occur at any time after 1800. Even Poole is sometimes impatient, and Dorothy Wordsworth's letters at the time of the quarrel over Montagu are painful to read. It is impossible to blame his friends, but it is easy in approaching Coleridge through what they say to blame him in the wrong tone of voice. Both these books give the impression of a man hunted by the people who wish him well. In their whole effect they perpetuate the pitying attitude that made Lamb so indignant; it is forced on them by documents which only a very bold writer would systematically treat as secondary. But in Coleridge's life personal relationships were secondary, and their great importance only shows the greater importance of other things. His friends judged him too much in terms of achievements—we must remember that Wordsworth professed to have published the first edition of *Lyrical Ballads* merely for money—and after a time began to dishearten him by anticipating failures: everybody tried to dissuade him from *The Friend*. Whatever he projected, somebody was sure to remind him that *Christabel* was unfinished.

He needed no reminding: he knew his own mind, and the

extreme illness of his own body, too, well enough: he knew all the differences of mood between free poetic creation and "game of far other kind". But he did need somebody who could take his philosophy seriously, whether it was to come out in verses or in the great work: and he needs for his final biographer somebody who is prepared to take the risk of starting at the philosophical end. For even within what is narrowly called literature it is that side of him that matters, and when it comes to assessing achievements his most important work, in the *Biographia* and in the notes now at last dug out of the pocket-books, is that he habitually thought of literature not departmentalised as a source of pleasure or instruction or as a technical trick of rhetoric, but as one of the best activities of a whole mind. In his own life it was.

COLERIDGE'S POLITICS

MANY people thinking of Coleridge's politics will remember that he "snapped his squeaking baby-trumpet of sedition" and lived to be called the procreator of spectral Puseyisms and ecclesiastical Chimeras. They feel a disconcerting difference between the man who trapped Mr Needham into saying that Jesus Christ was a *seditious Dog*, who put "Wherefore my Bowels shall sound like an Harp" as the motto to an essay on "National Fasts", and the don-like bogy who made his onset on Harriet Martineau with compliments and the words: "You appear to consider that society is an aggregate of individuals"; of whom Hazlitt had said: "Proscribed by court-hirelings, too romantic for the herd of vulgar politicians, our enthusiast stood at bay, and at last turned on the pivot of a subtle casuistry to the *unclean side*."

It seems affectation for Coleridge-students to say, as Mr Harold Beeley has said, that in politics Coleridge's "essential faith was unchanged"; and now for Mr White in his Introduction to this selection from the political writings, letters and table-talk*, to argue that artists never change their minds but "grow". For it must be plain to anyone not obsessed by a false notion of consistency that Coleridge did change his mind as radically, as carefully, and one might add as slowly, as perhaps a man ever has. The effective part of the process took about six years, and it involved, within his own mental life, a complete reaction (the word is Mill's) against the eighteenth century in politics as in everything else.

Pantisocracy was a typically eighteenth-century scheme: "The leading idea of pantisocracy", he wrote to Southey in October 1794, "is to make men *necessarily* virtuous by removing all motives to

---

* *The Political Thought of Samuel Taylor Coleridge*, edited with an Introduction by R. J. White (Cape). Reviewed *New Statesman & Nation*, 25 June 1938.

evil—all possible temptation." And later in the same letter come two important sentences omitted by Mr White: "All necessary knowledge in the branch of ethics is comprised in the word justice: that the good of the whole is the good of each individual, that, of course, it is each individual's *duty* to be just, *because* it is his *interest*. . . . In the book of pantisocracy I hope to have comprised all that is good in Godwin." It is important to realise that the revision of his whole philosophy, which involved the abandonment of these main principles, had begun before the great disillusionment at the French invasion of Switzerland in 1798, and before the visit to Germany.

For many Englishmen in the early nineteenth century the strongest influence working against perfectionism of the Rousseau-Godwin-pantisocratic type was Malthus's theory of population, by which a residuum would always be left on the misery-line; but Coleridge reached a similar position earlier by a "rediscovery" of the doctrine of original sin. He opposed Malthusian morals by insisting that morality and prudence were two distinct things: he set up against the Utilitarian calculus the moral will, "the worth and essential character of the *agents*". His positive political doctrine developed more slowly than his criticism of his contemporaries: but certain leading ideas show themselves early behind this criticism. He argues against Cartwright and the doctrinaire radicals generally that the logical concomitant of Universal Suffrage based on "Rights" is the equalisation or abolition of private property. Pantisocracy had involved complete "aspheterisation" and, of course, the absence of all government: when he wrote in 1799 (if the attribution of the *Morning Post* article is correct) that "for the present race of men Governments must be founded on property", he had not therefore necessarily changed his mind; but when he continues:

> That government is good in which property is secure and circulates; that government the best, which, in the exactest ratio, makes each man's power proportionate to his property,

there is a new emphasis and a new tone. This idea, repeated ten years later in *The Friend*, was the basis of his practical conservatism.

But his view of property was by no means rigid; he inclined to the view that private property in the fullest sense was limited to movable goods: he emphasised (and Mill said that this was his greatest service to politics) the idea of a *trust* inherent in landed property—which was part of his reiterated doctrine that rights imply duties: and he attacked the treatment of land as if it were an object of commerce. He had his eye on landlords of the Lord Marney type thirty years before Disraeli. All this, together with his conception of the "Nationalty", the property vested in a National Church which should be primarily a civilising institution, explains his influence on the later Christian Socialists, and it helps to explain also his defence of the Corn Laws. A State should first of all be self-supporting in essentials produced on the land and guaranteed by the landed classes; that was a condition of the security of its peculiar civilisation.

Mr White rightly emphasises in his Introduction and in his selections—especially in those from the superb journalism in the *Morning Post*—the growth of Coleridge's patriotic nationalism about the turn of the century, and he might have called attention also to the Imperialist implications of his attitude to trade. In an article of March 1800 he argues that if the French were left in possession of Egypt an expedition against them there would be "a just and necessary undertaking", as "they might in time expel us from our Eastern possessions, and annihilate our Indian commerce". Yet commerce was for Coleridge only a matter of luxuries. One has to remember that Joseph Hume made a quick fortune in Bengal.

It is easy to smile at Coleridge plunging enthusiastically down a blind alley loaded with the Fathers and Luther and Hooker and Kant, damning Malthus and shouting Jeremiads over the Reform Bill. But who was not in a blind alley in the twenties and thirties? John Mill knew he was, and admitted it was Coleridge who helped to get him out. I think that Coleridge's influence on the Christian Socialists and Young England and the Oxford Movement was less important in the long run than his influence on the Philosophical Radicals themselves. This influence was partly *per contra*, because

21

he and his followers forced the revision of the Progressives' first principles by their opposition; but it was also direct because he was so undoctrinaire. His *Grounds of Sir Robert Peel's Bill Vindicated* shows an enlightened and "progressive" (the word is Mill's again) attitude to social legislation compared with that of Benthamite sticklers who voted on the unclean side because of a principle of non-interference.

It is an unhappy feature of Mr White's otherwise interesting introduction to this very useful book that he cries up Coleridge at Mill's expense. The essay has signs of the fault that Mill was so scrupulous to avoid—sectarianism. Mr White does not fully show his cards because he promises a full-length book on the subject: but the many readers who may look forward to it must be allowed to hope that while dutifully allotting Coleridge to no old party he does not claim him for a new one; that the text of his quotations will be more carefully corrected than in the present book; and that the system of references shall not be designed to try their Christian fortitude.

THE OTHER SARA*

IT was awkward for Coleridge that after marrying one woman called Sara he should have fallen in love with another: to avoid confusion with the names he called the second "Asra". She was Sara Hutchinson, whose sister Mary was Wordsworth's wife. The book I am talking about this evening is a published collection of Sara Hutchinson's letters, 169 of them, all that are known to have survived, edited by the well-known Coleridge scholar, Miss Kathleen Coburn.

I opened it with some excitement. The letters of Sara the wife to Thomas Poole, edited some years ago by Mr Stephen Potter under the title *Minnow among Tritons*,† had shown, apart from all other evidence, some of the plain reasons why Coleridge's marriage broke down. She wrote, for instance, to Tom Poole that she had heard that her husband had changed his political sentiments, and said to Poole: "Pray furnish me". I was excited because I wondered what the other Sara was like: she had been a rather sketchy figure hitherto, seen mainly by people who might have been prejudiced about her.

The excitement was not merely that of inquisitiveness, a love of the "Higher Gossip", of "chatter about Harriet"; I thought that the letters might be of literary importance, perhaps in several different ways. It is a very delicate matter to determine how far biography is relevant to properly critical ends; each case sets different problems, and needs different methods. With the English Romantics the problems are specially complicated, both because so much of their verse was of directly autobiographical origin, and because so much is known about them. They lived among and fostered a cult of personality, and therefore people tended to keep the documents. It is easy to start with a proper desire to understand

* B.B.C. Third Programme, 20 May 1954.   † Nonesuch Press, 1934.

the circumstances of a poet's life and the quality of his mind revealed in them—and to do this is certainly relevant to many particular poems—but then to get led on into more and more irrelevant detail, till the works are lost under the washing-bills.

Sara Hutchinson has a very special place, both in understanding the general circumstances of the lives of both Wordsworth and Coleridge, and also in interpreting one of Coleridge's major poems. *Dejection: an Ode* was originally written to her as a long verse letter in April 1802, but was not published in anything approaching that original form until 1937. Criticism is doing only half its job on the Ode if it adopts the editorial rule that the *textus receptus* is the last version seen through the press by the poet himself, and exerts its energies only on this, ignoring all the others. For the two main versions differ not only a great deal in length and in detail, but even in their main mood and direction. The chief elements in the experience from which all the versions of the poem grew were the contrast between Coleridge's unhappiness in his own family life, and the happiness of the Wordsworth group of which Sara Hutchinson formed a part; together with the self-analysis which showed the lack of happiness and firm affections as a loss of the essential joy without which poetic creation itself was for him impossible. The published version and the original verse-letter differ from each other primarily in that the one gives its main emphasis to the losses, the misery, and the failure of creative power, while the other ends with a long strain of forty-four lines focused upon the active joy which Sara possesses. The comparison of the versions, when taken together with other writings of Coleridge, led me some time ago to begin at least tentative revisions of my views about his theory of poetry in general. Anyhow it is evident that over several years Sara Hutchinson provided a centre for his emotions, in a way which affected the development of his most serious thought. He wrote of her in one of his notebooks:

> Endeavouring to make the infinitely beloved Darling understand all my knowledge I learn the art of making the abstrusest Truths intelligible, & interesting even to the unlearned.

We had been warned, then, at least not to expect to find Sara a woman who was in any way Coleridge's intellectual equal. But yet I opened the book in some excitement, hoping to find evidence of a mind which could plainly be sympathetic to and interested in the development of such ideas as Coleridge's, evidence of a sensibility which could readily be in tune with his: perhaps even something that would help to the understanding of him.

But the disappointment in these respects is almost complete. It was not to be expected that there would be any letters to Coleridge himself; but there are no letters to anybody between 1800 and 1805, the first period of her close friendship with him, the time of holding hands by the fire, of the fowls with the white sauce, the "cheese, at Middleham, too salt"—things which helped Coleridge to formulate his theory of association: there are not even any glances back to what happened in those years; for Sara lived hard in her present. Even when they are meeting again in 1808–9 she has not much to say: there is his "great Canister" of snuff; she helps him to produce that misguided periodical, *The Friend*, and reports about his troubles with the printer: "He has had a vast of plague—more than suits one of his temper and habits." Over the break between Wordsworth and Coleridge the letters are either missing or almost completely silent. There is no sign of interest in Coleridge's works or intellectual development. In 1817 she writes:

Have you seen Mr Coleridges "Lay Sermons"? The first they say addressed to the higher classes is of all obscures the most obscure—we have not seen either and hear very little that is satisfactory of his goings-on—and especially that his health is much impaired.

This is either unfair, or else it shows that her source of news is out-of-date or inaccurate; she did not seem to know that his living at Highgate was already leading to recovery, and to a burst of publishing which included the *Biographia* and *Sibylline Leaves*. The next year it is sad to find her actually dreading that she might be involved in correspondence with him; she had just met him for a short time in London, and then wrote:

We see Coleridge both advertized & puffed in the *M.C.* I am glad to find that he intends publishing the Lectures & wish he may do it—

because then he will have his own—else it is scattering his knowledge for the profit of others—it is wonderful that the first Lecture was true to the Prospectus—but indeed he has exhibited many wonders lately—pray have you any conversation with him? & did he inquire after "my dear" or his other Friends—I was afraid that he would have favored Mrs C. or me with a Letter because he asked me the address, but I hope he has forgotten it—if he should ask you try to evade the question—for we are neither of us ambitious of the favor, especially as an answer *would be required.*

After seeing him at Ramsgate in 1823, she tartly reported that he "did not require us to exert ourselves for conversation". Just before his death she saw him again and softened to calling him "my dear old Friend"; and when he is dead she comments: "His own relations had more pride in him than Love for him—at least Pride was the foundation of their Love." But whatever the quality of her own love may have been, these letters do not reveal a breath or a shadow of it.

Nor do they reveal any qualities of mind of an uncommon sort; she enjoys things she sees, and conveys, in ordinary description of no special power, her pleasure in the simple good things of life. She was plainly a lovable and affectionate woman, with a talent for putting people at their ease and drawing them out, a natural confidante. Whatever else Coleridge's Asra became beyond this was projected onto her by him, and we still do not know what she thought about it.

She is obviously so nice that it is a pity this publication should make her seem a bore. For it is all very well to read such letters as these at intervals when the postman brings them—and she is constantly making little jokes about whether her letters will be worth the postage money on receipt—but to read 169 of them on end, in a heavy volume of 446 pages without the notes, is an experience of quite a different kind. The gossip streams on in an unending flow, punctuated with only full-stops and dashes, with more and more underlining as she grows older, about all the doings of the Wordsworth, Hutchinson, and Monkhouse families for generation after generation. The same few Christian names beat on in monotonous confusion; there are seven Johns, five Thomases, four Georges, four Henrys, three Williams, eight Marys, five Saras, three Dorothys, with abbreviations and nicknames abounding among them. The unfortunate editor has been forced to distinguish these same recurrent names by superior index-figures in the text, so that we get John squared and Sara cubed and so on, and William to the oneth is always William Wordsworth the great poet. For several years we hear about the stomach of Willy, or William squared, how it would not stand fruit or vegetables; yet how he was always greedy and made himself ill with gooseberries at the Lloyds' and with apples at the Clarksons'; and how a watch must be kept to make sure he doesn't overeat at Christmas. Or we hear often and often about the looks of Dorothy squared, or Doro, who in early childhood looked fine by candlelight, but day showed her up; and she got better as she got older. Then there is the bluestocking lassitude of Sara cubed, Coleridge's daughter, who cared for nothing but classical literature and personal beauty and wouldn't exert herself; right on from childhood till she was a mother who wouldn't rally after childbirth. Every form of deficiency or ailment is minutely described in children and adults—coughs, dysentery, rheumatism, cataract, smallpox and death. She is specially verbose about the troubles with her own teeth, and was once anxious after a visit that she had left her toothpick-case behind. And she doesn't stop with human beings: through several of the early letters her pony had a bad cough; and at one time all the horses round Sockburn have coughs.

Pages and pages of the book are taken up with ordering carpets, bonnets, hats, dress-material, knitting-wool and even sometimes books from London; two gentlemen's hats are to be sent "fashionable and hansome but not round tops 22 inches round the outside of the crown to be bought of Mr Idle". It is a matter of interesting relief to learn that the carpets should not have been sent by canal, because it was slow and inefficient, but by the wagon *via* Leeds. As a solid sample of the trivial stuff I will quote the final paragraph from a letter of April 1820:

Do not forget Henry Hutchinson when you have Willy with you—

And Dorothy must give Anne a call at Miss Babbington's in or about Sloane Street when she may chance to pass that way. I think I should have gone to Penrith this week to pay my long-intended visit if I was sure that A. Whelpdale was still there, because he sent so kind a message & offer of coming for me which I could not do when Dr W. was here and D. on the eve of such a long absence. Remember me very kindly to him & Mrs W. when you see them—We are all well except myself who am now writing with a distracting tooth and ear ache which I suppose I brought on yesterday by *walking* to Church—Farewell Kindest remembrances to Dorothy—Dr W. & Willy—Yours ever most truly S. H.

W. is just come from the post and has got the proof title page &c— So D. will have no care about that.

There are many pages that are no better, the kindly good-natured scribble of maiden-cousin and maiden-aunt.

There is perhaps one strong argument for having published all this stuff in bulk. It shows more convincingly perhaps than all the many other documents that show it, the restricting and almost suicidal narrowness, even self-centredness of the Wordsworth group. Happy they certainly were with each other; but it gives a special interest to Coleridge's poem *Dejection*, to see spread out at length the loving insistence on trivialities which bred within the charmed circle he thought so idyllic. He could never have belonged; and as Asra committed herself deeper and deeper with the years, he must have found the memories of 1801–3 more important than the current fact.

But for this one effect of the whole mass—and the whole mass costs two guineas—the valuable and interesting parts of these letters could have been produced in a careful selection costing ten shillings or even less. For I do not mean to leave the impression that there are not interesting things. There are amusing and astute passages of common human interest; and there are also side-views of literature and history. The intransigent Toryism of Sara's politics, for instance, comes out in curious ways. She mourns over the death of Bishop Watson as the passing of the head of a great Lake District landowning family, without a comment on his notorious pluralism and his nepotism and his long neglectful absence

28

from the Diocese of Llandaff; one wonders if she even knew that somewhere in Wordsworth's house lay the unpublished manuscript of his great attack on Watson written in 1793. After Peterloo she rejoices in the dismissal of the Lord Lieutenant of the West Riding of Yorkshire, because it proves that "Ministers are strong"; and she actually hopes for the suspension of Habeas Corpus. But even with all its Toryism she could not stomach *Blackwood's Magazine*, and there are several long and amusing outbursts against its scurrility, its inconsistency and lack of principle; she despises even its approval of Wordsworth. Yet when it comes to the Cockneys, she almost seems to be on *Blackwood's* side; for Sara Hutchinson once met Keats, and she has left for posterity her comment on the publication of *Endymion*:

> Little Keats too I see is in the publishing line—but the Title of his Poem has no charms for me—however beautiful it may be I am sure it cannot awaken my interest or sympathies—I wonder anybody should take such subjects now-a-days.

So far had a devoted sister-in-law and a very likeable woman imbibed the principles which William to the oneth had set out in the Preface to the *Lyrical Ballads*.

WORDSWORTH: THE TWO VOICES*

THE great Oxford edition of Wordsworth's poems, planned and all but finished by Professor Ernest de Selincourt, has now reached its third volume. When he died in May 1943, the copy for the last three volumes was almost ready for printing: their completion was left to Miss Helen Darbishire, who understood his methods and purposes; she had been consulted in all the earlier stages, and knew the material minutely. His death therefore meant no change, no break, no bathos.

This is obviously not an edition for every reader, or for any reader all the time. Arnold's principle remains true, that to be enjoyed and seen for the great poet he was, Wordsworth should be read in selections, "relieved of a great deal of the poetical baggage" which in full editions encumbers him.

> Two voices are there: one is of the deep;
> It learns the storm-cloud's thunderous melody,
> Now roars, now murmurs with the changing sea,
> Now bird-like pipes, now closes soft in sleep:
> And one is of an old half-witted sheep
> Which bleats articulate monotony,
> And indicates that two and one are three,
> That grass is green, lakes damp, and mountains steep:
> And, Wordsworth, both are thine.

In the Oxford edition, which retains Wordsworth's own final arrangement of the poems in what he intended to be a psychological system of grouping, the two voices are often speaking on the same page; the bleats interrupt the melody; and the *apparatus criticus* below reveals how the words of either voice were subject to revision. Even *The Solitary Reaper* sings with half a dozen variants.

Yet once the reader's purpose of straight immediate enjoyment of the great poems has been superseded, and questions begin to be

* *New Statesman & Nation*, 29 March 1947.

asked, this edition becomes absolutely essential. It will be remembered that Professor de Selincourt began his work with the edition of *The Prelude*, in which he printed for the first time in full the two versions, the original of 1805–6 and the published revision of 1850, running parallel side-by-side on opposite pages, so that either all the changes could be viewed comprehensively as one went along, or else one version could be followed through entirely by itself. *The Prelude* supplies the extreme example of what happened more or less to all the poems. A full variorum edition is part of the story of the "Growth of a Poet's Mind". *Louisa*, for instance, began in 1807, when it was first published, and up till 1832 continued to begin, like this:

> I met Louisa in the shade;
> And, having seen that lovely Maid,
> Why should I fear to say
> That she is ruddy, fleet, and strong;
> And down the rocks can leap along,
> Like rivulets in May?

Then in the edition of 1836 this opening is changed to:

> Though by a sickly taste betrayed,
> Some will dispraise the lovely maid,
> With fearless pride I say
> That she is healthful, fleet, and strong . . . etc.

Can it be altogether an accident that it is in exactly this year, 1836, that the historian of our nineteenth-century women's fashions notes an abrupt change, and remarks that "the design of the dress became mildly sentimental and lost its exuberant romanticism. A demure prettiness took its place"? And can it be of no significance at all that in 1845 the original text came back, but with the substitution of "nymph-like" for "ruddy", when timid, ringleted, bonneted, clinging, and fainting girls were before long to expire in the total incapacity of Dora Copperfield? The poet's mind seems to have been alert, in his later years, to the taste of possible readers.

In the past thirty years Wordsworthian scholars and critics have altered the old portrait of "Daddy Wordsworth" almost beyond

31

recognition; so that there is now perhaps a new danger that unwary readers may come to think that all the Daddyisms and bleatings belong to the period of decline and that the years before 1807 were purely golden. A new volume of the collected poems suggests again that all the later poems can well be left to curious anthologists, historians, and scouts for Museums of Taste; and that there is plenty in the early years alone to absorb a reader concerned about poetry, the problems of style and of creation. This third volume contains a great deal written after 1807—the whole of the *Ecclesiastical Sonnets*, the *Memorials* of the Tours of 1814, 1820, and 1837, the Duddon series, many later Miscellaneous Sonnets and so on—but leaving all this aside, and keeping to *The White Doe of Rylstone* and what was written before it, the two voices are still found talking side by side, not only on next-door pages, or on the same page, but even in the same poem: and unmistakably, without any possibility of confusion with anybody else, Wordsworth, both are thine.

A single group of poems will illustrate the problems which this volume revives. The *Memorials of a Tour in Scotland 1803*, as finally arranged, contain one of the best-known and most loved of all Wordsworth's poems, *The Solitary Reaper*. It was not in fact written till 1805; but few of the poems in the group were written in the actual year of the tour; they were mostly memorials in the sense of recollections; the original experiences belonged to the time of the tour and, in the case of *The Solitary Reaper*, were later reinforced by the manuscript of Wilkinson's *Tour in Scotland*. This poem cannot therefore be looked on as isolated by the time or occasion of its writing: it belongs with what surrounds it and there, judged as a complete poem, it stands absolutely alone, with qualities that the other poems do not even approach. There are certain preliminary gropings in the verses *To a Highland Girl*, which sway between cottagey detail and the imputed splendour which makes the *Reaper* so impressive:

> Thou art to me but as a wave
> Of the wild sea; and I would have
> Some claim upon thee, if I could.

The other poems of the group are in quite a different mood, as well as on another level of achievement. But one of them, *The Blind Highland Boy*, contains in itself so many contrasts, uncertainties and failures in proportion and taste, so much oddly assorted imagery, that it makes an excellent starting-point for reconsiderations.

This poem, it will be remembered, is presented in form as if spoken to children by the fireside at Grasmere. It is a simple tale of a boy, blind from birth, who is brought up on the shore of a sea-loch where ocean-going ships come in. He is fired, by sailors' stories and the sounds of ships, with a desire to go to sea himself; but his mother forbids him. Then one day, when he is ten, he secretly puts off from shore alone in a turtle-shell (or washing-tub); he is carried a quarter of a mile out by the tide; he has a moment of delighted ecstasy; he is brought back by men in a rowing boat and is thenceforth reconciled to living on shore. The poem is mostly in verse of appalling flatness and insipidity, helped out by little tricks of rhetoric designed to rouse the children's interest: but it contains two pieces of writing which have great beauties—the description of the sea-loch in lines 46–70 and a simile in lines 186–190, comparing the boy's rescuers to fowlers going out after wild duck. The first of these was quoted by Coleridge with approval in his examples of Wordsworth's most characteristically personal writing; and he then asked the very significant question: "Who but a poet tells a tale in such language to the little ones by the fireside?"

The question we would now rather ask is: "Who but Wordsworth would conceive and write this poem as a tale for the little ones at all?" For it is clearly a poem about his one great recurrent theme—the moment of visionary insight which, while it lasts, seems to contain the knowledge of all values, the meaning of life: the moment which always ends:

> You've often heard of magic wands,
> That with a motion overthrow
> A palace of the proudest show,
>   Or melt it into air;

So all his dreams—that inward light
With which his soul had shone so bright—
All vanished.

This poem was in fact written in the years between the first part
and the last part of the *Ode on the Intimations of Immortality*, and is
an exercise in expressing, through different imagery, one of the
main ideas of the Ode. Wordsworth's greatest literary problem
was to find the symbols appropriate to his own unique vision. He
is continually imputing something of it to children and simple
people: but in narrative and realistic settings the circumstances can
rarely live up to and carry the imputations. There is a constant
war raging between the studied simplicity in externals and the
complex innocent greatness which is supposed to belong to the
persons. The persons are always best when they are most detached
from physical details like cottages and armchairs. Not a single
adjunct of the solitary reaper is described. The original washing-
tub stanza in *The Blind Highland Boy* is a vivid case in point, and
I agree with Jeffrey against Lamb that it was intolerable for all
its truth to fact:

> But say, what was it? Thought of fear!
> Well may ye tremble when ye hear!
> —A Household Tub, like one of those
> Which women use to wash their clothes,
> This carried the blind Boy.

There is nothing inherently ludicrous in the boy using a washing-
tub: what is ludicrous is to make such a fuss about it; this explanation is studied and arch; it is consciously intended to startle the
reader at the homeliness of the thing, when he need never have
been startled. These are the words of a gauche man, insensitive
to the effects of his own writi g. No wonder the *Edinburgh* called
him "outrageous for simplicity", and begged leave to recommend
"the simplicity of Burns". It is typical of Wordsworth's deep uncertainties about this whole problem of simplicity that he was
prepared to accept Coleridge's alternative of the turtle-shell, an
object lifted out of Dampier which might, transfigured, have found

34

its place in a companion poem to *The Ancient Mariner*: it is merely an exotic absurdity grafted on where it is, a trailing irrelevance in eight stanzas.

The purpose of *The Blind Highland Boy* is explained in this one stanza:

> Thus, after he had fondly braved
> The perilous Deep, the Boy was saved;
> And, though his fancies had been wild,
> Yet he was pleased and reconciled
>   To live in peace on shore.

These few lines, in small flat language, might in any other poet be dismissed as the careless and impatient winding-up of a story which anyway had elements of comicality and bathos. But with Wordsworth they must be taken seriously, and one wonders at the utter failure to emphasise them by imagery or extension. For the matter is not a warning to Grasmere children not to have visions, but the possibility of an ultimate reconciliation with life, when visions have faded: towards that Wordsworth himself was trying to find his way.

His poetic character has been admirably described as the "egotistical sublime". The egotism had a number of very important effects. He was quite abnormally cut off from the ordinary business of living, except in the close circle of his own family and friends. His relationship with Dorothy, fruitful as it was, had round it the atmosphere of the "little secret". What in a close circle is full of profound significance and beauty may seem utterly trivial, meaningless and absurd when published to the world. Wordsworth could not always translate. Jeffrey, as might be expected, charged him with lack of *decorum*; and his offences were worst when the little language of the home was given out ungarnished and undeveloped. When Coleridge was sympathetic, big words like "interfused" or remote exciting objects like the tropical turtle-shell were liable to be worked in after a letter or some talk. Surroundings and habit fostered Wordsworth's egotism; and he himself cherished it; for, as he knew, he was creating the taste which would appreciate him: and who was then to know? The *Edinburgh* laughed at the awkwardly-managed washing-tub and the poems on the Grave of Burns, but did not even mention *The Solitary Reaper*.

In that poem the egotism rises to its full creative greatness. The self on which the poem pivots is now not a poet on a walking-tour or a family-man who has just put down Wilkinson's manuscript: he has forgotten all about the homely accidents of Highland life, and the little language; there is no sought-after description, no touching speculation about the girl's age or family, no Coleridgean philosophising. The circumstantial self has gone, with all his trivialities: the self is a seer. The girl, in a sense, is nowhere: everything is imputed to her and half of it is negative or doubtful. In the rich succession of images one Wordsworthian theme after another slips in unmagnified, unextended, unexplained, but each clear and pure and perfectly proportioned. After reading this poem one need ask no questions at all, need puzzle over nothing; but it seems as if, to reach this point, readers had to have *The Blind Highland Boy* to bite on.

There are indeed six variants to *The Solitary Reaper*; but not one of them disturbs the structure or completeness of the poem. The notes at the end of this volume give Dorothy's description of the reapers they had seen in 1803, the relevant quotation from Wilkinson's *Tour*, and a cross-reference to Wordsworth's poem *To the Spade of a Friend*. The two voices sound even through the commentary.

WORDSWORTH'S FAME*

THE Earl of Chesterfield, who had for neighbours in the country the Beaumonts of Coleorton, heard much from them of their admiration for Wordsworth's poetry. So one day in London—it was in about 1810—he went into his bookseller's and asked for the latest volume of these poems:

> When he asked for it, Paine, the Bookseller, was surprised, said he had it not, but if his Lordship was in earnest to purchase it he would get it for him. Lord Chesterfield said: "I gave seven shillings and sixpence for it, and anybody shall have it for the odd sixpence." He then expressed his surprise at the puerile nonsense in it, and Lysons, on looking into the volume, was equally astonished at such stuff being published.

Nothing could show more clearly the extent of the neglect, and the extent to which the then prevailing educated taste was quite unable to take in Wordsworth even at his best.

As one would expect, it was mostly the young people who were first to appreciate and love him; and from one group particularly his reputation spread out widely into the country. J. T. Coleridge, Samuel Taylor's nephew, had been sent by his uncle a copy of the *Lyrical Ballads* and some of Wordsworth's other poems. He got to know them well and when he went up to Oxford he passed on his enthusiasm to his friends at Corpus. In 1811, a boy of sixteen called Thomas Arnold came up from Winchester and joined Coleridge's set. They all, J. T. Coleridge said, felt the "truth and beauty" of Wordsworth's poems, and became zealous disciples of his "philosophy": and he added:

> This was of peculiar advantage to Arnold, whose leaning was too direct for the practical and evidently useful—it brought out in him that

---

* B.B.C. Third Programme, 10 Dec 1947.

feeling for the lofty and imaginative which appeared in all his intimate conversation, and may be seen spiritualising those even of his writings, in which, from their subject, it might seem to have less place.

Through Arnold perhaps more than through any one other man the love of Wordsworth, and what was thought to be the Wordsworthian spirit, passed into Victorian culture. The very words "lofty", "imaginative", "spiritualising" show how the poems came to be regarded as producing a sort of noble mood, a high seriousness. Through Arnold's pupils at Rugby this taste and this mood were diffused; Arnold's sons, Matthew and Thomas, each in his own way, became exponents of Wordsworthianism; and the family was even partly brought up in the Lakes, at Fox How, not far from Rydal Mount. Wordsworth in old age was their close friend.

His reputation rose sharply in the thirties, and increased as that of Byron declined. A peak point in merely public fame came in 1839, when he was given an honorary degree at Oxford. The Professor of Poetry greeted him then in elegant Latin as the man who

> of all poets, and above all, has exhibited the manners, the pursuits, and the feelings, religious and traditional, of the poor . . . in a light which glows with the rays of heaven. To his poetry, therefore, they should, I think, be now referred, who sincerely desire to understand and feel that secret harmonious intimacy which exists between honourable poverty and the severer Muses, sublime Philosophy, yea, even our most holy Religion.

Such strange praise was not just a formal academic tribute; it was also a direct expression of personal love and indebtedness: for the speaker was John Keble.

Already by the early forties Wordsworth was being claimed by the new Oxford High Churchmen as *their* poet. This was due in part to the ecclesiastical slant of the later works; but they also found in him a restatement of transcendentalism; and they turned his love of the simple into the spirit of the *Magnificat*: "He hath put down the mighty from their seat: and hath exalted the humble and meek."

38

I met a little child in Rydal vale,
With a huge bunch of daffodils; a posy
Large as the child herself, who was but frail,
And hot with climbing; and in all the rills,
With both hands clasped, she dipped her daffodils. . . .

My sainted Mother! was I once like this,
A creature overflowed with simple bliss?

The writer of these sentimental lines on Wordsworthian themes
was Frederick William Faber, who later, as a priest of the Oratory,
sentimentalised the cult of the Virgin. Nor was Keble himself just
touched by Wordsworth's ecclesiasticism; *The Christian Year* is
drenched in Wordsworthian sentiment and imagery:

Shame on the heart that dreams of blessings gone,
Or wakes the spectral forms of woe and crime,
When Nature sings of joy and hope alone,
Reading her cheerful lesson in her own sweet time.

Such verses derive directly from Wordsworth; but they break completely from his central experience, and point towards that view of
Nature as providing an automatic sort of psychotherapy, the view
that is so clear in Tennyson's *The Two Voices.*

It is plain from *The Prelude* that Wordsworth's total experience
could never be repeated or imitated: his experience of the interaction of the human mind and Nature was unique and individual.
In the *Memorial Verses* Matthew Arnold said to the River Rotha:

few or none
Hears thy voice right, now he is gone.

Wordsworth's purely poetic influence—especially on the loose,
dissipated, careless structure of verse—was bad. Poems such as
The Scholar Gipsy and *Thyrsis* could not have been written but for
Wordsworth, but they owe little to him technically or even verbally.
In those lines of Arnold that owe most perhaps of all to Wordsworth:

Calm soul of all things! make it mine
To feel, amid the city's jar,
That there abides a peace of thine,
Man did not make, and cannot mar:

the very form of the prayer shows that the central experience is missing, however much desired. For none of the Victorians caught or repeated the essence, though all felt its effects, acquired some part of its adherent moods. From the thirties onward the minds of all Englishmen were modified; fresh habits of vision, new stimuli to feeling, altered tastes, changed directions of moral purpose can be attributed very largely to Wordsworth. Life often imitates Art; and long before critics had attempted to isolate and describe his peculiar experience and poetic sensibility, Life had begun to imitate Wordsworth. Though his experience could not be repeated, he seemed to have contributed a new dimension in which experience was possible. It is an extraordinary tribute to the strength and also to the indeterminateness of his influence that he modified the attitude to the world of such diverse people as Thomas Arnold, Keble, Faber, Newman, John Stuart Mill, Gladstone, Kingsley, Matthew Arnold and Clough.

It was said of Clough that few looked on Nature "more entirely in the spirit" of "his favourite Wordsworth". Gladstone, aged twenty-three, noted that "One remarkable similarity prevails between Wordsworth and Shelley; the quality of combining and connecting everywhere external nature with internal and unseen mind. But . . . it frets and irritates the one, it is the key to the peacefulness of the other." And Kingsley, who said his own soul " had been steeped from boyhood" in Wordsworth's poetry, proclaimed that he "had learnt from it how to look at and feel with nature" and had been preserved by it from "shallow, cynical and materialistic views of the universe".

Of all the records left by these men none is clearer or more startling than the account by John Stuart Mill of his experience in 1828, when he had reached a phase of extreme gloom and dejection both about himself and about human happiness in general. He tried Byron, but found there nothing but the burden under which he himself laboured. "But while Byron was exactly what did not suit my condition", he wrote, "Wordsworth was exactly what did":

What made Wordsworth's poems a medicine for my state of mind, was that they expressed, not mere outward beauty, but states of feeling, and of thought coloured by feeling, under the excitement of beauty. They seemed to be the very culture of the feelings, which I was in quest of. In them I seemed to draw from a source of inward joy, of sympathetic and imaginative pleasure, which could be shared in by all human beings. . . . From them I seemed to learn what would be the perennial sources of happiness, when all the greater evils of life shall have been removed.

That phrase "a medicine for my state of mind" is a clue to much of the Victorian love of Wordsworth; it was often less concerned with the beauty of the verse than with its psychological, almost its moral, effects. His was "a soothing voice":

> He spoke, and loosed our heart in tears.
> He laid us as we lay at birth
> On the cool flowery lap of earth,
> Smiles broke from us and we had ease.

And others spoke of his consoling power.

Mill made the point that Wordsworth may be said to be "the poet of unpoetical natures, possessed of quiet and contemplative tastes", and that it is exactly such people who most need poetic cultivation. Wordsworth, for instance, was notably not Keats's poet, but was Thomas Arnold's poet. The "egotistical sublime" poet has qualities of mind and character which more especially appeal also to the man of affairs and action. Wordsworth taken broadly as a whole did suggest that he strove to be like his own Happy Warrior,

> Whose powers shed round him in the common strife,
> Or mild concerns of ordinary life,
> A constant influence, a peculiar grace;

to be "the generous spirit. . . . among the tasks of real life". His conscious attempt to reform poetic diction, to use what he called "the very language of men", may have contributed something to his ultimate success with this class of readers; but I do not think it was so important with them as his other principle of illustrating "the primary laws of our nature". The persons in his poems are never vivid individualised portraits; they are broad generalisations, and become the symbols of moral moods. The leech-gatherer as an individual is never clear, and even he fades out till

> the whole body of the Man did seem
> Like one whom I had met with in a dream;

and yet by some mysterious alchemy there come from this dim figure words which "give me human strength by apt admonishment". This use of human beings as ethical symbols had a particular appeal in the age dominated by the contest between philanthropy and doctrinaire utilitarianism. Wordsworth became, in a way that Shelley could never have become—for his diction and imagery were too strained and loud—the poet of that widespread generalised benevolence which was so prominent in the moral mood of the Early Victorian Age. Wordsworth countered the broad generalisation of economic man with a broad generalisation of moral and sentient man. He did not "neglect the universal heart":

> Our life is turned
> Out of her course, wherever man is made
> An offering, or a sacrifice, a tool
> Or implement, a passive thing employed
> As a brute mean, without acknowledgment
> Of common right or interest in the end.

It is hard for us, who have known at least bits and pieces of Wordsworth from childhood, who see Nature after a hundred and fifty years of him; for us who have been to the Lake District and stumbled, cursing Wordsworth, on the screes of Great Gable; for us whose hearts regularly leap up when we behold a rainbow in the sky; for us for whom every Spring the heart with pleasure fills and dances with the daffodils—for us it is very hard indeed, even after careful historical searches, to say that just at such-and-such a time, exactly in such-and-such a way, Wordsworth modified the prevailing taste and vision of Englishmen.

A writer remarked in the *Saturday Review* in 1858:

> It is odd enough that Wordsworth's personal influence with his friend Sir George Beaumont did not lead him to see—or if he saw, to repent

of—the falsity of the conventional brown tree, for Wordsworth's was a life-long protest against the brown tree in poetry.

He helped to give people new eyes, and he, more than any one other man, changed their taste in landscape. It would be wrong to say that nobody would ever have come to like mountains or have gone for a holiday to Snowdonia or the Lakes if Wordsworth had never lived. But as Wordsworth did live and write, the two things grew up inextricably intermingled. And the very railways that Wordsworth cursed for breaking his mountain seclusion made available to tourists, as they thought, the spiritualising, ennobling influence about which the poet himself had so much to say. It was an awkward paradox, that in the Wordsworth household, when the terminus of the railway was at Birthwaite, the phrase "people from Birthwaite" should have been used to convey horror and contempt, while it was the poet's works more than anything that had brought them there. In Mrs Wordsworth's widowhood there was a flagrant case; some young strangers actually got into the garden, and the old lady in the well-known tone of recognising evil said, "Boys from Birthwaite"; a chase was made, and the centre of the party was found to be the Prince of Wales; so far had Wordsworthianism penetrated by 1857.

By 1864 a Wordsworth anthology appeared, *Our English Lakes, Mountains and Waterfalls*, with all the most obviously descriptive local passages chosen. Each was illustrated by an actual photographic print stuck into the book—those wonderful early photographs, revelling in the detailed clarity of fern and leaf and falling water. The "dear native regions", to which even the schoolboy Wordsworth had thought always to look back, had become a national source of secondhand uplift through the medium of sun-pictures. And every summer from Oxford and Cambridge came the earnest young men on reading parties, from Arnold's Rugby, and Jowett's Balliol, and the John's which had the Pickersgill portrait of the poet that had made the servants weep, young men ready for fishing and walking and swimming and taking headers, ready to fall, perhaps, like Philip Hewson for a "lovely potato-uprooter" and the simple life, rather than for the sweet young things in elastic-sided boots whose hearts were leaping up as they were ferning by the waterfalls or scurrying back to the farm for rum-butter at tea. For these young men there was Aristotle in the morning, or Herodotus on Egypt, but in the afternoons there was the enjoyment of just that one thing which all the wealth of ancient literature, all Homer and Virgil, all the Greek dramatists, all Horace and Catullus, all the pastoral poets like Theocritus and even the Virgil of the *Georgics*, all Hesiod of *The Works and Days*, had somehow failed to provide—that one unique, inexplicable, unintelligible sense

> sublime
> Of something far more deeply interfused,
> Whose dwelling is the light of setting suns,
> And the round ocean and the living air,
> And the blue sky, and in the mind of man:
> A motion and a spirit that impels
> All thinking things, all objects of all thought,
> And rolls through all things.

That sense seemed to them something quite new and quite unique in all the literature of the world.

Not even the clever reviewer, Mr Dallas of *The Times*, could explain it in the sixties: even he, who had seen the social import of the later Ruskin, who had judged the Wordsworth cult of Nature and solitude and simple things for the element of "misanthropy" which lay within it, even he could not explain this magic appeal of Nature to Wordsworth's hidden soul, giving him a "vague hint of a world of life beyond consciousness, the world which art and poetry are ever working towards". He saw that Wordsworth revealed the essential "secrecy of art", that in *Tintern Abbey* and the *Ode on the Intimations of Immortality* he "is describing, with all the clearness he can command, the know-not-what—the vanishing effects produced in his consciousness by the veiled energy of his hidden life".

This is a language which I think we now understand more clearly than that of the Reverend Stopford Brooke in his very intelligent and interesting lectures on the Theology of Wordsworth,

44

given in St James's Chapel in 1872. It is a language which one
other Victorian writer would also have most deeply understood,
a writer who, as a Roman Catholic priest, had no bias towards
Wordsworth's philosophy or later religion—I mean Gerard Manley
Hopkins, whose critical insight has even now not had its due. He
was one of the young men of the reading-party kind in the sixties—
he just missed the Lakes one year and went to Horsham instead.
Then, in his maturity, he wrote in 1886 about Wordsworth, thinking mainly of the *Ode on the Intimations:*

> There have been in all history a few, a very few men, whom common
> repute, even where it did not trust them, has treated as having had some-
> thing happen to them that does not happen to other men, as having *seen*
> *something*, whatever that really was. Plato is the most famous of these.
> ... Human nature in these men saw something, got a shock; wavers in
> opinion, looking back, whether there was anything in it or no; but is in
> a tremble ever since. Now what Wordsworthians mean is, what would
> seem to be the growing mind of the English speaking world ... is that
> in Wordsworth when he wrote that ode human nature got another of
> those shocks, and the tremble from it is spreading. This opinion I do
> strongly share; I am, ever since I knew the ode, in that tremble. ...
> Wordsworth was an imperfect artist, as you say: as his matter varied in
> importance and as he varied in insight ... so does the value of his work
> vary. Now the interest and importance of the matter were here of the
> highest, his insight was at its very deepest. ... For my part I should
> think St George and St Thomas of Canterbury wore roses in heaven for
> England's sake on the day that ode, not without their intercession, was
> penned.

PETERLOO I*

A HUNDRED and twenty years ago today it was fine and hot in the country round Manchester. In the early morning in many towns and villages men began to form up, in order to march to the greatest meeting for Parliamentary Reform that there had ever been.

They were working men, almost all of them—weavers, spinners, fustian-cutters, hatters—belonging to the various trades that even then made South Lancashire famous all the world over. They were poor and anxious; they were hard hit by the post-war slump; wages were miserably low and thousands were unemployed, without a dole.

But they were hopeful and happy; some marched to a bugle, some to a band; all carried banners, woven by their friends and bearing such mottoes as these: "No Corn Laws", "Universal Suffrage", "Annual Parliaments", worked in bright colours; one only was black, and bore the legend: "Equal Representation or Death", and before it danced a diminutive surgeon singing a song of triumph.

In some of the marching parties were Unions of Female Reformers, dressed in an elegant uniform of white and blue, while in others the women marched beside the men and took their children with them. Some wore laurel in their hats, as a sign of peace. All came in a gay spirit, as if it were a Reformers' Easter.

But the magistrates and other authorities of Manchester looked on the day in another light: this was a dangerous invasion of their town from the country districts. For four years past they had assumed that every movement for Parliamentary Reform had bloody revolution at its heart.

Their spies and informers had exaggerated every whiff of discontent that suggested physical force: only two years before,

* *News Chronicle,* 16 Aug 1939.

46

Habeas Corpus had been suspended mainly on their evidence, and peaceful honest men had been sent to gaol without trial. They had persistently discounted all good that might be said for the Reformers, and in a narrow spirit of loyalty to Church and King had been only too ready to believe the worst.

They had even raised a Corps of Volunteer Cavalry to help their inadequate and venal Police: and the Manchester Yeomanry—dull sons of merchants and shopkeepers, employed on August 16 in a stupid mood of vengeance and local pride—have won for battle-honours the execrations of history.

Among the Reformers were a few who believed that violence was their only hope of redress. Trade unions were illegal; the Parish Relief for the unemployed was hopelessly inadequate and badly administered; the wolf was at the door.

It would be easy to make out a defence of violent measures: but even so, the great majority were intent on peace, and marched to Manchester in the naïve belief that a "Radical Reform in the Commons House of Parliament" would automatically cure the multiform and ghastly ills they suffered under.

This belief had been encouraged by some of the best men of the time. In 1816–17 Cobbett's *Political Register* had been read with almost religious reverence in chapels and gardens on Sunday afternoons; old Major Cartwright, who had been a Reformer since the 1770's, seemed a fusion of Jeremiah with Job: and other less convincing and less dignified leaders had urged opinion to the same ends.

Of these other leaders the most popular was Henry Hunt, who was to be chairman of the great Manchester meeting of August 16. His sincerity was the better half of his vanity; but he had caught the popular imagination so far that a young wife, watching her husband taken to prison by armed guards, could stand on the door-step shouting "Hunt and Liberty!"

On the 16th he arrived in a long and slow procession at "the area near St Peter's Church" over an hour late; and the waiting bands, which had been playing to the crowd of 60,000 people such tunes as "God Save the King" and "Rule, Britannia", struck up

47

"See the Conquering Hero Comes". He came to the hustings: the crowd pressed up closer to hear him, wedged one against another almost to suffocation.

But he had scarcely begun to speak when there was a disturbance on the far fringe. A troop of the Manchester Yeomanry had ridden round a corner with drawn swords.

The crowd cheered, and the Yeomanry had scarcely cheered in answer when they began to ride for the hustings. People fell in front of them, some trampled by the horses, others cut by the swords. They had been ordered by the magistrates to execute a warrant of arrest against Hunt and others on the platform.

Many of these amateur soldiers were drunk; they could not ride; they could not manage their swords; and when the arrests were made they lost their tempers, cried "Have at their Flags", and ran amok among the crowd.

Then a body of the 15th Hussars, whose Waterloo medals flashed in the sun, came up at the magistrates' orders and charged across the ground to "rescue the Yeomanry".

The crowd could not escape: jammed by their own numbers and jammed by the narrow exits, they were caught either by the sober and disciplined advance of the Hussars or by the captious fury of the Yeomanry. Eleven were killed and nearly five hundred seriously wounded. There were women and children among them.

When the trumpets sounded for the troops to re-form, there were literally heaps of hurt and struggling people on the ground. The Prince Regent, through his Home Secretary, Lord Sidmouth, sent his congratulations to the magistrates and to the Manchester Yeomanry.

The historical importance of Peterloo cannot be exaggerated. It was the death of the reactionary system that had grown up in the Napoleonic wars, and almost at a single stroke it won over the middle classes to Parliamentary Reform and made their triumph in 1832 possible. By an irony of history the men who marched to Peterloo put their employers (not to say their enemies) into power.

Its importance to us is hardly less; for the disaster of that day is a classical example of executive mismanagement. The Home

Office had both misunderstood the state of opinion in the country and also misunderstood its local representatives, who are today the Police.

If Peterloo, because of its famous nickname, remains in every schoolboy's memory, it should remind him always in after life that an executive which is not submitted to severe and informed criticism in every move it takes verges towards both incompetence and tyranny.

PETERLOO II*

A CLEARLY defined historical incident like the "Peterloo Massacre", an incident which, though its antecedents and consequences may have the widest bearings, was itself confined to a short space of time and a limited area, under the eyes of many witnesses, can have an inestimable value and interest to the student of literature as well as to the historian. For the whole conception of what the "incident" was, is built up in the words of those who wrote and spoke about it. Literature, so to speak, makes the event; it is in its literary forms that the incident is afterwards accessible.

The literature of Peterloo is magnificently rich; in newspaper reports, speeches, memoirs, autobiographies, pamphlets, poems, the reports of trials, letters official and private, and in memoranda of every conceivable kind the events of that day were described, argued about and refined to the last possible legal quibble. There can be few such short episodes in English history so thoroughly and so ably documented ; we have the words of the most exalted and the humblest kind of people in the country, people speaking in their own idiom faithfully recorded, people writing under the stress of great emotion with all the resources of experienced rhetoric. There is extant about Peterloo almost every kind of language, used with almost every kind of purpose, expecting almost every kind of response in those who read or heard it. The eyewitness accounts alone have this range.

A mere bibliography would stretch to many pages: here it is possible only to hint at the depths of interest that the comparison of these accounts contains. One of the fullest and best of them all is given by Samuel Bamford in his autobiography *Passages in the Life of a Radical*, a book which still currently passes for famous, but is far less well known than it deserves to be. Bamford was a

* Not published before.

Middleton hand-loom weaver (though he had done many other jobs in his time), and was the leader of one of the parties that marched in to the meeting from the country. He had written a number of verses and songs, and was known as the poet of radicalism. Immediately after Peterloo he was urged, he said in the *Passages*,

> to write something, in the metrical way, about the Manchester affair, but I never did; it never presented itself, as it were, to me in the form of poetry; it was too overpowering, too brimful of affliction, to be measured in verse. I made several attempts that way, but it would not do, and I never sought to describe it in any other form until this present publication.

In fact he published nothing in the first rush of controversy, and his book appeared as reminiscences, twenty years later, when he saw the booksellers' windows filled with *Pickwick*, *Nicholas Nickleby*, and *Jack Sheppard*, and he believed he could do something better than "the trashy, unreal novels which the press deigned to extol". He was to compete, not with Shelley, but with Dickens.

The *Mask of Anarchy*, recommending a sort of Gandhi-like passive resistance, had imaged the ideal behaviour of a crowd when charged by cavalry:

> Stand ye calm and resolute,
> Like a forest close and mute,
> With folded arms and looks which are
> Weapons of unvanquished war,
>
> And let Panic, who outspeeds
> The career of armèd steeds
> Pass, a disregarded shade
> Through your phalanx undismayed.

And Bamford put in prose what happened as he saw it:

> On the cavalry drawing up they were received with a shout of goodwill, as I understood it. They shouted again, waving their sabres over their heads; and then, slackening rein, and striking spur into their steeds, they dashed forward and began cutting the people.

"Stand fast," I said, "they are riding upon us; stand fast." And there was a general cry in our quarter of "Stand fast". The cavalry were in confusion; they evidently could not, with all the weight of man and horse, penetrate that compact mass of human beings; and their sabres were plied to hew a way through naked held-up hands and defenceless heads; and then chopped limbs and wound-gaping skulls were seen; and groans and cries were mingled with the din of that horrid confusion. "Ah! ah!" "for shame! for shame!" was shouted. Then, "Break! break! they are killing them in front, and they cannot get away"; and there was a general cry of "break! break." For a moment the crowd held back as in a pause; then was a rush, heavy and resistless as a head-long sea, and a sound like low thunder, with screams, prayers, and imprecations from the crowd-moiled and sabre-doomed who could not escape.

This seems in Bamford's account to fuse together the first advance of the Manchester Yeomanry in their hopeless attempt to arrest the speakers and the later charge of the Regulars. And here is the same part of the day's business described by W. J. H. Jolliffe, who was then a Lieutenant with the detachment (four troops) of the 15th Hussars:

We advanced along the south side of this space of ground, without a halt or pause even: the words "Front!" and "Forward!" were given, and the trumpet sounded the charge at the very moment the threes wheeled up. When fronted, our line extended quite across the ground, which, in all parts, was so filled with people that their hats seemed to touch.

It was then, for the first time, that I saw the Manchester troop of Yeomanry: they were scattered singly, or in small groups, over the greater part of the field, literally hemmed up, and hedged into the mob, so that they were powerless either to make an impression or to escape: in fact, they were in the power of those whom they were designed to over-awe; and it required only a glance to discover their helpless position, and the necessity of our being brought to their rescue. . . .

The charge of the hussars, to which I have just alluded, swept this mingled mass of human beings before it: people, yeomen, and con-stables, in their confused attempts to escape, ran one over the other; so that, by the time we had arrived at the end of the field, the fugitives were literally piled up to a considerable elevation above the level of the ground.

This was part of a formal statement written twenty-five years later, which was printed in full in the *Life of Lord Sidmouth*.

Even Bamford writing his account was writing consciously for publication, and he knew that he had some literary skill. It is in the crowds of witnesses in the Trial Reports that the freshest and most spontaneous eyewitness accounts are to be found; these reports bring us as close as any historical document can to the actual spoken idiom of the ordinary people who saw the events of Peterloo. Various shorthand methods were employed in the reports; but on internal evidence alone it is possible to see that some do give a very close approximation to the exact words spoken in Court. You can catch almost the intonations and hesitations; this is something no editor could supply; the style of such reports is their own authentification. The *Report of the Proceedings in the Cause Redford v. Birley and Others*, taken from the shorthand notes of Farquharson and published by Wheeler of Manchester, is one of the best of them. This was a test action for damages brought by one of the wounded people against members of the Manchester Yeomanry; the hearing began on 2 April 1822.

Here is Shelley's stanza from *The Mask of Anarchy* about the cavalry using their swords:

> Let the horsemen's scimitars
> Wheel and flash, like sphereless stars
> Thirsting to eclipse their burning
> In a sea of death and mourning.

And here is part of the evidence given in *Redford v. Birley & Ors.* by John Jones, fustian-cutter, of 14 Windmill Street, Manchester:

Q. Did you see the Yeomanry Cavalry come into the field?
A. I did.

       *   *   *   *   *

Q. Did the people try to escape?
A. The people fled in all directions, they were riding over men, women, and children.
Q. Did you see any thing more?
A. There came a great mass of people against my door then—they were jammed against my door; the Cavalry came up and struck them;

53

the people were groaning and skriking, till an officer came up and said
"gentlemen, forbear, forbear; the people cannot get away."

Q. Did you see any stones thrown at the Yeomanry?

A. I saw none, but one; and that was when they were scouring the
croft.

Q. Did you see any provocation given to the military that day?

A. No sir, I did not; at my door there was a woman killed, and a man
suffocated.

Jones was then cross-examined about what had happened earlier
in the meeting:

Q. Now as each of these divisions came on the ground, there was a
great shout?

A. There was, I believe; there were shouts many times.

Q. And a tremendous shout when Mr Hunt came?

A. I believe there was.

Q. And when the Cavalry came on the ground?

A. A shout from the Cavalry, and then from the populace.

Q. From the Cavalry first?

A. I cannot say if the Cavalry shouted first; but when they came, they
flourished their swords round, and then there was a shout.

Re-examined by Mr Evans

Q. Whichever shouted first, the Cavalry shouted as well as the
people?

A. They might have shouted; they brandished their swords—it is all
the same.

> Let the horsemen's scimitars
> Wheel and flash, like sphereless stars
> Thirsting to eclipse their burning
> In a sea of death and mourning.

"They might have shouted; they brandished their swords—it is
all the same." "At my door there was a woman killed and a man
suffocated."

It is no serious objection to Jones's evidence that he was speaking
over two years after the events. It is true also that his wife had
been a witness for the defence in the trial of Henry Hunt and

Others in 1820. But however much a witness is primed, however much he has talked and read about a case, he cannot possibly rehearse the exact words and idiom and rhythm of his answers, least of all in cross-examination and re-examination, where the questions may be unexpected; and it is exactly in the words and rhythms that Jones's answers are so effective and so moving. Much of the substance of them he must have said before, and heard and read before: but the precise way of putting things was his own and extempore, and it cannot have been invented for him by the shorthand-writer or the editor. The exact method of reporting by verbatim question and answer has here done more than preserve evidence on which to form considered judgment and to make a summary for a history text-book; it has perpetuated a whole attitude to the event as sensitive and as clear as a highly-wrought and intelligent poem.

Now the Shelley poem is a long privately-mythological exhortation to the people of England. Though Shelley himself said that two of his chief abominations were Lord Eldon and didactic poetry:

> Next came Fraud, and he had on,
> Like Eldon, an ermined gown;
> His big tears, for he wept well,
> Turned to mill-stones as they fell:

yet *The Mask of Anarchy* is in effect a didactic poem, and his wife described his motives in writing it:

> The news of the Manchester Massacre . . . roused in him violent emotions of indignation and compassion. The great truth that the many, if accordant and resolute, could control the few, as was shown some years after, made him long to teach his injured countrymen how to resist. Inspired by these feelings he wrote the *Mask of Anarchy*, which he sent to his friend Leigh Hunt, to be inserted in the *Examiner*, of which he was then the Editor.

Leigh Hunt did not insert it, and did not publish it till 1832, because he thought "that the public at large had not become sufficiently discerning to do justice to the sincerity and kind-heartedness of the spirit that walked in this flaming robe of verse".

55

There was also, of course, the risk of prosecution for libel or seditious libel.

This whole episode makes one wonder whether Shelley's professed hatred of didactic poetry was not wiser than his practice; for though the purpose of *The Mask of Anarchy* was to rouse pity and indignation for the past and present, and political hope for the future, it is just the "flaming robe of verse" that obscures these purposes; there is no coalescing imaginative adjustment between the imagery and the facts. The refrain addressed to the English people illustrates just this weakness:

> Rise like Lions after slumber
> In unvanquishable number,
> Shake your chains to earth like dew
> Which in sleep had fallen on you—
> Ye are many—they are few.

As one reads Bamford's autobiography, the evidence of John Jones and his wife, the account by Prentice in his *Historical Sketches and Personal Recollections of Manchester*, and so on, all these Lancashire people do not appear much like lions, and not at all as if they had been slumbering; the old image of the chains is stale and feeble compared with their vigorous descriptions of their lives and troubles and sufferings. Jones's evidence rouses in me far more pity and indignation than *The Mask of Anarchy*: and it has this effect just because of its style.

To say this is not to express a crude preference for the literal to the metaphorical, for the direct over the oblique; it is not just to fail to try to understand what poetry is aiming at: it is rather to say that this particular poetry, which claims to have a bearing upon action, fails of its own purpose just because its imagery does not imply the imaginative assimilation of the facts with which that action would have to deal. Generous indignation and the "flaming robe of verse" are not enough. The men of England to whom this poem is addressed are a thin fiction:

> And at length when ye complain
> With a murmur weak and vain

> 'Tis to see the Tyrant's crew
> Ride over your wives and you—
> Blood is on the grass like dew.

This view of the weakly, vainly murmuring sufferers is a myth about ghosts when put up against the characters in Bamford's *Passages*. "Doctor" Healey dancing and singing his song of triumph at the head of his detachment on the march to Peterloo would not at all like to have been told that his song was "a murmur weak and vain". And against the etiolated democrats of Shelley's "slaves" and "lions after slumber", it is good to put the case of Thomas Blinstone, as reported by Prentice. He was an old man of seventy-four who stood at the edge of the crowd as a spectator when the Yeomanry first came round the wall; they rode over him, broke both his arms, badly bruised his body and disabled him for life. When he was interviewed by the Relief Committee he said:

> And what is wur than aw, mesters, they'n broken my spectacles, and aw've ne'er yet been able to get a pair that suits me.

It is a speech, and a kind of speech, that Shelley never heard, and all his poetry suffers for it. But Shakespeare knew about this sort of thing, and in his history plays we have just the multiform variety of idiom and rhythm and vocabulary that the documents for Peterloo provide.

SHELLEY I*

FOR thousands now alive a passionate love of Shelley was a major experience in their young development—a love not only for particular poems, but for an idea of Shelley and the Shelley style; yet there are few in whom this passion has lasted into later life. This is acknowledged even by Mr Lea, who is opposed to all that it implies. The common view is, briefly, that the delight does not last because there is something immature in the poetry itself. This is not new; it was well and clearly stated by J. A. Symonds in 1878:

> There was no defect of power in him, but a defect of patience; and the final word to be pronounced in estimating the larger bulk of his poetry is the word immature.

That was written before Dowden's *Life* and before Arnold's essay, which was a review of it; before the "inspired child" critiques of the nineties and all that derived from them; it was written, in fact, in the middle of a century in which, according to Mr Lea, eulogy was the rule, and long before 1933, when he says "a Bull was published declaring Shelley to be bad, after all". He adds, that disparagement now carries the day, and that "no satisfactory full-length study of either Shelley's work or his life has so far appeared in this country, making use of all the available material". But there have been good books and better essays on Shelley in England which do not all get caught on the dilemma of false eulogy or disparagement which Mr Lea has prepared for them.

The immediately relevant question is: Why should it be thought any disparagement at all to say that Shelley is adolescent and the bulk of his work immature? For it is surely just this that gives it its unquestioned power, its unique character in our literature. His

* *New Statesman & Nation*, 1 Dec 1945, reviewing *Shelley and the Romantic Revolution* by F. A. Lea (Routledge).

58

poetry enthralls boys (girls rather less, I fancy) as no other poetry enthralls them—the rush of images based on light, sea, clouds and mountains; the impatience with authority; the "passion for reforming the world"; the "idealisms of moral excellence"; the unflagging fantasy; Greece for the classical side, astronomy and botany for the modern, and even for the Army Class the series of dream girls (in *Alastor*, *Epipsychidion*, etc.) who exalt Narcissistic imaginings into regions of beautiful mystery. The vagueness, profusion and complexity of the images are among the greatest attractions; it is indeed poetry "not perfectly understood"; but it is poetry loved with greater intensity and passion than any poetry afterwards. The strongest evidence of Shelley's essential immaturity is his unfailing popularity with the young. But adolescence is never wholly superseded in any man, not even in those who (to quote Mr Lea) "have left behind with their youth less of their intolerance than their generosity". Not only can past experience be recalled by Shelley with peculiar vividness; but there is an immature element in most adult situations, and Shelley is the supreme poet of exactly that.

I find it hard to appraise this book because, of the two later phases of response to Shelley which Mr Lea describes, I have experienced only one, and that imperfectly. Even in adolescence there seemed to be "an element of supreme value in *Adonais*", and I agree that Phase 2 is an attempt to explain whence this value derives; but I cannot agree that this attempt, by inducing us to follow Shelley into "an intellectual mysticism that leads straight to despair", must make Phase 2 intolerable as a lodging-place. For the contradictions and despair in face of death which *Adonais* expresses are only one mood of human feeling among many. We do not go to *Adonais*, or to Shelley at all, for a system, or for a final answer about anything, but for an experience. To be committed neck and crop to a considered philosophy of despair by reading the works of one poet is simply not a normal response at all.

In Phase 3, Shelley becomes for Mr Lea not a man or a poet but a "pure phenomenon" (of the kind that D. H. Lawrence became for Mr Middleton Murry, whose work colours all Mr Lea's judgments) "all equally significant, because of the order to which he belongs". Here I resign; I claim to be temperamentally disqualified; and suggest the banal alternative that to understand Shelley we must see him whole and see him plain. To this end it is important to follow the way he seized on certain philosophical ideas and the use he made of them in his verse: Mr Lea's book is for this purpose a useful and, so far as the matter permits, lucid guide. The genesis of these ideas is described more fully than before, with good quotations, especially from the less well-known prose. But the philosophical understanding is far less than in Miss Powell's admirable essay in *The Romantic Theory of Poetry* (1926); and not all Mr Lea's honest and painstaking revelation of contradictions, unresolved problems, imperfect arguments and uncorrelated experiences can convince me that Shelley was as great a philosopher as he was a poet.

SHELLEY II

If last week a boy had said: "I love what I've read of Shelley's poems and want to know something about his life, the sort of man he was and what he did", what could one have honestly recommended? Dowden, with simpering flights of imagination where evidence failed? Walter Peck, with two vast fascines of fact bound in pedantic American haywire? Arnold, with "What a set!"? Maurois, with paper boats right up to the last? All quite unsuitable: even Shelley's own letters wouldn't do, as collected in the Ingpen edition. In feeble doubt one might have given him Symonds's book in the English Men of Letters series or Olwen Ward Campbell's *Shelley and the Unromantics*. Now, for several generations, there will be no doubt.

This book * is not only a great achievement in itself, but an event in the mental history of the future. Wherever English is spoken or taught, Shelley is with the young a focus and stimulus of enthusiasm for poetry and for politics: to the young they are both modes of imaginative activity, and Shelley thought of them always as closely linked. Much therefore depends on the idea of him that is formed.

Mr Blunden starts with the belief that Shelley was one of the plainest examples of "the supreme capacity called genius", and that "his adventurous and many-sided life" was "unified by a deepening faith in the artist's duty and power in human advancement". Even by Regency standards his life was odd, and Mr Blunden's triumph is that he has made this oddity human, credible and sympathetic; he has neither exalted nor toned down, vulgarised nor explained away. By deliberately compressing his work into one volume he has been able to bring out the unity he stresses: every sentence

---

* *Shelley—A Life Story* by Edmund Blunden (Collins). Reviewed *New Statesman & Nation*, 11 May 1946.

tells, and the book is full of vitality. He is, perhaps, the only man living who could have done this, because of the quality of his knowledge; it is altogether scholarly—he moves with ease this way and that through the unholy jungle of documents, complicated by biased reminiscence, false gossip, suppression and forgery: he knows not only Shelley but the period, the other people and the places—but beyond scholarship he has a deep, familiar, imaginative understanding which brings Shelley into intelligible relations with a full and vivid world. The reader feels confidence in his rightness and integrity from the start. The home life at Field Place, Sir Bysshe, the family connection with the Dukes of Norfolk, the Horsham tradesmen, the local traditions of St Leonard's forest, all slip at once into convincing perspective. The legend that life at Eton was an unresting orgy of flogging and fisticuffs quietly gives place to a portrait of a living and exciting school where Shelley suffered persecution and misery certainly, but where he also had some success, some happiness and fun, a school which actually taught him very thoroughly what it claimed to teach! For Eton must have its share of credit for Shelley's absorbing, infinitely fruitful love of the Classics.

The book's next great merit is its re-distribution of emphasis. Mr Blunden has refused to measure the importance of an episode by the amount of evidence about it that happens to have survived, or the amount of others' speculations. Thus, the Oxford chapter, though clear and full enough, is short: Miss Hitchener and Fanny Imlay take properly minor places: Hogg, who later imposed himself grandiosely on Shelley literature, is reduced in stature without being slighted. The treatment of the Godwins is ingenious: there is no full-dress description of the Skinner Street household; even the crucial meetings with Mary are done very economically; but Godwin runs all through the book like a malaria which, once caught, may suddenly without warning bring on horrible fevers. Perhaps the biggest positive change of emphasis is in the importance given to Leigh Hunt and "the Hampstead set". This is no fanciful predilection of Hunt's biographer; but his knowledge makes possible a fresh and necessary view of Shelley, showing how the Hampstead evenings saved him when his nerves were bare to every breeze during the crisis of Harriet's death and the Chancery suit; and also how through them his literary isolation was modified and his range of sympathies increased. Mr Blunden is specially good in suggesting the reasons why the acquaintanceship between Shelley and Keats never matured, and in the biographical analysis of *Adonais*. In all the later chapters the balance between the Hunt group and the Byron group is nicely kept, each contributing so much to Shelley, and each receiving so much from him.

The poems are treated throughout as incidents in the life, and are criticised mainly from that angle. Mr Blunden exerts his sharpest and most moving writing to describe the local and emotional settings which stirred Shelley to creation. The avoidance of ambitious speculative interpretations is a guarantee that this book will last; skill and judgment have controlled it everywhere, but it is mostly Shelley who speaks, or his friends who speak about him, or a scene is calmly and impersonally reconstructed. There is some lyricism, but no indecent ecstasy. Some readers may complain that there is not enough about Shelley's ideas, his philosophical reading, his intellectual development: they are deliberately excluded except as affecting what he did. For this is " a life story", a "narrative", and it is wiser to sympathise with the author in his hard decisions about what to exclude than to blame him for not doing what he never meant to do. Only a lifetime of familiarity with the sources could have made these decisions so sure, and in result so splendidly effective.

One major exclusion must have cost Mr Blunden many qualms: there are no references of any kind, no footnotes and no bibliography. The book thus looks clean and attractive to the general reader, and tells its own tale; but thousands of readers will regret it. Let us hope these thousands will be able to get a copy, too; happily the state of the text suggests that the Collins Clear-Type Press has been misprinting at high pressure to meet an inevitable huge demand.

SHELLEY III

FEW of those who write about Shelley treat him primarily as a poet. Professor Hughes calls him without question "the supreme lyrist of our tongue"; yet no line of argument in his book leads up to this tremendous conclusion, nor does he even say directly which poems he thinks supreme. Shelley is himself partly responsible for the way his critics treat him: he gave little concentrated thought to problems of expression, language, style and all the methods of poetry. On his own theory the term "poetry" could cover much else besides creative literature. Few artists of his stature have said less about the difficulties of their medium; and few men so interested in philosophy, so acute even in philosophical argument, have seemed less disturbed by the logical problems of language.

.Professor Hughes's book * is in the main another study of Shelley's metaphysics, religion, ethics, and politics. In order to demonstrate the growth of his ideas, it includes a detailed biography up to the spring of 1831, the time of *Queen Mab*. The book makes jerky reading; the car moves on through air-pockets of awkward rhetoric; around its way innumerable influences roll and countless sources are diffused, "an ever-varying glory". The journey is uncomfortable but rewarding. What is one shown at its end?

> Shelley died [says the guide] a troubled spirit, in the midst of upheaval, in a defiant faith and wild and pining hopes. . . . He dreams a young man's dream. And in an age awakening to intimations of a spiritual immanence alike in Man and Nature he is among the writers most conscious of it. Nothing in English poetry is quite like the little lyrics that distil his melancholy each in a handful of notes and blend him with the life of things, or his repossession of the fancy—or more than fancy—that made the primal myths and bore the seed of all idealisms. The denizens of his earth and heaven are a host of Shelleys.

---

* *The Nascent Mind of Shelley* by A. M. D. Hughes (Oxford). Reviewed *New Statesman & Nation*, 26 July 1947.

But what the guide points out is not always what the tourist best sees; and by some curious accident of arrangement I saw at the end of this journey a Shelley who was primarily a man of action. Mr Blunden has lately done all that can be done to bring the young farmer to life and kill the ineffectual angel; and here he gets unexpected support. For poetry was to Shelley a form of action, and he took to it because he found it was the form of action he was best at. Public speeches, pamphlets, literature dropped in "a woman's hood of a cloak", money spent on dykes and drainage, dinners with the Duke of Norfolk, had proved ineffectual indeed; but something had to be done and done at once. It is the restless urge to achieve, to influence, to convince, that strikes out from Professor Hughes's demonstration of the dates and fluctuations and inconsistencies of Shelley's philosophical ideas. The aim is certainly to make "the denizens of his earth a host of Shelleys". But how can they now respond?

All Shelley's poetry is in some sense or degree didactic; even the ending of the *Ode to the West Wind* begs the wind to be the "trumpet of a prophecy". The proper status for the reader of didactic poetry is to be a pupil, willing and convinced or not, as one is with Lucretius. But the reader of Shelley is forced, by the style and drive and method, to identify himself with the poet. The effect is an experience, not a doctrine communicated. Shelley's success or failure in any poem is to be measured by the extent to which the essential experience is accessible. And in nearly every case the experience *includes* the desire to convince others of its validity for them. Shelley is always insistently personal, even when detachment is his theme. That is why Professor Hughes is right to link the ideas to the life; but he gives the external events in more circumstantial detail than is necessary to stress the psychological peculiarities in Shelley's personal relationships.

Bradley said of Wordsworth (and by implication also of Shelley) that his natural religion was "more profoundly expressed in his descriptions of his experience than in his attempts to formulate it". The attempts at formulation are not properly philosophy so much as an inferior kind of imaginative literature. The great terms,

"Intellectual Beauty", "Liberty", "Spirit of Nature", and, most of all, "Love", which Shelley used to describe ultimate and perfect Being, have immense emotive power, but, unless the context of the poem limits and controls the emotions they awaken, each reader is at the mercy of his own associations. A knowledge of the historical background and sources of these terms may lead to the acceptance of a faith in natural mysticism of the kind that Shelley himself was trying to formulate; but the substance of such a faith is not to be found in Shelley alone, nor, as Professor Hughes points out, did he reach a formulation which satisfied himself. The perfect literature of "The One" is exquisite, harmonious silence. There never was a less silent poet than Shelley.

> Teach me half the gladness
> That thy brain must know,
> Such harmonious madness
> From my lips would flow
> The world should listen then—as I am listening now.

The desire was to become ever more vocal, to convince ever more hearers.

SHELLEY IV

THE recent run of books about Shelley does not seem to be caused by any revived, fresh or unexpected interest in his poetry. All have assumed that he was a great poet and have professed that only for this reason is his life worth studying or writing about at all. But there has been no serious critical survey of his poetry for its own sake. It may be that there is nothing new to say, that its qualities are self-evident and that criticism is best dumb. But the peculiar way in which he is approached suggests that there are more complicated motives in the minds of those who write about him.

Many have complained at the "chatter about Harriet" and at that kind of interest in Shelley which centres on the fact that he had two wives; but still it seems to be the interaction of his work and life, rather than his work alone, that causes the strong attraction of such various writers. There is little sign that his poetry is more widely, or more attentively, or more lovingly read than it used to be; he is probably far less read for pure pleasure than Keats or Wordsworth; the three great Coleridge poems are probably read more often than any three by Shelley. Shelley is mostly read for some oblique purpose; his poems demand reference to things outside them—to his life, to the reader's life, to causes, to the past and the future, and the fate of the world—to almost anything. As poetry they are very hard to assess, even to enjoy without such references. Trelawny spotted this very early when he wrote: "To form a just idea of his poetry, you should have witnessed his daily life; his words and actions best illustrated his writings." Such a remark would be almost meaningless applied to, say, Keats or Coleridge. Coleridge's actions would form a remarkable series of illustrations to *The Ancient Mariner*.

Trelawny may have been a liar or embroiderer; but many of his Shelley stories do in fact read like prose drafts of Shelley poems, or like episodes out of symbolic journeys. He tried to teach Shelley to swim:

> He doffed his jacket and trowsers, kicked off his shoes and socks, and plunged in, and there he lay stretched out on the bottom like a conger eel, not making the least effort or struggle to save himself. He would have been drowned if I had not instantly fished him out. When he recovered his breath, he said: "I always find the bottom of the well, and they say Truth lies there. In another minute I should have found it, and you would have found an empty shell. It is an easy way of getting rid of the body."

It is like acting a piece of *Alastor* or *The Revolt of Islam*. This and other stories—the discovery of him in the wood by the lake; the reading at the mantelpiece while his dinner was untasted; the plan to solve the great mystery altogether with Jane Williams; the attack at Tanyrallt, to mention just a few—these are things that belong to the world of the poems. All his love affairs are ambiguous in the same sort of way.

It is this ambiguity, this living only partly in the normal world of the senses and of common human acts, that has led so many of his most ardent admirers to talk of angels, eternal children, ethereal beings and so on. It has led others to say flatly that he was mad. Even those like Edmund Blunden who aim to bring out in fullest relief the normalities in Shelley's life—his practical charity, his gaiety of manner when he was happy, his interest in dykes and crops—are labouring to protect him from the grotesque exaggerations of spiritualisers, rather than to deny or to explain away the oddities. It is exactly the interaction of the oddities with the normal, of the poetry with the life, of the idealisms with the fleshly Harriets, Marys and Janes that makes his whole career so interesting and attracts such diverse comments. He epitomises more than any other single Englishman the hungry searching after the infinite, the desire of the moth for the star, which is so typical of Romanticism and of youth. His search lay in a full context; he had not only a well-informed mind, so that history and the writings of others were always ready to hand for use, but he also had such personal charm that his life was full of friends and women onto whom he could project his images of perfection in every phase. Because his life was so full in these two ways there has been much to discover about it and much to say.

Its fullness and its fascination even for unexpected types of mind could not be more clearly shown than in the two immense volumes by Newman Ivey White * which have just been published for the first time in England. Mr White is an American Professor of English who has spent over twenty-five years studying Shelley; he has "had access", as his publishers say, "not only to the source material known by his predecessors but to a great deal of his own discovery". His book, which first appeared in America seven years ago, is an academic biography which consciously and deliberately makes dullness its aim; for Professor White is very honest:

> Attempts to be witty or profound [he writes] commonly warp the straight grain of truth and justice. Cleverness and brilliance usually score their points *for* the biographer and *against* his subject. The "style" may indeed be the man, but it is too often not the man for whom the reader's interest has been engaged.

Yet it is humanly impossible to write in any language without a "style". The ideal of styleless biography for a scholar is to print nothing but the source documents; any linking or commentary must have a style. Scholars can have good styles, as Bentley and Housman have shown; Masson has shown that they can have bad styles. For a writer on Shelley, of all people, to minimise the importance of style is bad enough; but it is far worse than to employ a bad one. Professor White often paraphrases his sources in such a way as to kill their essential quality; and his own links and comments have none of the virtues of the best American prose, which is at least brisk. I have not checked any of his quotations or references as to their accuracy; but his machinery inspires confidence, and his fullness of treatment demonstrates the fullness of Shelley's life. All the ambiguities and oddities remain essentially untouched, unexplained, unspoiled by Professor White's judicious consideration of the facts.

* *Shelley* by Newman Ivey White. 2 Vols (Secker & Warburg).

Nobody need try to defend Shelley for his blunders; but we do need to understand. Such understanding can be achieved in two ways. It can be achieved first by considering what was positive, clear and unproblematic in Shelley's life, by considering his simpler loves and enthusiasms and happinesses: and, secondly, by recognising that his problems were peculiarly those of an adolescent personality displayed with all the complexity and vigour of a man of genius. An understanding of one positive side of Shelley has just been helped by Mr John Lehmann's Introduction to his anthology called *Shelley in Italy*.* He links Shelley to the Mediterranean and Renaissance tradition in our culture, by stressing first the importance of his Latin and Greek, especially his Greek reading. He says that his language "showed the strength of the latinate diction of the eighteenth century softened by Athenian grace and sparkle". How fairly welcome such phrases fall after Professor White! It seems that we are back in a world that has some significance for ourselves; it is that part of Shelley's world that Peacock most appreciated. Of the journey south through Italy in November 1818 Professor White can say:

> Whoever wishes to see the effects of such a journey upon a lively and intelligent mind should read Shelley's detailed account in the letters, which even the usually unenthusiastic Peacock thought exceptionally fine.

Details follow, but the resonances are all lacking; it is for writers like Mr Lehmann to supply them. They may not know to the last document what Shelley did on any special date, but they can appreciate the beauties and virtues of Shelley's great letters to Peacock, and can relate them to the traditions in which Shelley read and lived. Given Professor White's scope there are, of course, long extracts, but they seem deprived of their sense and fire because of the detail in which they are embedded, and the lack of just that sense of history which Shelley took for granted and Mr Lehmann can appreciate.

* *Shelley in Italy*, an Anthology selected with an Introduction by John Lehmann (Lehmann). Reviewed *New Statesman & Nation*, 1 Nov 1947.

But neither Mr Lehmann nor Professor White faces all the implications of Shelley's journey to Italy in 1818. It was almost as much an escape as was Byron's self-imposed exile. Shelley travelled in the style of a gentleman with his own servants, less formally than his father on the Grand Tour, but in the same expectation of deference. His most furious radical poems of the Peterloo year come from Italy with a smug tinge; and they were never published till after his death. For all his intentions to be practical he was completely out of touch with the politics of the years following the suspension of Habeas Corpus. His living in Italy was itself one of the ambiguities which need understanding; it was a release into a world gloriously rich in association, but removed from responsibility; its scenery was like the succession of his own poetic images; the ruins of faiths and empires were there daily to view; one could eat grapes sitting on the fallen monument of a tyrant; the sky was like Panthea's eyes. "This Poem", he wrote of the *Prometheus*,

> was chiefly written upon the mountainous ruins of the Baths of Caracalla, among the flowery glades, and thickets of odoriferous blossoming trees, which are extended in ever winding labyrinths upon its immense platforms and dizzy arches suspended in the air. The bright blue sky of Rome, and the effect of the vigorous awakening spring in that divinest climate, and the new life with which it drenches the spirits even to intoxication, were the inspiration of this drama.

Italy did not so much enrich Shelley's life as order a richness that was already there; it showed himself to himself; that is one of the gains of escape into exile.

He no more than others could escape from his own character and from memory; but in Italy even the violent swinging from extreme to extreme in his personal relationships began to be more controlled; Mary became of more importance to him. His disillusioned comments on Emilia lack the ghastly and intolerant venom of his attacks on Eliza Westbrook and Miss Hitchener; the old situations recur, but with lessened consequences. Shelley had a power ⸒ cause others unhappiness in proportion to his power to charm them; his cruelties grew out of his highest aspirations; he loaded people with his own most passionate ideals and hopes, and hated when they faded. Even before *Epipsychidion* he showed that he knew well enough what he was liable to do:

> I fear thy kisses, gentle maiden,
> Thou needest not fear mine;
> My spirit is too deeply laden
> Ever to burthen thine.

> I fear thy mien, thy tones, thy motion,
> Thou needest not fear mine;
> Innocent is the heart's devotion
> With which I worship thine.

These small casual verses show an awareness of his own attitude to people; they express a clarity of intention which his actions, as he knew, belied. He did burthen people, and then resented it. All his doctrine depended on the innocent devotion of the heart, not only on its possibility, but on its reality. His life was a succession of starts to realise it, all intense. This is what makes it so fascinating. One can see, even behind Professor White's huge façade of "Shelley scholarship", the yearning boy whose painful hopes to do good in the world are lit by Shelley. It is a light which biographers must refract.

PART TWO

VICTORIANS

ARE THE VICTORIANS
COMING BACK?*

THE answer to this catchpenny question is plainly "Yes". I have
lived all my life in a world in which either, in my immediate surroundings, some clearly definable Victorian things had not yet
gone out or, in some other context to which I was at least near
enough to have news of it, some other Victorian things were already
coming in again. In childhood I achieved a confused sense of
relationship (not to say identity) between my grandmother and
Queen Victoria herself, because she dressed in her widowhood like
the portraits in the memorial volume called *Sixty Years a Queen*,
a survival of the Jubilee which had by my time been demoted to
the children's bookshelves. And this sense of relationship was so
deep and secret that I did not know of it myself till a young school-
master after the Kaiser's war—I think in the Summer of 1921—
suddenly spoke in a history lesson of Queen Victoria as "a little,
fat, dumpy German woman". I immediately found myself blush-
ing, with one of those dreadful, irrepressible, infinitely expanding
childhood blushes which run down into the neck when the face
can no longer hold them, and force a pressure that can only burst
into tears. The master noticed this, and turned to me and said
some sarcastic thing so painful that I have never exactly remembered
it, a taunt about my feelings for the Queen which felt like a cut at
Grannie and at my then self-pitying self.

He had obviously just been reading Lytton Strachey or, more
likely, a review of Lytton Strachey; for *Queen Victoria* was published in April 1921, though *Eminent Victorians* was as early
as 1918.

Much of the present interest in the nineteenth century is often

* First given as a paper to the Girton College English Club on 5 May 1948,
but later revised and altered. Not published before.

written and spoken of as a reaction against Strachey; but I do not at all feel it so. I first read those two books twenty-five years ago; and I now feel my interest in the Victorians as a continuation of the admiration I then had for them. Their effect was not trivial mockery, cheapness, quick and false judgments. One effect on me, at least, of Strachey's essay on Manning was to make me read Newman's *Apologia*; I wangled off compulsory cricket to get on with it and lay, absorbed in the book, all a summer's afternoon under a hedge of flowering dog-roses in the meadows by the Trent. Which fitted neatly, of course, onto the essay on Thomas Arnold. An almost passionate love of my so-called Public School was won by going behind its Victorian expansion. But by a perverse cycle of reading I came at the Middle Ages through the Oxford Movement. Even F. G. Lee's *Directorium Anglicanum*, discovered in the school library, at the age of fifteen or so, when the library was still a glorious dusty jungle, set going a train of historical and ecclesiastical reading that played a great part in my life. Such things superseded an earlier love for Froude's *English Seamen in the Sixteenth Century*, which had once almost made me want to go to Dartmouth, with some vague ideas about "the devildoms of Spain".

The views of history with which I grew up were almost entirely created by Victorians; and Strachey did not necessarily contradict them; he directed attention to a rather different Victorian field, and he also woke me up to the possibility of treating the Victorians themselves as interesting, problematical, extremely relevant to my own life and the general life I was born into. Next, in time and value, in this process was Harold Nicolson's *Tennyson*, published in 1923. These three books did not seem sneering; they were the source of a humane, critical, historical attitude. Something of the sort was particularly needed with Tennyson. The collected edition of Tennyson I still use was given by my father to my mother before they were married: they were not people who could be said to have had "literary tastes" in any special way. But I have a brother called Lancelot, a sister whose second name is Elaine, and my own first name is Arthur. In a very intimate sense the Victorians did not "go out"; revision of opinion about them was partly an internal matter in the process of growing up.

By chance it had been to the part of the world we lived in that Millais brought down his wife in December 1862, to what they called a "wayside hostelry"; perhaps it was the Royal Oak. He had stood her shivering at night-time in the James I bedroom at Knole to paint his picture from Keats's *Eve of St Agnes*; and like a good practical Victorian he observed that moonlight was not strong enough to shine through stained glass and throw warm gules on Madeline's fair breast; and that therefore Keats was wrong. Back in London he used a bullseye lantern for the moon. When the thing was done, and shown in the Academy of 1863, Tom Taylor came up to him and said: "Where on earth did you get that scraggy model, Millais?" His answer is not recorded; but if he had said that the first sitter had been his wife, Taylor must have known at once that she had been Ruskin's wife, and that the marriage had been annulled because it had never been consummated. But neither could have mentioned it. You all know about it now; but it could not possibly have been mentioned to your predecessors, the first students of this college at Hitchen in 1869. But I can mention it now without batting an eyelid; and I think it is an immeasurable gain that I can do so, a victory of sanity and honesty and healthiness over all their opposites—a victory the Victorian minority was fighting for, but one which the Victorians in general would never have allowed and were fighting against.

This Ruskin-Millais affair, which has just been publicised in the book called *The Order of Release*, is one instance among many of an important change: it shows that we are far enough removed from the lives of the great Victorians for documents to be made available which have for years been kept back or suppressed by their families. Dickens's letters to his wife were published in 1935, and a new collected edition of his letters in 1938; and though I believe there are many more letters to come, it is now possible to get a clearer view of his life and character. A large number of new Thackeray letters have been released by his descendants, and the beginnings of a collected edition have appeared, with an unbelievable display of editorial pomp. The Chapman diaries have already altered our view of George Eliot's early life, and her letters are being edited at Yale. Various other collections of papers are being released or discovered for the first time.

This is important; for one of the most marked features of the Victorian *ethos* was its quite abnormal reticence about certain things; therefore every scrap of evidence that comes from behind the barriers they built round themselves has a necessarily disproportionate value—a value it would not have had if the barriers had never been there. I do not at all agree with those who have tried to decry the publication of the details of Ruskin's marriage to Euphemia Gray as mere vulgar scandal-mongering, smirching a great man; it is only necessary that we should also have the papers that are said to represent the other side of the case. Such knowledge is necessary for understanding a whole personality; and with the Victorians—thinkers, artists, poets, novelists, architects, churchmen—the whole personality does need understanding before the work can be properly understood. Their specific works are often liable to hopeless misinterpretation when they are considered by themselves, without reference to the whole life and the whole environment. Thus it is only with the fullest possible knowledge that we can hope to keep our bearings in the jungle of their productiveness.

The evidence that a general interest in the Victorians has immensely increased during and since the war both here and in America is available at every turn. It is apparent in illustrated articles in popular papers like *Picture Post* and *Illustrated*; in the B.B.C. Programmes it has appeared not only in the long series of talks called "Ideas and Beliefs of the Victorians", but also in an amazing number of talks on the Third Programme and the Home Service about isolated Victorian subjects and people—talks about Mill, Ruskin, Darwin and so on. For years the *Architectural Review* has been running articles and illustrations on various aspects of Victorian architecture and applied art, calling attention to qualities that had been ignored or despised. The new edition of the Victoria and Albert Museum's Small Picture Book called *Victorian Paintings* takes up a completely new attitude. The popularity of Trollope's novels in the war was rather a special case, but the present popularity of George Eliot has wider implications. In more academic style such earlier books as H. V. Routh's *Towards the Twentieth Century* and Lionel Trilling's *Matthew Arnold* point to the same conclusion. I shall discuss the question of reprints later, but it is notable that last year three different selections from Tennyson were published within a few months of each other.

The Victorians are coming back all right: but the important thing is that we should discriminate between the returns which may be valuable and those which almost certainly will not. For the danger in this whole situation is that it may be considered indiscriminately as a necessary swing of taste, a process of opening the eyes of this generation to virtues and beauties hidden from its immediate predecessors by the inevitable reaction against what was too close; that the "relativity of taste" may be played up so as to lead people into accepting almost anything. But it will be dis-astrous if the Victorians' stupidities, vulgarities, failures and un-happinesses are minimised or explained away, or accepted as some-thing else. For many Victorians were in many respects stupid, vulgar, unhappy and unsuccessful; and these aspects of the age remain visible in the objects, the buildings, the pictures and the literature that have been left to us. The peculiar vulgarities, un-happinesses etc. of the Victorian Age can partly be explained as exceptional, and peculiar to the age, for historical reasons; they are not typical of English life in general. If there is a change of attitude towards the Victorians that attempts to establish their general and typical set-up to life as admirable, it will be a dangerous thing. So many of their problems are still ours that we cannot afford to be uncritical and swallow them whole.

There is a good deal of evidence that the process of playing on the idea of a necessary and proper "swing of taste" is already far and subtly advanced. I do not mean just the fluctuating fashions for wax fruit, samplers and so on: I have myself a black papier-maché stereoscope inlaid with mother-of-pearl and decorated with lilies-of-the-valley, which I am rather fond of. One may possess and even collect typically interesting Victorian objects without being seriously involved in any major errors of judgment: but there is a real risk that what may seem at first just an "amusing" fashion (that is a word that has been current in this context on and off for nearly thirty years) may by various means, and even by the disproportionate influence of a few individuals, develop into something more through the failure of alertness and discrimination.

This process has been more apparent in the *Architectural Review* than in any one other publication known to me, and it has there lasted over a considerable period. A very clear statement of the kind of arguments that are used appears in the issue for April 1944. The following passage (p. 86) is part of an introductory note (written apparently with the editor's authority) to an article on some architectural and decorative features in the village of Canford Magna, near Wimborne, Dorset, which were in danger of being destroyed:

> Probably orthodox good taste is not yet ready to swallow the architecture of Canford Magna. To those for whom Culture means Augustan good manners, and Bad Taste the rustic work of John Hicks of Kinson, Lord Wimborne's model village will seem an outrage. . . . An appeal to public opinion has often to be made long before the general taste is in a state to appreciate the value of the objects appealed for. For public opinion invariably has a blind spot for the recent past, a blind spot whose course can be traced through history, turning a sightless yet at the same time hostile gaze on the works of the immediate predecessor, whoever he may be. Thus the Wrens and the Joneses could not be satisfied until they had torpedoed the English vernacular tradition in favour of a self-conscious style . . . the Victorians, although it had by then become a second vernacular, eagerly broke up the Georgian front; and we in our turn are doing what we can in our own small way to do the same to the Victorian. There is obviously no way of reversing the spirit of an Age, and yet to set out, as we do, to destroy the whole output of the preceding generation because of an antipathy which is in the nature of things, and in the nature of things will pass, seems unnecessarily barbarous. A better course, surely, would be to apply to the unpopular period certain universal criteria which might be expected to reveal its essential quality.

Or, best of all, since universal criteria do not always turn out to be so universal, make the necessary effort of imagination and put oneself outside the aesthetic prejudices of one's own day. . . . Once it is realised that an Age, the Victorian for instance, is dead, and must not be revived or imitated, its activities begin to gain significance, begin to look like its art. And all manifestations of art are worthy of affectionate study as well as of critical analysis.

The closing sentences of this quotation display a remarkable form of argument, a sort of Glide. It runs thus:

> An age is dead.
> It must not be revived or imitated.
> Its activities begin to gain significance.
> What gains significance begins to look like its art.
> All manifestations of art are worthy of affectionate study.

Running through this glide of statements is a principle—that, when an age is dead, all its activities begin to look like its art; and this principle is said to apply equally to the Victorian Age, as to any other.

The full logical consequence of this principle and its application is that *everything* produced in the Victorian Age is now "worthy of affectionate study as well as of critical analysis". The process of drawing-together is made more important than the process of discrimination. Every scrap of commercial stained-glass in a Gothic-revival District Church; every stud-box with a cheap little coloured print of the Royal Family on the lid, under glass; all the portraits of Gladstone and Tom Sayers printed on silk; all the tortuous fire-irons, metal bedsteads, woollen-tasselled bell-pulls, fringed tablecloths, prints of *Dignity and Impudence* and *Bubbles*; all the advertisements for Rowland's Macassar Oil and all the antimacassars which so perversely helped the advertising campaign; beer-bottle labels, match-box tops and moustache-cups—all these things are to be "worthy of affectionate study as well as of critical analysis", because the age is dead.

But what sort of affection is this to be? When these objects are said to "look like" the art of the Victorian Age, are we being asked to give them the same kind of affection that we give to the indisputably great works of art of other ages, such things as Salisbury Cathedral, the Duccio altar-piece at Siena, and *King Lear*? Are we even being asked to give them the same kind of affection that we may give to *The Scholar Gipsy* or *Middlemarch* or Gerard Hopkins's drawing of an iris? If you object that it is unfair to compare great things with small, I reply that that is exactly what, by implication, the article in the *Architectural Review* is doing. It *is* asking us to give the same kind of affectionate study to the rustic work of John Hicks of Kinson (including porches decorated with stuck-on fir-cones) that we give to a church by Wren. In another hundred years the same kind of affection may be demanded by the successor of the *Architectural Review* for a 1948 garden stuffed with cast cement elves, toadstools and rabbits.

Affection, and affectionate study, can be deeper or shallower, more serious or more trivial. I may say I have an "affection" for a favourite fountain-pen or a favourite pair of socks or a toothbrush even. From such purely private likings one can shift outwards into affections for things with family-associations, to hymns sung at mother's knee, or to the hideous little Gothic school chapel begun as a memorial to the great Victorian Headmaster, the Second Founder. But to confuse these affections with the affections which can be roused by a great and serious work of art is the typical symptom of a brash and ignorant mind; often a symptom of mere sentimentalism masquerading as the latest thing in taste.

You will have noticed, in the passage from the *Architectural Review*, that "affectionate study" is spoken of as something distinct from, almost opposed to, "critical analysis". But the great task of an educated person is always to control and order his affections by his critical sense. In the ideal man of perfect judgment the two are never in conflict. We never expect to reach that ideal. But all education—and education in this sense is unending—is a process of striving towards it. To set up the two in opposition is to open the way for an attitude we know to be less serious, less exacting, less involved in all the deepest parts of the personality; it opens a way for the preference of the "amusing" to the great.

82

It seems to me an essential starting-point in the study of the Victorian Age and of its products to recognise that it was an age which saw a more fundamental break with the long traditions and methods of the past than any preceding age in history. The Victorians themselves realised this; the greatest of them foresaw its implications. They saw that the violent break with traditional designs and craftsmanship, the proliferation of cheap machine-made goods and shoddy commercial "novelties", was impoverishing life rather than enriching it. They did what they could to save the serious richness of the past. Are we to exalt the trivialities they despised?

The *Architectural Review* has shown us one process of sly suggestion by which a supposed great shift of taste may be imposed upon us. Let us turn to some rather more general, literary evidence.

The clearest statement, in general terms, of what is happening was made by Professor Basil Willey in a Third Programme talk in December last year, the text of which was printed in the *Listener* dated Christmas Day. This talk is an outstanding example of the suggestion—for it does not rise to becoming an opinion or a belief—that the Victorians may have something to give us of great value and importance which has in the last two generations been missed—something to give us in the Arts, in Thought, and in style of life and attitude to all the business of living, something that is not to be found elsewhere.

The opening paragraph of Professor Willey's talk is this:

After the first world war we were all "debunking" the nineteenth century: after this one we are deferring to it, and even yearning after it nostalgically—*tendentesque manus ripae ulterioris amore*. Books and articles on its great thinkers, novelists and poets, and reprints of their works, pour from the press in as vigorous a trickle as present shortages will allow. In our own unpleasant century we are all displaced persons, and some of us feel tempted to take flight into the nineteenth as into a promised land, and settle there like illegal immigrants for the rest of our lives.

Deference and Nostalgia are then, according to one who is in a position to see and know, two elements in an attitude to the Victorians now become so widespread that such broad generalisations as these can safely be made about it as a matter of course. But before I deal with deference and nostalgia there is one particular question among those mentioned by Professor Willey that must not be forgotten in this appearance of revived interest. In the present shortage of paper, with other difficulties over labour and material in the making of books, commercial publishers have fallen back on the device of issuing a large number of reprints. A short preface, for which the writer is paid a not very rewarding lump sum, gives a slight dash of novelty: beyond that, the book is quicker and cheaper to produce than a new work; and there is less risk attached to it if the reprint is of something that has been called a "classic", or of something about which a specious argument can be spun that it is a "forgotten" or "minor" classic. With books short as they are, the quick sale of such reprints may not really indicate a strong genuine demand for exactly those works; it may indicate the vague general need for "something to read", and the special desperate needs of the Christmas and Birthday market. Many such reprints have been of Victorian works now out of copyright.

I don't mean that all these reprints are of books not worth reading at all; but that their sale does not represent an existing taste for works of exactly that kind; yet just because other books are so scarce and made scarcer by the publishers' policy, these reprints are willy-nilly helping to form the taste of a large number of readers whose judgment is immature, feckless, weak or nonexistent.

The point is this: that Victorian reprints do not, in Professor Willey's words, "pour from the press in as vigorous a trickle as present shortages will allow": but for the exactly opposite reason, that their production is the best way of making money in a time of shortage which does *not* allow the publication of countless other things for which readers and students are crying out, and authors panting to see in print. It is no satisfaction to be presented with three new selections from Tennyson at five shillings or eight and six when you can still buy the Moxon first editions in original green cloth for sixpence or a shilling and happen badly to want Hutchinson's edition of George Herbert or Miss Bradbrook's *Themes and Conventions*. The reprints of Victorian works do sometimes, as in the case of Tennyson, meet a reviving and justifiable interest; but the danger is that they may foster a careless taste, with no increase of understanding.

Now for Deference and Nostalgia. Let us take Nostalgia first. The clearest expression I know of a deep longing and preference for Victorian life has been made by Mr G. M. Young; in him it was no part of a post-war mood. But his own writing about the Victorians has probably done more than that of any other man to prepare the ground—to make remarks like Professor Willey's possible. Personally I owe Mr Young a great deal, not less because I sometimes disagree with him as flatly as possible. At any rate he committed himself before the war to the opinion that if he had the choice of all time and all space in which to live another life he might well choose England in the 1850's.

He knows his period too well to be under any illusion that the Victorian Age was all of a piece, that stability and order were its marks in contrast to the flux and uncertainties of our own time. He knows that a feeling of "security" was not characteristic of it. It was far otherwise. But there was a central period, very short, rather less than twenty years, in the fifties and sixties when an appearance of security, stability and order gave confidence and continuity to life and allowed those who did not look too far beneath the surface some happiness and quiet and fullness of enjoyment according to their tastes. It is not an accident that the craze for Trollope had some nostalgia in it: for the Barchester novels all fall in that period—*The Warden* was finished in the autumn of 1853 and *The Last Chronicle* was published in 1867; where there was nostalgia, it was for Barsetshire. Nobody could be nostalgic over *The Way We Live Now*. And it was in a Barsetshire mood that Mr Young wrote, now many years ago:

> Yet in the far distance I can well conceive the world turning wistfully in imagination, as to the culminating achievement of European culture,

85

to the life of the University-bred classes in England of the mid-nineteenth century, set against the English landscape as it was, as it can be no more, but of which nevertheless some memorials remain with us today, in the garden at Kelmscott, in the hidden valleys of the Cotswolds, in that walled close where all the pride and piety, the peace and beauty of a vanished world seem to have made their last home under the spire of St Mary of Salisbury.

The Cathedral Close at Salisbury is indeed beautiful; one reason for its beauty is a negative one—the almost total absence of Victorian architecture. But the grotesque perversity of bringing it in as the climax to an already perverse theory about Victorian civilisation does reveal an important fact: the Close at Salisbury is in no way Victorian; but the Victorians liked it, and liked it partly because they too were nostalgic. The world of Trollope in the fifties and sixties was already a dying or dead world; the Barchester novels are backward-looking, full of a nostalgic spirit: that is partly why those suffering from nostalgia in our own time find them sympathetic.

If, then, our attitude to the Victorians is to be nostalgic, it must recognise their nostalgia. We know nostalgia to be a fruitless mood, partly because they indulged it so fruitlessly. We can see the thwarted, stifled element in Thackeray's longing for the eighteenth century: it brought him sometimes even to writing pastiche prose. We can see Pugin and Carlyle and F. G. Lee and Ruskin and Morris and countless others hankering after the Middle Ages. We have inherited from the Victorians a historical method, a historical way of seeing things; and we must be very feeble creatures if we learn nothing from their failures in that style of vision. Professor Willey himself looks on the nostalgic attitude as a temptation.

So we come to Deference. To what are people deferring? I should say quickly here that I defer myself to Victorian scientists and engineers so far that I shall not much mention them; with many various qualifications deference can be given to the professional historians. But in what *other* fields is deference being given? I must here quote another sentence from Professor Willey's talk:

86

Much that we used to mock at in "Victorianism" may now show a different face to us: its prudery may seem reticence or refinement; its hypocrisy, true virtue; its sentiment, fine sensibility; its idealism and optimism, genuine faith; its domestic cohesiveness and parental tyrannies, something precious that we have let slip to our cost.

Here is a full programme of possible deference in taste and ethics and religion: you will notice that it is introduced cautiously with a "may": each proposition, you will notice too, is framed as a semi-humorous near-paradox, coming to a deliberate climax in the suggestion that parental "tyranny" can be "precious". The cautious, indirect way of putting these propositions forward is meant to indicate that the speaker himself does not (yet, at any rate) accept them; but that it is not unreasonable to suppose a time may come when what has been called prudery will come to be seen as reticence and refinement; when what has been called hypocrisy will come to be seen as true virtue; when what has been called sentiment will come to be seen as fine sensibility, and so on. Thus the way is subtly prepared for an utter reversal of major judgments in ethics and aesthetics on a prodigious scale. The main suggestion that I miss is the suggestion that what has been called ugliness may come to be seen as beauty; when "Evil be thou my good" is already the motto of the New Look.

In examining this programme of deference I want to begin with the visual arts, partly because the campaign for a New Look is at present more vigorous than that for a New Listen or a New Feel, and partly because the evidence is daily under our eyes.

You who live on the northern outskirts of Cambridge suffer, in this respect, from one disadvantage. When you first go into the town in the early part of the day with your senses alert and your mind unjaded, you approach King's Parade from the Trinity Street end: but we who live in the south, and come at it by Trumpington Street, take the last gentle bend by the University Press with a different kind of expectation. There is before us one of the most beautiful streets in Europe. Among the many things that make it beautiful one always strikes me particularly—that is the harmony of a whole made up by buildings of different periods, in very different styles, standing happily together because each is good in its own kind. A general presiding wisdom seems to have reigned there from the end of the fifteenth century, right up to the 1820's or 30's. But to this general harmony there is one exception, a thing that stands out, from the southern approach, like a deliberate insult to the harmony, a self-conscious flouting of the wisdom: I mean, of course, the Waterhouse buildings of Caius; and their date is 1868–70. I don't see how by any standards, universal or relative, these buildings can be seen as anything but a hideous mistake. In their proportions to their surroundings they are wrong—to the rest of Caius, to the Senate House, to the old University Library; in their general outline they look raw, incomplete and deadly stiff; their detailed ornamentation, including the statues, is fussy, ambitious and ill-placed. The building looks like an ill-mannered *parvenu*. Will time, or changes in taste, change that look?

The same architect was responsible, in just the same period, for the new Broad Street front of Balliol College, Oxford. In intention it is as different from the Caius building as possible—for its style is a mixture of a sort of Scottish baronial and a sort of Gothic; but the same kind of deathly stiffness is there; it is a meaningless, ambitious exercise. In five years Waterhouse had ruined two of the finest short streets in Europe.

Si tertium monumentum requiris, circumspice.

The other day I was talking to a pupil about tragedy; about Aristotle and then about the undeserved death of the innocent and the positively good. We mentioned, quite reasonably, Cordelia. I then showed him a black-and-white reproduction of Paul Falconer-Poole's picture (1858) called *The Death of Cordelia* and asked him, without special warning or introduction, what he thought of it. He said the grouping and expressions of the figures made Cordelia's death look like an unsuccessful suicide or an accident, as if somebody had been run over by a cart. We then turned back to the Introduction to the new Victoria and Albert Small Picture Book No. 10 and I showed him that in its author's opinion this picture of Poole's "is no unworthy parallel to the mystery and primitive wildness of Shakespeare's starkest tragedy". He laughed.

This Introduction is a document which deserves very close attention. It is an official publication with Crown Copyright, "Published under the Authority of the Ministry of Education". Its author is official and anonymous, a Civil Servant. We therefore have a strong right as taxpayers (or future taxpayers) to be concerned about what it says. It begins as follows:

> The introduction to the first edition of this picture book truthfully recorded that "for a long time Victorian Art in all its manifestations has remained under a cloud" but prophesied that "some day in the curiously changing cycle of critical opinion more light will shine through". Already, twenty years later, that prophecy is in a fair way towards being fulfilled.

That is a familiar attitude after what I have said earlier. Two paragraphs lower down the Introduction goes on:

> Nothing could be further from the truth than the common impression that the Victorians, when faced with profound emotion, could only rise to mawkish sentimentality.

It then says, to illustrate the point, that the picture reproduced as Plate 7 "is heart-rending in the simplicity of its absolute grief".

And what do you think Plate 7 is? It is a Landseer picture of a dog "with human eyes". And which, you ask, of all the many Landseer pictures of dogs with human eyes?—*The Old Shepherd's Chief Mourner*.

The coffin in the cabin covered with shawl and plaid; the empty chair, the abandoned crook and hat; the Bible on the stool; the beam of light struggling in from an invisible source; detailed leaves strewn; the sheep-dog crouching, with its dreary muzzle propped against the coffin. *That* is the picture that "is heart-rending in the simplicity of its absolute grief". That is what we now pay our taxes to be told with Crown Copyright under the authority of the Ministry of Education is "heart-rending in the simplicity of its absolute grief". It is not merely sentiment, but the abysmal anthropomorphic sentimentalising of animals, that is already being proclaimed as "fine sensibility". Professor Willey's prophecy came true within three months of being made.

I take it that Ruskin's opinion, as much as any one other, is responsible for *The Old Shepherd's Chief Mourner* becoming "one of Landseer's most celebrated works". Though Ruskin's two main discussions of it in *Modern Painters* are rather difficult fully to reconcile with each other, he is at least clear-headed in seeing that the picture cannot be generally appraised without raising the question of Landseer's emotional treatment of animals, or his interpretation of animals' emotion. A modern judgment of the picture which fails even to hint at the existence of this major problem in the criticism of Landseer does not reach the level of awareness that a museum-goer would find helpful. Grief cannot be "absolute"; it must be relative to the griever and the grieved-for. As the griever is in this case a dog, very special questions are raised— about animal psychology, about Victorian attitudes to animals, about Landseer's peculiar knowledge of animals, and so on. As it stands, the phrase "heart-rending in the simplicity of its absolute grief" suggests that the only proper or possible attitude to the picture is to swallow quite uncritically Landseer's treatment of animal emotion, together with all the obvious but sophisticated devices (the abandoned crook and hat, the Bible marked with spectacles on the stool, the empty chair, the concealed source of light, etc.) which he uses to enforce it. No alert spectator can regard these things and the kind of grief with which they are associated as merely "simple". I have known the picture for about thirty years, and my heart has never been rent by it, nor has the heart of anybody to whom I have ever talked about it. The views of all the people whose judgment I value are either that the picture is funny or that it is an example of that very "mawkish sentimentality" which the Introduction denies to it. The mere rhetorical reversal of this current opinion may still make some people laugh, but it is likely to bewilder or mislead others.

To say of Poole's picture *The Death of Cordelia* that it is "no unworthy parallel to the mystery and primitive wildness of Shakespeare's starkest tragedy" shows a complete inability to appreciate the depth and complexity of Shakespeare's *King Lear*, and Poole's failure to illustrate any aspect of it adequately. This phrase also is a rhetorical play with words and contains no serious critical judgment; but it might dangerously suggest to the unwary that a serious and detailed comparison between these two works is possible, and that they are to be thought of as almost equal in artistic importance. The sentence hinges on the equivocal word "parallel". Would the authorities of the Victoria and Albert seriously and at length maintain that Poole's picture *The Death of Cordelia* and Shakespeare's play *King Lear* are of anything like comparable artistic importance?

Not all Victorian tenderness is sentimental; but that *The Old Shepherd's Chief Mourner* should be picked out and praised as avoiding "mawkish sentimentality" makes one simply ask: "Where then is mawkish sentimentality to be found?"

In the exhibition of Pre-Raphaelite pictures now at the Whitechapel Art Gallery, there are several paintings by Arthur Hughes; and within his work alone it is possible to distinguish the uncertainty of Victorian mood, and make some very relevant distinctions. In the picture *April Love* there is a kind of sentiment which does not become offensive by underlining and excess. But in a rather similar picture called *The Long Engagement* a falsity of tone appears. There is a violet-eyed curate with ginger whiskers, and a silver-birch tree on which the ivy has grown up above the word "Amy" carved there presumably by him in the engagement's early days. The writer of the Introduction to the Catalogue of this Exhibition puts the matter very well:

> Hughes, at his best, is capable of a gentle, exquisite tenderness, a lyrical innocence, which make him, in spite of a certain technical feebleness, the most charming of the group. He is perpetually on the edge between sentiment and sentimentality.

That is the vital point. How is one to judge what is and what is not over the borderline between sentiment and sentimentality, between a tolerable and an intolerable tenderness? Can the line shift with no more valuable significance than a waistline or the hem of a skirt? Is all this just a matter of fashion, with no more to it than that people like change, or at best that a new look, or a new occasion for tears, gives the illusion of making a new woman?

This question cannot be answered easily: any theory that sounds convenient is liable to major disputes involving the use of philosophical and psychological terms. Those I must avoid, if only because I am incompetent to use them.

In approaching an answer I want to revert to something I said earlier. When I was discussing the increasing knowledge we now have of the Victorians and their lives, I said that it was of great importance, because it was necessary in understanding and judging them, to know all that we could of their personalities and environment. Equally it is true that the whole personality of the judge must be involved: the judge himself must be an educated, humanely developed personality. The appeal is similar to that which Aristotle is continually making in the *Ethics* to the "good man in action". And just as in Greek ethics there was an emphasis on the element of *knowledge* in the good man, so here, emphasis is necessary on the element of knowledge in the person fit to make these judgments of taste.

Looking back into the further past beyond the Victorian Age it is plain that the whole style, not only of literature and art, but of personality can change in an incredibly short time. The most striking example is what happened in England within the seventeenth century. Before the end of the century in which Shakespeare died, we find Dryden saying of him that his language was partly coarse, partly unintelligible, and altogether too "pestered with figurative expressions". It is a judgment we find hard to sympathise with; yet I think that much of the historical and critical work on the seventeenth century has contributed to explaining how it happened. But this is still a matter I am personally only on the edge of beginning to understand.

With the Victorians I think the matter is easier; and certainly the evidence is fuller, evidence provided by themselves and by their immediate predecessors and successors. It is possible for historical reasons to isolate and describe what is *peculiar* to the Victorian Age: and it is this that I want to emphasise in the ending of this paper.

They themselves knew that they were peculiar; they were conscious of belonging to a *parvenu* civilisation. At one moment they are busy congratulating themselves on their brilliant achievements, at the next they are moaning about their sterility, their lack of spontaneity. In either mood they are all agog at being modern, more modern than anyone has ever been before. And in this they were right. They took the brunt of an utterly unique development of human history; the industrialisation and mechanisation of life meant a greater change in human capabilities in the practical sphere than had ever before been possible. The task of assimilating this change meant a total disturbance of the traditional tempo and rhythm of life, an upset of all balance.

On the one hand you had an extreme literalness and matter-of-factness; on the other hand a sort of hysteria. I have elsewhere tried to define Victorian sentimentality as being largely "the imposition of feeling as an afterthought upon literalness". These terms do not carry the analysis of the situation very far. But they do indicate something of the dilemma we can so plainly see in Victorian art and literature. Matthew Arnold was right to stress in his contemporaries generally the lack of the "spontaneity of consciousness": and his whole attack on the one-sidedness, the lack of tradition, the crudity of Philistine taste, has lost nothing of its point. The alarming thing in current attitudes to Victorians of the kinds I have been describing is that they utterly ignore the central criticism which the great Victorians themselves applied to their own age. It was, as Arnold said, typically (and at its best) a critical age: and it is typically as critics that we must approach it.

THE MOOD OF DOUBT*

VICTORIAN thought was dominated by the idea of history as a sequence of events in time. The sequence was imagined in terms of space. The whole human condition and the whole condition of the universe were imagined as either being or following a horizontal line ever getting longer and longer. Sometimes this line was thought of as ending at the present moment, like the line of purple ink on a barograph. Sometimes the line was more like railway lines along which the human race or the universe was travelling, lines already laid down by natural law or by God. I can best indicate the preponderance of this horizontal spacial imagery by two of the most hackneyed quotations from Tennyson: "The one far-off divine event, to which the whole creation moves" clearly employs the figure of spacial progression for the whole cosmic process. And "Let the great world spin for ever down the ringing grooves of change" was in fact an image taken from the railways; for when Tennyson first travelled by train he thought the wheels travelled in grooves instead of on lines. Or again, Matthew Arnold writes in one of his moments of agnostic determinism: "We, in some unknown Power's employ, move on a rigorous line": but he more often made the comparison with a stream or a river, which is still the imagery of linear movement through space.

This temporal-historical-linear habit of thought was on the whole shared by optimists and pessimists alike. It was common to religious thinkers and scientists, used by Newman in his *Development of Christian Doctrine*, and by Jowett interpreting the Bible, as much as by Huxley defending Darwin. It is partly an accident of language that the word "progress" has come to imply improvement while "process" has remained neutral. Most of the significant Victorian writers as well as ordinary educated people were deeply

* B.B.C. Third Programme, 9 Feb 1948.

94

involved in *processive* habits of thought, though they might not at all agree that a process in time always involved amelioration. One effect of this was that they were all acutely conscious of their own unique position in the linear sequence of time. They never could forget what John Stuart Mill called "the consciousness of living in a world of change". The phrase has now been a piece of stock-in-trade with preachers for a century; but then it stood for a vivid and inescapable new mood. Tennyson caps the argument again: "I the heir of all the ages, in the foremost files of time".

The muddle of the image here does not destroy the proud consciousness of modernity. You find that consciousness just as plain in the first chapter of *A Tale of Two Cities* as in the third chapter of Macaulay's *History*. Dickens had a lot of dummy books with facetious titles to decorate his study: among them was a series called "The Wisdom of our Ancestors" and the titles of the volumes included *Ignorance, Superstition, The Block, The Stake, The Rack, Dirt, Disease.*

This acute consciousness of modernity did not by any means lead to any assurance that the future was secure. During the years 1820–70 there were many moments when, for external reasons alone, the future seemed very insecure indeed. Major epidemics of cholera in 1832, 1848–9 and other lesser outbreaks; chances of revolution in 1832, 1839, 1848; great disturbances in parts of the country in 1850, and riots that thoroughly disturbed Matthew Arnold in 1866. Major scares of foreign invasion in the fifties from Napoleon III, and in the seventies from Prussia. If anyone believes that ordinary life for the early- and mid-Victorians was comfortable and secure, let him look up in the index of Irving's *Annals of our Time* the following heads: Colliery Accidents; Collisions at Sea, Railway Accidents, Riots, and Shipwrecks.

And further, the tempo of life increased so much and so suddenly, and the multiplication of novelties and problems came so fast, that experience could not be quickly enough assimilated, assessed, or related to other experience. This caused, both in the lives of individuals and in the political life of the nation, further difficulties and also discomfort, uncertainty, doubt and hysterical

95

impatience leading almost to despair. The expression of these moods was not confined to the Cassandra-wailings of Carlyle or the melodious whine of Matthew Arnold. A hundred years ago this July in the year of revolutions in Europe, just after the great Chartist demonstration had failed to become the English revolution, Thackeray wrote to his mother of "a society in the last stages of corruption, as ours is. I feel persuaded that there is an awful time coming for all of us." The words are like those of Marx in his speech at the meeting called by the *People's Paper* in 1856.

I need not even recapitulate here the tale of horrors brought about in the new towns and factories by the developments of the industrial revolution, the tale of poverty, disease, lack of sanitation, child labour, overcrowding, long hours, barbarism, illiteracy, drunkenness. But I think that those who have presented the Victorian case for progress have minimised these evils, and have minimised the degree of indifference to them. Computations of an average rise in real wages and a comparison of artisans' food and clothing with those of their grandfathers do not outweigh the evidence of contemporaries as various as Disraeli, Engels, Kingsley, Dickens, or Mrs Gaskell, to name but a few. These writers either used or independently confirmed the huge reports of Commissioners, Inspectors, and Doctors, and they add to that evidence a contemporary sense of moral horror, both at the sufferings themselves and at the indifference so often shown to them.

Even if real wages were higher, what was the quality of life which those who earned them could enjoy? Cobbett, Wordsworth, Southey and Carlyle, all saw and deplored the decay in the general quality of life before the beginning of Victoria's reign. Macaulay had the opportunity to see and understand what was involved, when he reviewed Southey's *Colloquies on the Progress and Prospects of Society* in 1830; but he did not even try to understand Southey's point of view. Southey, for instance, compares some country cottages with a row of new industrial cottages, and asks: "How is it that every thing which is connected with manufactures presents such features of unqualified deformity? From the largest of Mammon's temples down to the poorest hovel in which his helotry are stalled, these edifices have all one character . . . and they will remain always as offensive to the eye as to the mind." Macaulay either cannot or will not see the point; he merely jeers: "Here is wisdom. Here are the principles on which nations are to be governed. Rose-bushes and poor-rates, rather than steam-engines and independence." And he talks of an "enthusiast" who "makes the picturesque the test of political good". I am not qualified to judge the merely statistical parts of this essay of Macaulay's, which read so convincingly, but I am sure that with a prim and shallow confidence he has utterly missed the essential truths that Southey was trying to express—truths which Ruskin and William Morris laboriously recovered thirty years later.

In another essay, that on Sadler's *Law of Population,* I think Macaulay failed to appreciate, or deliberately shirked, one of the greatest problems, one of the greatest causes of pessimism. Sadler's book was a hideously rhetorical and rather crazily argued attack on Malthus. Macaulay jeers Sadler out of court, but he never comes to grips with what lies behind him—the theory which overshadowed and darkened all English life for seventy years. Malthus's famous book was first published in 1798 as a direct counterblast to the anarchistic optimism of Godwin's *Political Justice.* Even its author admitted that it cast over human affairs a "melancholy hue". In effect his doctrine boiled down to saying that poverty, squalor, disease, starvation and war were always necessary and ordained by God, except in so far as the lowest people in every society could be restrained from breeding. This meant in application that a certain substratum of poverty was always necessary and incurable.

In a letter of 1848, Thackeray, pouring out his baffled complexities in the face of the French revolution, said: "the question of poverty is that of death disease winter or that of any other natural phenomenon. I don't know how either is to stop." All the orthodox arguments of the time led to the same conclusion. Coleridge, Carlyle and Dickens launched attacks on the implications of Malthusianism. Mr Micawber is a deliberately anti-Malthus character; Dickens had another dummy book called

Malthus's Nursery Songs. But emotional outbursts and jokes did no good. The theory was never systematically disproved; the Poor Law of 1834 was based on it; and its acceptance underlay much of the dull mournful acquiescence in misery which the age so freely produced.

Another common mood was that of frustration at men's bewildered incompetence to find answers to the age's countless problems, both practical and speculative. I can take here only a few examples. Faced with the problem of relations between employers and employed, Dickens, at the end of *Hard Times* (1854), could offer no solution more hopeful than the reiterated comment of Stephen Blackpool that "'Tis a' a muddle." His treatment of the trade union in this book was neither dramatically nor factually convincing, for he was never prophetic, though in some things he did advocate what turned out to be the winning cause. He maintained with vigour, over many years, that it was useless to talk of education and morality to the poor until they had good houses, good drains, good water, light and air. A hundred years ago this year, the first English Public Health Act was put on the Statute Book; but it was totally inadequate. It broke down on political disputes over centralised control, the use of public money (the old cry for economy!), and the propriety of compulsory powers. It failed. Dickens is still found in the fifties screaming ever more shrilly for good houses, good water, good drains, light and air. He shows more clearly than any other man the frustrations caused by current political theory. He set up a sort of plain man's cry for administrative responsibility and efficiency by whatever means it was reached. On Public Health he shouted for centralisation and compulsion. But what would centralisation mean if there was nobody but the Tite Barnacles in Whitehall? "'Twas a' a muddle." Nothing is plainer than the growing despondency and bitterness of Dickens's later books. If progress was the rule of life, progress in Reform was abominably slow, in comparison with the progress in vulgar ostentation of the middle classes. Matthew Arnold took up where Dickens left off. Though the State may not be able to assimilate its indigestible problems of poverty, squalor and recurring unemployment, there may perhaps be some hope if the Philistines can assimilate the best that has been thought and said in the world.

Arnold felt, fully and sensitively, the effects of the speculative problems of the time. As we look back now, one of these shows the Victorian dilemma more plainly than any other—the great problem of the Immortality of the Soul. This is utterly central; for it raises the question whether life is worth living at all. The common approach was in the temporal linear habit of thought: Where are we going? Where do the lines lead? There were few men alive, whether utilitarians or religious people, who then thought of the goodness of an act as being in the act itself or in the will that willed it; all was in the consequences, whether happiness tomorrow, or the "life hereafter"; both were matters of future reward. *In Memoriam* was popular chiefly because it worried at the problem of immortality. I will not quote the all-too-familiar passages in which doubts and fears work round to a faith that is a sort of desperate hope. But this is what Tennyson said in a talk about "Immortality" to Knowles and William Allingham in 1872: "If I ceased to believe in any chance of another life, and of a great Personality somewhere in the Universe, I should not care a pin for anything." This sentence is an appalling confession. Kingsley, too, wrote in 1850, that if God were a deceiver, "I'd go and blow my dirty brains out and be rid of the whole thing at once, I would indeed." When irresponsible, suicidal cynicism is the other side of a religious medal, the religion is not now to us attractive. And the war passages in *Maud* show again the moral irresponsibility to which the suicidal temptations of a great Victorian could lead.

But it is impossible now to sneer. We are in a position to begin to understand the depths of psychological disturbance which the whole change of human tempo, the change in the content of human experience, brought on. The more I read of the early- and mid-Victorians, the more I see anxiety and worry as a leading clue to understanding them. They were not complacent compromisers. They were trying to hold together incompatible opposites, and they worried because they failed. They clung to an immortality that

99

should not include the possible justice of Eternal Punishment; they wanted a system of administration which should be efficient without expense; in face of repeated and ferocious strikes and riots, they clung to the doctrine that the interests of employers and employed were identical. They knew such things as these were incompatibles; they worried because they could neither reconcile them nor move on to other terms of thought. They worried about immortality, they worried about sex, they worried about politics and money. They were indeed caught between two worlds. It fell to them to begin the adjustment of the whole complex human organisation, personal and political. It fell to them to adjust it to an environment that was utterly new in the history of the race. It is not surprising if, to support life at all, they turned to (among other things) an intensification of personal relationships and an unbalanced exaggeration of domestic virtues.

> Ah, love, let us be true
> To one another! for the world, which seems
> To lie before us like a land of dreams,
> So various, so beautiful, so new,
> Hath really neither joy, nor love, nor light,
> Nor certitude, nor peace, nor help for pain;
> And we are here as on a darkling plain
> Swept with confused alarms of struggle and flight,
> Where ignorant armies clash by night.

THACKERAY'S LETTERS*

FOUR volumes at six guineas the set, not sold separately. A total of almost three thousand pages. Edited in all the complex panoply of American scholarship by Professor Gordon N. Ray; checked and supervised by Howard Mumford Jones with three research assistants. Printed at the Harvard University Printing Office; published here with the imprint of the Oxford University Press; illustrated with portraits, drawings and facsimilies. This is how, after eighty years of restraint, mystery, piecemeal printing and piecemeal suppression, a great bulk of the letters of Titmarsh, Yellowplush, Your Fat Contributor, William Makepeace Thackeray, now first comes before the public.

The impact of his personality is buffered by 173 pages of prefatory matter and cushioned by footnotes stuffed in often more thickly than the text. The shock is finally allayed by twenty-eight appendixes, six genealogical tables, and a various array of indexes. Professor Ray speaks of his edition as occupying a place "in the development of Thackeray scholarship", of the care taken in preparing it: yet it has many errors, in the texts and in the notes.

How Thackeray would have smiled at all this! And if he was really nervous about Posterity reading his letters, as he sometimes made out, he would have smiled again at the fact that hardly any of posterity can afford to buy them, and that even the review copies have been given out with a very sparing hand.

For though he was too easy-going and unmethodical to be a good businessman, he thought and cared a great deal about money and about all the details of the trade of literature. He frankly wrote and drew and lectured and edited for money, and when in the

* B.B.C. Third Programme, 2 Sep 1947, reviewing *The Letters and Private Papers of William Makepeace Thackeray,* collected and edited by Gordon N. Ray. 4 vols. (Oxford).

early days a publisher paid him for a job in pounds instead of in the promised guineas he firmly wrote:

> Such rich men as you and Mr. Tilt must not rob me of my shillings —Twenty guineas, and of course no bills.

Immediate success, and the money success could earn, was a far greater spur to him than any visionary hopes of fame or any ideals about his art. While *Vanity Fair* was still being written he said:

> I don't profess to write for posterity and have a much greater value for pudding yet I don't mind saying that especially of latter years (for I look upon the first efforts as jokes, and schoolboy exercises as it were) I have done my best to work as an artist telling the truth, and morbidly perhaps, eschewing humbug.

In 1849 he wrote to Arthur Shawe:

> Your brother-in-law the writer of the present . . . is become quite a lion within the last 2 years, dines with a lord almost every day, and is rather prosperous as times go. But though I am at the top of the tree in my business and making a good income now (near upon £2000 let us say)—yet it is only within the last few months that I have got to this point.

This theme, with variations according to fame and circumstances, runs through all the letters up to the final editorship of the *Cornhill* and the unfinished story of *Denis Duval*.

For Thackeray was very much a man of the world, "a lazy epicurean nature", he said. Food recurs here at every age, from oranges and "Gooseberry pyes" at seven, through a pottle of strawberries at Charterhouse and the bad meat at Trinity, Cambridge, where "Men eat enormously, I am not much behind hand", to the long series of heavy dinners in clubs and inns and great houses which were the exhausting routine of the years of fame—"the old routine of the world and its vanities and three courses and claret almost every day". Somebody called him as a boy not greedy but "gustative". And he also liked his drink. He is already writing to his mother from Cambridge: "The Sauterne is greatly admired— Five men came in here uninvited on purpose to drink thereof this afternoon, so I just pretended to go & speak to a man in the court"; this from the rooms of which "Men will say someday, that Newton & Thackeray kept near one another!" On a water party with the *Punch* people with their women-folk in 1846, which he describes in one of the short snatches of diary, "Champagne began the instant we got on board". There was much singing and banter, and on the way home "many instances of Bacchic fury occurred"; the famous publishers were particularly under the weather: "Young Bradbury was rolling about on the box of the fly, so helplessly bespattering himself—Evans by his side—but only cheerfully drunk."

There is the famous story of the dinner with Tennyson—Tennyson who had a period of gloomy drinking of heavy port—the dinner after which Tennyson said: "I love Catullus for his perfection in form and for his tenderness, he is the tenderest of Roman poets" and quoted

Quo desiderio veteres renovamus amores

and other verses in his big lilting voice; and Thackeray said: "I do not rate him highly, I could do better myself." Then next day he sent a letter beginning:

My dear Alfred,
    I woke at 2 o'clock and in a sort of terror at a certain speech I had made about Catullus. When I have dined, sometimes I believe myself to be equal to the greatest painters and poets. That delusion goes off; and then I know what a small fiddle mine is and what small tunes I play upon it.

These were the passing exaltations of a very nice and very honest man, whose love of food and drink helped to kill him early. He often writes of pills and doses, of soda-water for breakfast; and for years he had a recurrent painful stricture in what he called the Hydraulics.

He was not by birth a Victorian, being in fact eight years older than the Queen. He grew up in the Regency, became legally a man in the year of the Reform Bill and was married in the year of Victoria's accession. Part of the threaded, various fascination of these letters is to see how a man of his alertness, gaiety and love of life, absorbed and forwarded the changes in manners and morals and style which crept across English social life in what should, perhaps, be called the Albertine age. In these changes Thackeray was a central, exceedingly important personality, one of our greatest leaders of moral fashion: his lecture on George IV expresses perhaps more clearly than any other single document the changes in morals and manners which distinguish the Albertine age from the age before it. The strong influence most commonly described by social historians to account for these changes is that of the Evangelical party; yet by this Thackeray was almost wholly untouched, and he noted that the Simeonites among his acquaintances in Cambridge were a bit ashamed of their allegiance, at least when he was there. His mother did indeed become in middle life a devout fundamentalist, and something of a puritan. She even tried to convert William, and to persuade him to use his writings to propagate her doctrine. But oddly enough she seems to have reached this phase of belief not through any English teacher so much as through the French Protestant pastor Adolphe Monod, whose church she attended in Paris. Thackeray's own children even were sent to Monod's classes and the worldling's daughters remembered sitting in a sort of stern stupor under his repeated exhortation: "Ah, mes enfants, fuyez, fuyez ce monde!" while in a corner by the window holding up a small Bible was the great Prime Minister Monsieur Guizot.

Thackeray's own religion was a sort of Liberal Modernism based on an ethic of sentiment and affection, and a belief in Providence almost fatalistic, not in individual fortunes and misfortunes, but in the general ordering of the world:

O enormous various changing wonderful solemn world! Admirable providence of God that creates such an infinitude of men—it makes one very grave and . . . full of love and awe.

His religion too was worldly, and he had a real hatred of "a blasphemous asceticism . . . which is disposed to curse hate and under-

value the world altogether". About the *De Imitatione Christi* he
wrote to Mrs Brookfield:

> Why, you dear creature—what a history that is in the Thos a Kempis
> book. The scheme of that book carried out would make the world the
> most wretched useless dreary doting place of sojourn—there would be
> no manhood no love no tender ties of mother & child no use of intel-
> lect no trade or science—a set of selfish beings crawling about avoiding
> one another, and howling a perpetual miserere. We know that deduc-
> tions like this have been drawn from the teaching of J.C.: but Please
> God the world is preparing to throw them over.

Mrs Brookfield had evidently been touched sentimentally by the
revival of ascetic ideals by the Puseyites; and Thackeray wrote,
long after the main crisis in their affections:

> She is a woman quite capable of skipping into a Chapel, popping into
> a confessional before a priest who would hear her, soothe her, absolve
> her, baptise her and send her home engaged to Catholicism before she
> knew where she was; and then she would tell her husband; and then it
> would be bon jour; and away would go Magdalene and Arthur and the
> Inspector in one cab; and she in another to Our Lady of Sorrows and
> two guineas a week for her board; and good-by to the children, and to
> friends whom she loves as a sister, and to those who have loved her as
> women are not loved every day. I can see Aubrey de Vere coming in
> with his sanctified smirk to visit her afterwards and the rest of the shave-
> lings coaxing and squeezing her hand and giving her precious conversa-
> tion and dainty little penances, and making much of her.

How full of life and observation and movement these few
sentences are! and what a judgment on the character of the
woman whom for years Thackeray himself loved "as women are
not loved every day"! It is easy to see how he got a reputation for
being cynical. But his eye was every bit as quick for the absurdities
in himself as for those in others. The best of the caricature
drawings scattered so generously through these letters are the self-
portraits; the broken nose and spectacles and fatuously childlike
cheeks crop up with the great body in every sort of trivial social
posture; and in the letters and diaries themselves his own gaffs and

errors and wrong-doings, repentences and regrets are treated more harshly than those of others; he was never smug, cruel or ungenerous.

In an odd way it was his sense of absurdity as much as anything else that made him a leader of moral fashion. He was nothing of a reformer: huge sanctities, sacrifices and heroisms, causes for which one may die or causes for which one may arduously live, were not for him. Carlyle once said: "I wish I could persuade Thackeray that the test of greatness in a man is not whether he would like to meet him at a tea-party." Thackeray is not a rejector, scorner or renouncer of the world; he is an accepter of the world as it is: but it has absurdities and he can't help pointing them out. Coarse manners and debauchery make men ridiculous, and in the long run repulsive. Even in his oat-sowing days he could not take vice with its grossness. "Thank God", he wrote in one of the scraps of diary, "that idle & vicious as I am, I have no taste for scenes such as that of last night."

It was his sense of absurdity and of the need for decorum and balance (one of his self-caricatures showed him as "Equilibrist and Tightrope dancer in ordinary to the nobility & the Literati") that made him a leader in the snob-hunt. The new industrial fortunes and the growth of the middle class put his subjects under his eyes. In one of these letters he records a meeting with

> Mrs Lock the Engineer's wife ... not quite up to her present aggrandized fortune ... [in] a blew satting gownd wh. it was a most estraordinary raiment indeed—

That is a condensation of hundreds of his humorous social papers which are indeed nowadays not very funny, though in their day they played so great a part in building up the Victorian conception of a gentleman.

There can rarely have been a man who was so much a social animal and so little a political animal. His family were Whig-Liberal and his mother even radical. In 1831 he himself wrote to Edward FitzGerald:

I am glad the last King of England is a good one really & truly I believe he will be the last. Brougham will be Lord Guardian or Lord Protector or something like——

and at the side is a drawing of a remote and ineffectual king shuffling on a throne, as a huge candle-snuffer is lowered upon him by a misshapen hand.

Over the bedchamber crisis of '39 he let himself go to his mother in a way that gave an inkling of the Queen's character:

> The Queen has no business to be a woman. She is a machine worked by ministers, and a set of Whig chambermaids about a dull, obstinate, vain, silly creature like this little Vick are enough to pull down the institutions of the whole country. The rascally, lying, pettifogging Whigs were beaten—never mind by whom—but deservedly beaten and they came back—how? upon the shoulders of the maids of honour. Fye psha, pooh, nonsense, for shame, humbug: I am furious at the cant which makes a saint out of the self willed vulgar little mind.

Then in 1840 he did a wickedly funny drawing of the Queen and Prince Albert at Covent Garden, the chinless Queen with a vast top-heavy crown, in a sort of stubborn gaping alertness, ignoring Albert's Germanic blandishments.

In America in 1856 he was "speaking of Queen Vic in the very handsomest manner". "How this country whiggifies me", he wrote. "The rabble supremacy turns my gorge." He had become a Victorian.

Apart from the curious episode when he stood as an independent Liberal candidate for Parliament for Oxford city, he took no part and showed very little interest in the public affairs of his time: his books rarely touch on politics: he was a private, family, dining-out man. And within that limited sphere his avid, experiencing, gustative, sensual, tender nature had all its happinesses and trials.

The insanity of his wife, and the course of his friendship and passionate love for Mrs Brookfield, are the subjects of painful and terrible letters, never admitting all the depths they reveal. It seems clear that he believed he could have a deep, pervasive, all-satisfying mutual love for a woman who should meet every need of his nature and follow every phrase of his mind: at times Jane Brookfield gave him what he wanted and became the last compounding chemical in his work. But all the circumstances broke up the relationship, made its fruition and its endurance impossible. At the crisis he wrote to his mother:

> Very likely it's *a* woman I want more than any particular one: and some day may be investing a trull in the street with that priceless jewel my heart. . . . What can any body do for me? Nobody can do nothing: for say I got my desire, I should despise a woman; and the very day of the sacrifice would be the end of the attachment.

He was doing himself wrong in a bitter mood when he wrote that. He was not crying for the moon; he was caught by circumstances and suffered for it; and it was not just a piece of Victorian prudery which withheld him from doing what some people might now call the obvious thing to cut his way out.

Carlyle's most serious judgment on Thackeray is perhaps the best comment on these wonderful letters, which (for all the defects of their editing) do present him as he has never been seen before:

> A big fellow, soul and body; of many gifts and qualities (particularly in the Hogarth line, with a bit of Sterne superadded), of enormous *appetite* withal, and very uncertain and chaotic in all points except his *outer breeding*, which is fixed enough, and *perfect* according to the modern English style. I rather dread explosions in his history. A *big*, fierce, weeping, hungry, man; not a strong one.

QUALITIES OF
GEORGE ELIOT'S UNBELIEF*

THE Victorians had a genius for getting themselves into memorable situations, and also for recording such moments—vivid and relevant, pathetic or funny—in the lives of themselves or others. Newman weeping over the gate at Littlemore; Thomas Arnold the younger, on the eve of election to a professorship that required him to be an Anglican, overheard by his family once more saying his prayers in Latin; Mark Pattison meeting Newman in a train just after the publication of *Essays and Reviews*; Digby Dolben mobbed in Birmingham for wearing a Benedictine habit and sandals; Holman Hunt dressed like a nervous bandit painting the shore of the Dead Sea a goat, to become *The Scapegoat*; Margot Tennant on her knees in prayer with General Booth in a railway carriage; the Prince of Wales riding into Jerusalem, under the guidance of Dr Stanley, on the route of the Triumphal Entry; Marian Evans toiling in her study at Coventry over the last chapters of Friedrich Strauss's *Life of Jesus*, distressed at the analysis of the story of the crucifixion, looking up at an image of Christ to gather the endurance to go on with it.

Leslie Stephen, in telling the tale of Strauss and the Christ image, added: "To others the image might perhaps have suggested rather remonstrance than encouragement." But it was entirely characteristic of Marian Evans that it gave her encouragement; for she can scarcely be called typical in anything. Her skull measured $22\frac{1}{4}$ inches in circumference and was said to be broader from brow to ear than any other recorded skull except Napoleon's. She openly lived, right through the mid-Victorian age, with a man who was not her legal husband. Even without the novels, she was not a typical

* B.B.C. Third Programme, 15 Mar 1948. Printed in the *Listener*, 25 Mar.

person. Yet her intellectual and spiritual and moral history exemplifies many trends and qualities of Victorian thought.

It is characteristic of her that she lost her belief in dogmatic Christianity in rather a conservative style, in rather an old-fashioned context. The first phase of her infidelity was not brought on by Strauss or any other German rationalist, nor by fossils and monkeys and shellfish; it was rather brought on by the literary-historical tradition of the English eighteenth century. In spite of a few references to geology and to a reading of Mrs Somerville's *Connexion of the Physical Sciences*, it seems that there was very little in the sceptical side of her early thought that would have been unfamiliar to Hume or Gibbon. What would have been unfamiliar, and indeed uncongenial, to them was the intense laborious earnestness with which her scepticism was reached, the moral tone of it. Some causes of this different temper and tone, operative in the country as a whole, can be seen peculiarly active in her own early life.

Evangelicalism, more than anything else, changed the whole temper of society; and though the religion of her immediate family was a tepid and conventional Church of Englandism, Marian Evans came under powerful evangelical influence from three different directions—from an aunt, and from mistresses at her two schools. She developed very puritanical habits and a strong sense of sin and justice and judgment: she abjured worldly pleasures and, after reading a life of Wilberforce, determined upon a life of good works as well as good faith, so that she should be "sanctified wholly". It is not quite clear whether in these years she herself held the typically Calvinist doctrine of election; but it is certain that she lived much among Calvinists and that she often saw immoral consequences of this doctrine in persons of the Holy Willie and Justified Sinner kind. A woman convicted of lying said: "I do not feel that I have grieved the spirit much." This not only turned her against Calvinism, but intensified her own passionate love of truth and consistency. She carried the high moral purposes of her belief into the critique of it. In this, more than anything else, she differed from the eighteenth-century rationalists. She was passionate and earnest and dutiful where they were amused and easy.

Her literary tastes removed her still further from their mood. In her sternest religious phase she had rather ironically an admiration for that part of Young's *Night Thoughts* called "The Infidel Reclaimed". But this was soon replaced at the age of twenty by a love for Wordsworth. She then bought the collected works and set herself down to read them through. "I never before", she said, "met with so many of my own feelings expressed just as I could like them." This very sentence shows her unconscious stress on the importance of personal feeling. Years later, in the only full-length essay she ever published about a poet—it was in fact a merciless attack on the *Night Thoughts*—her judgment of Young proceeds by implicit reference to Wordsworthian standards. She focuses on Young's neglect of the "true qualities of objects described or the emotion expressed"; on his lack of allusions that carry us "to the lanes, woods, or fields"; and above all on the fact that he is not "true to his own sensibilities or inward vision". There was a strong strain of Wordsworthianism in her earnestness and in her tendency to treat her own emotions as something sacred. She was never led into the utilitarian error of underestimating the importance of feeling or into an estimate of ethics as a calculation of pleasure and pain: the inward claims of the sense of duty were overriding and paramount.

She was deeply affected by the sense of history prevailing in her youth. The view of history as linear in time was curiously expressed in a fashion for historical charts. Dr Stanley made a chart of Early Church History at Christ Church, and Marian Evans in Coventry was quite independently working on another, a thing of incredibly ambitious size in about eight parallel columns to cover a period of at least six hundred years. She even planned to publish it; but long before it was done one was actually published which she thought far superior to her own: as she put it herself, such a chart was "thus evidenced to be a desideratum". And indeed, if one was to read Joseph Milner's evangelical *History of the Church of Christ* and the Oxford tracts and Isaac Taylor's answer to them—all of which Marian Evans read or planned to read—some pictorial guide through the wilderness of Fathers and schisms and sects and heretics and councils and emperors was almost essential. And it seems quite clear that this study of early Christian history in a hunt for the true form of the visible Church, for pure and authentic original Christianity, was the beginning of her religious doubts. She found that even the early Church was ambiguous and often corrupt. This is a matter of the greatest importance for the history of the thirties and forties, because it shows how closely linked were the studies and frame of mind of those who became technically infidels and many of those who became technically Roman Catholics. The quickest way to appreciate the closeness of this link is to read Milman's review (reprinted in *Savonarola, Erasmus and Other Essays*) of Newman's *Development of Christian Doctrine*. Newman had stressed the silences, contradictions, imperfections of the early Fathers on vital matters of dogmatic theology in order to argue for the necessity of an infallible Church.

> We are told that God has spoken. Where? In a book? We have tried it, and it *disappoints*; it disappoints, that most holy and blessed gift, not from fault of its own, but because it is used for a purpose for which it was not given.

These are the words, not of Francis Newman, but of John Henry. It is small wonder that Milman commented: "Not content with the Trinity, he fairly throws over the New Testament."

And so Marian Evans too, after getting bogged in the early Fathers, pushed further back to the critique of the canon of Scripture. She had moved by this time with her father into the town of Coventry, and somehow there came into her hands a copy of Charles Hennell's book *An Enquiry concerning the Origin of Christianity*, which marked a turning-point in her life. It is of great interest that Hennell's book, first published in 1838, was written with little knowledge of the school of German Rationalist Protestants that had flourished for the past two generations. Their lines of thought had themselves in fact derived from Hume and the British Deists. In Britain itself this development had either been forestalled by the biblical fervours of the Evangelicals, or had been driven, for political reasons and through the slumbrous Toryism of the universities, into the byways of national life. The eighteenth-century rationalist tradition ran on through such men as Godwin, Tom Paine, Priestley, Richard Carlile and Shelley—most of all through the Liberal Unitarians—and it was in this context that Marian Evans met it in Coventry with Hennell's book. Within a short time of reading it she met the author at the house of his brother-in-law Charles Bray. These two men and their wives and sisters and friends determined the main direction of her thought for life.

The two men were complementary; Hennell was primarily interested in history and Bray in philosophy. The main argument of Hennell's *Enquiry* is directed to meet the common orthodox theory that the rise of Christianity cannot be explained except on the supposition of its miraculous divine origin. He explains the life of Jesus in the religious context of the Essenes and the political hopes of Judas Maccabaeus. Under the influence of the Messianic expectation, he says, Jesus came to believe that he was the promised one; he was put to death by the Romans for political reasons on the advice of the Jewish authorities anxious to preserve the public peace. The middle part of the book is a discussion of the dates and credibility of the Gospels, emphasising their "scantiness and mixed nature". Underlying the statement that they are "loaded with miraculous additions" is the principle that "those miracles which cannot be resolved into natural events probably owe their miraculous part to the exaggeration or the invention of the narrators".

Now such a principle plainly implies not only a historical belief in the necessity of evidence, but also a belief in the *a priori* unlikeli-hood of miracles; and it seems improbable that Marian Evans would have fallen so easily to Hennell's history if Bray's philosophy had not been there to support it. Bray was a necessitarian who had been influenced by Shelley's notes to *Queen Mab*. His views on the connection between physical and mental behaviour had been much affected by a belief in the phrenology of George Coombe, a belief which Marian Evans for a time at least shared. Exactly how far she ever accepted Bray's whole philosophy it is hardly possible to be sure; but she seems to have accepted the principle of an "undeviating law", that is an "invariability of sequence", in both the material and the moral world; but such steps do not lead far towards a full philosophy.

At least she accepted once and for all the hypothesis that miraculous interventions do not occur in the course of Nature. With this, through the lines of argument developed by Hennell, fell the whole structure of dogmatic Christianity, Incarnation, Resurrection, Trinity, Atonement and all. Sitting on the bearskin under the acacia on the lawn at Rosehill, Coventry, a young Victorian had lost one faith. Her eyes glowed with the faith and hope that she had gained. For it was to her a great release, a great advance, a great moral triumph. It was victory for the virtue she held dearest of all —the love of truth, of truth dependent on the empirical study of evidence, of truth, too, dependent on fidelity to one's own feelings.

Before long the chance came to use her new-won experience for the benefit of others: in the cause of truth she could employ her knowledge of German. She undertook to continue the translation of Strauss's *Leben Jesu*, which one of her new friends had begun. Strauss was then the latest representative of the German school of rationalistic protestantism in fear of which both H. J. Rose and Pusey became in effect the founders of the Anglo-Catholic revival. He rejected as crude the theory that Jesus and his disciples were deliberate deceivers, because it failed to take into account the characteristics of the religious mind. He also rejected the theory (chiefly associated with Paulus of Heidelberg) that all the miracles can be explained on purely naturalistic grounds. He maintained that the Gospels contained a nucleus of historical fact, but that the miraculous elements had been imported in the spirit of the religious thought of the time in which they were written. The early disciples unconsciously attributed to Jesus miraculous powers and supernatural claims, in order to glorify him as their teacher and vindicate him as the fulfiller of prophecy. The Gospels thus showed the early stages of the growth of a great religious myth. The historical man Jesus was elevated into the Christ; and Christianity was built on the "Christ Myth". This thesis is plainly similar to

Hennell's, and Strauss in fact arranged for Hennell's *Enquiry* to be translated into German, and himself wrote a preface for it.

George Eliot, broadly speaking, accepted Strauss's view, however much she disliked the details and tone of his book. She found the relentless unemotional debunking of miracle after miracle unsympathetic to her sense of beauty and to the symbolic fitness of things. It upset the strain in her that loved Wordsworth and valued the feelings. In February 1846 she said she was "Strauss-sick", that it made her ill dissecting the beautiful story of the Crucifixion; and that she could only endure it by looking at the Christ-image. In the last hundred pages she felt that Strauss had had his say, and that even he himself was fagged. In March she wrote: "The Crucifixion and the Resurrection are at all events better than the bursting asunder of Judas."

And then, in a letter dated July 30, 1863, when Renan's *Life of Jesus* had just been published and she herself was a famous woman, she wrote: "For minds acquainted with the European culture of this last half-century, Renan's book can furnish no new result; and they are likely to set little store by the too facile construction of a life from the materials of which the biographical significance becomes more dubious as they are closely examined. It seems to me the soul of Christianity lies not at all in the facts of an individual life, but in the ideas of which that life was the meeting-point and the new starting-point. We can never have a satisfactory basis for the history of the man Jesus, but that negation does not affect the idea of the Christ either in its historical significance or in its great symbolic meanings." The new humanism had thus incorporated the world religions. For George Eliot Christianity had lost its basis in history and it had lost its claim to dogmatic certainty, but it remained the most relevant and moving symbolism for the mysteries of life.

CHARLES DARWIN

In 1927 Darwin's old house at Down, in Kent, was presented to the British Association and became a shrine.

When one visits it, the strongest impression has little to do with the two books which turned the whole conception of human history upside down; there are no skeletons, no brilliant diagrams of comparative anatomy, no pickled foetuses, no copy even of the famous portrait of a "Chimpanzee disappointed and sulky. Drawn from life by Mr Wood". The imaginative pilgrim is brought back from remote eras of geological time plumb into the weight and consequence of prosperous Victorian family life. Here is the vast polished dining-table; here a top hat and account-books; here, in the drawing-room, the sofa on which father lay in the evening when novels were read aloud, but only novels with a happy ending; and from the windows the garden, with the ilex on the mound and the tree-fringed meadow beyond, seems less the site of vital observations on the action of earthworms than the playground of first the children and then the grandchildren, while the head of the family took his daily exercise round the Sand Walk. Science seems to have been a mere incident in this household. It is true there is the study with a microscope and a huge, low, wheeled stool drawn up before it; a little lavatory in the corner boarded off and hung with grey wallpaper; bottles, instruments, files for papers, a large part of the original furniture and library; but the children used to burst in even here to borrow the scissors or the ruler.

The portraits, too, are of a patriarch. Male Victorian faces should be judged from likenesses taken before the Crimean War, when beards came in. Here the huge bearded figure, in oils and photographs and caricatures galore, completely holds the walls and gives a quite lop-sided version of the life. Yet there is one drawing of Darwin clean-shaven in his youth. No one knows for certain

who did it, and it is a little lifeless, so that the impression of a set
and almost stolid face may be quite false; the jaw is square and determined; the mouth has some simplicity and sweetness; the nose is
lumpish and odd, but not yet over-fleshy; everything is dominated by a prodigious brow coming to a climax, whether by means
of hair or skull or mere error it is impossible to say, in an extraordinary pointed gable. This was done soon after his return
from the voyage of the *Beagle*, and it gives a ludicrous appositeness
to the remark of his father when he first saw him again: "Why, the
shape of his head is quite altered!"

No words or portrait could better symbolize what that five years'
voyage had meant. Darwin's experience of any branch of science
before 1831 had been desultory, unsystematic and amateurish; even
his general intellectual training had been commonplace. Yet one
propensity was from earliest boyhood very strong in him, and he
believed it to be innate—"the passion of collecting, which leads a
man to be a systematic naturalist, a virtuoso, or a miser". He also
had great keenness and accuracy of eye and capacity for observation,
and an unusual power of inspiring confidence. His first regular
experience of training in method came in his friendship with J. S.
Henslow, Professor of Botany at Cambridge, and this friendship
determined his fate. Henslow persuaded him to spend the summer
of 1831 in serious geological work.

The survey-ship H.M.S. *Beagle* was due just then for a long
tour of work on the coasts of South America, and her captain,
FitzRoy, applied for permission to take a naturalist with him who
should pay all his own expenses. On these terms likely starters were
few. Henslow himself refused the job and finally suggested Darwin,
not as "a *finished* naturalist, but as amply qualified for collecting,
observing and noting anything worthy to be noted in Natural
History". It was a wide enough field. There was a flutter in the
family; his father objected that it was a wild, useless, dangerous,
unsettling scheme, "disreputable to his character as a clergyman
hereafter". With admirable tact and wisdom his uncle, Josiah
Wedgwood II, won the doctor over, and Charles was allowed to go.
The ship's officers affectionately nicknamed him "Philosopher".

Behind the published versions of the *Journal of Researches* lay a whole history of minute and concentrated work, and also a history of even, thorough and revolutionary intellectual development. On expeditions he carried pocket notebooks in which he entered everything indiscriminately on the spot. From these he wrote up, as leisure on board or on shore allowed, the first draft of a general Diary and also separate, more technical, records of his scientific work and specimens. After the voyage the first proposal was that his material should be interwoven for publication with that of Captain FitzRoy. It seems that Darwin's sisters played a big part in squashing this dreary plan, and his work first appeared as a separate, third, official volume. This was prepared from all the sources; much material was not used at all; all was adapted and rewritten. It is now possible, thanks to one of his grand-daughters, Lady Barlow, to see all the stages of this work paraded in open order. In 1933 she published a splendidly edited transcript of the manuscript Diary, which had for frontispiece a reproduction of the drawing with the gabled head. She has now printed a number of chosen extracts from the pocket-books, together with a series of thirty-seven long letters, written during the voyage, to his family.*

Darwin admitted he hated writing letters; yet these are vigorous, cheerful, affectionate, even though he was sometimes miserably seasick, and towards the end more miserably homesick. They are, for all the hardships, illness and accidents they describe—the trials of the Captain's temperament alternating with praise of his efficiency and goodness—almost incredibly equable; there are few fluctuations of mood, or moments of despondency, no self-mistrust or self-analysis: the eye is always turned outward with that "enlarged curiosity" noted by his uncle. Towards Nature in her finer moods and products there is a kind of Wordsworthian reverence; an unaffected horror at the first sight of naked savages. Most striking of all is the modesty. There never can have been a man of great genius who in his youth dwelt less upon the prospect of success and

---

* *Charles Darwin and the Voyage of the Beagle*, edited with an Introduction by Nora Barlow (Pilot Press). Reviewed *New Statesman & Nation*, 6 April 1946.

fame; he still expects to be a quiet country clergyman; he is really surprised and pleased to be told that the specimens he has sent home have proved useful and interesting.

The significant intellectual development is better traced in the notebooks. There he can be seen month by month progressively bringing everything into comparison with something else; wringing out more and more meaning from the comparison of items not superficially connected; asking innumerable questions to determine beforehand what to look for (he wryly recorded in later life how in 1831 he and Professor Sedgwick had geologised in the valleys of North Wales quite blind to the evidence of glacial action staring them in the face); framing and testing at all stages provisional hypotheses to account for what he finds. In the unwearying application of such methods the spark of genius suddenly flashes. When he first grasped the central idea of *The Origin of Species*, Huxley thought: "How extremely stupid not to have thought of that!"

Huxley also said that these particular manuscripts were worthless because of Darwin's lack of training in biology. Many entries certainly have a vivid unscientific appeal:

Twiners entwining twiners—tresses like hair—beautiful lepidoptera —Silence—hosannah—Frog habits like toad—slow jumps—iris copper-coloured, colour became faint. . . .

Miss Martineau—: Charity everywhere. I doubted it at first. Byron and the Fuegian woman. Have any other associated animals charity? Cows not. Wild cattle? Porpoise?

What is so fascinating is to see a mind of great freshness, not yet canalised by special training, unburdened by too much scholarship and precedent, still free to own a sense of wonder and beauty, learning almost the elements of a science at the same time as it collected new facts and asked the boldest questions. When Darwin started, his main interest was in geology, and it was the discovery of certain animal fossils which first seriously turned his attention to the problem of species. In her earlier book Lady Barlow traced his growing interest in it, and she now shows how the zig-zag course of the *Beagle*, from islands to mainland and back again, kept the variations and distribution of species dramatically under his eye, and the problems in the front of his mind. He opened his first notebook specifically on the "Transmutation of Species" in July 1837.

There is perhaps no essential mystery about Darwin's later life, but there are several problems. Why, for instance, did he delay so long before publishing *The Origin of Species*? Lady Barlow is clearly right in ascribing the delay largely to his extreme intellectual caution; for years he collected "facts from seedsmen, facts from animal fanciers, facts from farmers, besides his own observations and those derived from other scientists" before his case seemed clear enough to make public; but it is perhaps going rather far to suggest that his allegiance to FitzRoy, who became as time went on a more and more dogged champion of the "fundamentalist" view of creation, was another reason for delay. The possibility of an almost neurotic element in his own caution would seem to explain more than any reference to the susceptibilities of others. For he was, on the whole, quite indifferent to the kind of religious controversy the book was bound to cause. Unlike Huxley, he was not interested in scientific propaganda or the "mission" of science. He always professed to have no ability for speculation and abstract thought; he said he reached only one of his major conclusions by "deduction".

His forty years' illness, too, has never been quite explained. Yet, besides rigidly dictating the routine of daily life, keeping him from public engagements and intensifying his love of home, this semi-invalidism must also have had deep effects on the habits of his mind. In his youth he was very fond of poetry; at school he loved Shakespeare, Thomson, Byron and Scott; he carried Milton with him wherever he went from the *Beagle*; on getting home he had a period of passionate delight in Wordsworth and Coleridge. But in later life he wholly lost "all pleasure from poetry of any kind, including Shakespeare"; it even gave him positive pain. His difficulty in writing, too, increased rather than diminished as time went on; the verbal facility and inventiveness which appear here and there in the *Beagle* pocket-books never matured.

A combination of conditions—the five years of abnormally intense work and receptive observation in his youth, the illness, the

modesty amounting almost to diffidence, the strong family affections
—seems to have intensified his earliest "passion for collecting" till
he did in fact become a sort of virtuoso or miser, lovingly lingering,
to the atrophy of all other intellectual interests, over the ever-
growing accumulation of detail, all but reluctant to part with it to
the world. If this was, in one sense, his weakness, his triumph was
that he did not succumb to it. The asking of questions, the framing
of hypotheses went on; his insight never failed. For all its privacy
and homeliness and patriarchal atmosphere, Down House—where
now the *Beagle* pocket-books and Diary are on view in a glass case
—was the scene of portentous conclusions. The wise pilgrim will
be glad that all the technical manuscripts have gone to Cambridge;
for Down is also the shrine, as this book and much else can witness,
of a very remarkable family.

TENNYSON
AND THE SPIRIT OF THE AGE*

THERE have been two main strands of thought about Tennyson's relation to his age, both agreeing at least in this—that he was a poet very closely and specially bound to the intellectual and social conditions of his time, specially fitted to be its laureate.

One line of thought has stressed his position as the "Poet of Science" and of the reconciliation of science with religion. As a spokesman of this view none is handier than Sir Oliver Lodge, who wrote:

> By the term "Poet of Science" I understand one who assimilates the known truths of Science and Philosophy, through the pores, so to speak, without effort and with intuitive accuracy, one who bears them lightly and raises them above the region of bare fact into the realm of poetry. Such a poet is one who transfuses fact with beauty, he is ready to accept the discoveries of his age, no matter how prosaic and lamentable they seem, and is able to perceive and display the essential beauty and divinity which runs through them all and threads them all together.

and again:

> The glory of Tennyson's faith was that it never led him to be unfaithful to the kinds of truth that were being revealed to his age. That, too, was an age of revelation, and he knew it; the science of his epoch was true knowledge, as far as it went; it was over-emphatic and explosive, and to weaker or less inspired minds was full of danger, but it was genuine cargo, nevertheless, which must be taken on board; there was a real overload of superstition that had to be discarded; and it was his mission, and that of a few other noble souls, to help us to accomplish with calmness and something like wisdom the task of that revolutionary age.

---

* B.B.C. Third Programme, 3 July 1950.

The other line of thought is in direct opposition to this, and maintains that Tennyson's alertness to contemporary ideas was superficial and a cause of poetic weakness. This view was put in the middle of his lifetime even, as by a critic of the *Enoch Arden* volume in the *North British Review* for October 1864:

> We think that Mr Tennyson's remarkable subjection to present and external influences explains, in some degree, both his empire over some, and the indifference to his poetry of other by no means less able judges. . . . His taste follows the fashion of the time, whether for great exhibitions or Gothic manor houses. . . . His preaching—and he is fond of preaching—is tinged by the cheerful paganism of muscular divinity, while his exaltation of doubt above dogma betrays the temper of modern criticism. In short, the age governs Mr Tennyson's utterances, which are the accepted expression of its complex fashions.

This is the view which also underlies the best of the modern books on Tennyson, that by Harold Nicolson. He there argues, and argues very persuasively, that the whole conception of a poet's "mission" was overlaid on Tennyson by the circumstances of his time, was urged on him unduly by some of his friends, and that it diverted him away from his own greatest poetic strength. The Victorian preacher never quite swamped, but was always in danger of swamping, the great lyrical poet of lonely melancholy, the poet of "the cold, the half-light, and the gloom".

These are then, broadly, the two opposed views that have been current for the past hundred years. I don't mean now to try to argue them out or reconcile them; but, keeping them in mind, I want to try to edge behind them and focus on one or two aspects of the evidence on which they have been built.

In the first place both sets of opinion agree upon the fact that— whether it was praiseworthy or not—Tennyson did in his poetry make a great deal of use of the science of his time; and I want to argue that his consciousness of scientific developments was in several ways important in forming the fundamental conditions out of which his poetry grew.

Towards the end of his life, when he was nearly eighty, Tennyson wrote a poem called *Parnassus*: it is not a great poem, and it leaves on the reader that unfortunate impression of being in part a mere metrical exercise, which was the price he often had to pay for his dexterity. It describes a vision of Parnassus with the Muses, and with the poets raised by them to the heights of the mountain. Tennyson aspires to join them, with his head in the zenith,

> and roll my voice from the summit,
> Sounding for ever and ever thro' Earth and her listening nations,
> And mixt with the great Sphere-music of stars and of constellations.

But overtopping the poets and the Muses and Mount Parnassus itself are "two shapes high over the sacred fountain", "ever spreading and heightening": they seem to blast the poets' evergreen laurels. Tennyson asks what they are, and the answer is given:

> These are Astronomy and Geology, terrible Muses!

Then he ends the poem with these four lines:

> If the lips were touch'd with fire from off a pure Pierian altar,
> Tho' their music here be mortal need the singer greatly care?
> Other songs for other worlds! the fire within him would not falter;
> Let the golden Iliad vanish, Homer here is Homer there.

This short poem expresses very plainly one important side of Tennyson's relation to his age. Two elements in it are quite clear: Astronomy and Geology had, in his younger manhood, not only revolutionised the whole conception of the universe, and of the time-scheme of the universe, and of man's place in it; but they had also forced a ghastly searching into the ultimate origins of traditional human values and suggested the possibility that even the greatest achievements—even the achievements of immortal verse—were nothing but tiny transitory incidents. The ending of this particular poem, written by an old man, full of honours for writing poetry, after a lifetime of doing nothing but write poetry (as FitzGerald complained) or else get ready to write poetry, is almost despondent or at least inconclusive. In the lines just before those I have quoted he had been told to "sing like a bird and be happy"; but he cannot take the advice in that form, nor can he even advise himself, like

Byron, to write because he wants to be a moment merry; he has to try to generalise the matter "in the light of modern knowledge" and form a principle. The poem should have developed from the phrase "sing like a bird and be happy" instead of focusing on the loss of Iliads: it should have realised the satisfaction, the self-justification, of spontaneous song. But if it had done so, it would not have been a poem by Tennyson. For so great a poet, for a man as intelligent as he was, he seems to have lacked to quite an extraordinary degree a genuine internal conviction of the value of what he was doing. Compared with Coleridge and Keats, say, Tennyson never felt on his pulses that the poetic activity, the exercise of creative imagination through words, contained the ground of its own justification. He felt the poetic vocation as something external calling him on to do he hardly knew what, not as an internal principle working itself out. This is quite plain from that other late poem called *Merlin and the Gleam*, which is patently autobiographical. Much has been added to the understanding of it by Sir Charles Tennyson's recent biography. But the point I want to emphasise at the moment is that "the gleam" as an image of the poetic vocation is something outside him always leading him on, as if it were out of his control, and leading him into mysteries which he can only dimly apprehend beforehand. To him the gleam means restlessness and searching; the poem is a counterpart to the early poem *Ulysses*:

> my purpose holds
> To sail beyond the sunset, and the baths
> Of all the western stars, until I die.
> It may be that the gulfs will wash us down:
> It may be we shall touch the Happy Isles,
> And see the great Achilles, whom we knew.

The ultimate resolution is "to strive, to seek, to find, and not to yield". Life, even the poetic life, is an endless journey and an endless search.

But these journeys are not, like the journeys in Keats's *Endymion* or the voyage in *The Ancient Mariner*, journeys which symbolise the development of internal experience; they are imagined as journeys out into a real external world, a world in which the dead Arthur Hallam may truly be seen again, as Achilles, a world where "the border of boundless Ocean" is a bound across which some ultimate revelation about the character of the universe may be sought, about the universe not as "in the mind of man" but as something that can be looked at through a telescope. They are journeys governed by the concept of space, not journeys like those in *Endymion* governed by the psychology of dreams. They are journeys governed also by the concept of time, not measured as in *The Ancient Mariner* by the intensity of an agony of purgation, but time as it is measured on clocks and calendars and by the movement of the heavenly bodies.

Tennyson was haunted by the sense of time. His more immediate reference-point might be the constellations:

> The brook shall babble down the plain,
> At noon or when the lesser wain
> Is twisting round the polar star.

> Many a night from yonder ivied casement, ere I went to rest,
> Did I look on great Orion sloping slowly to the West.

And beyond the daily, monthly or yearly movements was the time of History, over which Tithonus brooded as he heard

> Apollo sing
> While Ilion like a mist rose into towers.

> Man comes and tills the field and lies beneath,
> And after many a summer dies the swan.

And beyond that again was the vast sequence of time which the "terrible Muses" had revealed: Geology has taught him that "the Giant Ages heave the hill and break the shore", and that

> Many an Aeon moulded earth before her highest, man, was born,
> Many an Aeon too may pass when earth is manless and forlorn.

And Astronomy added:

> But if twenty million of summers are stored in the sunlight still
> We are far from the noon of man, there is time for the race to grow.

A lesson from Geology could provide an image like this:

> The moanings of the homeless sea,
> The sound of streams that swift or slow
> Draw down Aeonian hills, and sow
> The dust of continents to be.

All through Tennyson's work sounds

> Aeonian music measuring out
> The steps of Time.

He was an Aeonian poet; one on whom the consciousness of time bore like a burden; that is why Geology and Astronomy were "terrible Muses". The sense of the Aeonian music and of the twenty million summers reinforced his native individual nostalgia; and it is in *Locksley Hall*, where the bitterness over his own personal past, "the 'Never, never', whisper'd by the phantom years" links to the moving of Orion through the sky, and to the dip "into the future, far as human eye could see", that all the consequences of his obsession with time become most apparent, with the great world spinning for ever down the ringing grooves of change.

Locksley Hall shows also how the time-consciousness on the cosmic scale leads into the excessive consciousness of modernity:

> I the heir of all the ages, in the foremost files of time:

and it was this consciousness of modernity which Tennyson shared so acutely with his age (and felt so bitterly) that led him into that side of his work which has been called "preaching" and the "mission"; for he had to leave his mark upon the age in some kind of practical consequences. He had to contribute to the time-process he saw being worked out. The passages from *Locksley Hall* that bring the themes together are too well-known to quote again; but there are other poems in which their connection is just as plain; notably they appear in the poem called *The Day-Dream*. This is a poem set in a framework of modern love and a proposal of marriage to "Lady Flora". The central matter inside the framework is a version of the story of the Sleeping Beauty, a story which leads straight into the theme of time. When the story has been told Tennyson asks:

> Were it not a pleasant thing . . .
> To sleep thro' terms of mighty wars,
> And wake on science grown to more,
> On secrets of the brain, the stars,
> As wild as aught of fairy lore;
> And all that else the years will show,
> The Poet-forms of stronger hours,
> The vast Republics that may grow,
> The Federations and the Powers;
> Titanic forces taking birth
> In divers seasons, divers climes;
> For we are Ancients of the earth,
> And in the morning of the times.

Here is the same double consciousness as appears in *Locksley Hall*, the consciousness of being at once old in experience and knowledge and yet very modern indeed. Here too is the vision of the future growth of science, especially in psychology and astronomy, the hopeful prospect of political federation and the expectation that even poetry itself will become something bigger and better:

> When will the hundred summers die,
>   And thought and time be born again,
> And newer knowledge drawing nigh,
>   Bring truth that sways the souls of men?

Men's souls have to be swayed, and it is for the poets to sway them. I am suggesting that this view of poetry as a form of action is a direct consequence of the forms of Tennyson's thought, governed as they were by the idea of the time-process and the evolutionary idea which accompanied it. And if poetry is a form of action then poetry that celebrates action—like *The Revenge* and *The Charge of the Light Brigade*—and poetry which urges to action—like *Riflemen Form!*—are obviously important kinds of it.

But the awful doubt still remains whether, in the aeons upon aeons of geological, astronomical time, all human action, poetry included, may not be so utterly trivial as to be worthless, whether golden Iliads may not perish by the dozen. And that way lies the suicidal Tennyson of *The Two Voices* and *Despair*, the man who has to be rescued by desperate assertions of almost hopeless faith. This brings me to the last point that I have time to make. Many of Tennyson's poems—*Maud* most notable among the longer ones— totter on the edge of madness. Constantly the one rallying-point in them as poems is the description of external things. There is not time to give examples of the many various ways in which the main descriptive passages are used; but it is obvious to any reader who has ever known Tennyson well that it is often the descriptive passages that stay in the mind rather than the poem's main theme; description is his greatest poetic strength. Galahad's purity is never realised, but the fighting is:

> The hard brands shiver on the steel,
> The splinter'd spear-shafts crack and fly.

And it seems to me that in a number of poems he uses description as if it were in itself the final aim of poetic art. For instance, *The Golden Year*, *Godiva*, and *Edwin Morris* all end on a passage of tremendous physical description which overbalances all that has gone before. Like this:

> and, high above, I heard them blast
> The steep slate-quarry, and the great echo flap
> And buffet round the hills, from bluff to bluff.

This emphasis on description, and the use of it to perform so many different functions, is another consequence of Tennyson's commitment to a "scientific" mode of thought. He was widely praised for his "accuracy", his fidelity to detail—and in this his work led into that of the pre-Raphaelites; but I think these descriptions also had for him a central emotional importance. They stabilised his mind in the contemplation of unending processes, and allayed the restlessness of the searching and journeying involved in his view of what poetry should do.

IN MEMORIAM*

I HAVE chosen to talk on *In Memoriam* in this series, not because it is primarily a philosophical poem in any strict sense of the term—in fact Tennyson himself made it quite clear that he did not intend it to be so; but because it represents so very clearly the mood of its time in relation to some great problems which border on philosophy; because that mood gave it a popularity which few long English poems have ever had; and because I think it is a poem which many modern readers find it very difficult to be clear-headed about.

In Memoriam was not originally planned as a single long poem at all; it was a series of short poems in the same metre, which gradually grew in bulk over a long period. Up to quite late Tennyson was speaking of his "Elegies" in the plural. Some were certainly written to form short groups with others; some ran straight on from the one preceding. But the idea of working them all into a sequence under a single title was strictly an afterthought. This fact is a main cause of the difficulty we now have in reading the poem; it is impossible to apprehend it as a unified whole; for it is not a whole; and it fluctuates waywardly. It *is* possible, of course, with the aid of Bradley's famous *Commentary* to see that the poem does fall into four main Parts, divided by the Christmas Poems; to see that each of three of the Parts does have a predominant mood; and to see that there *is* a development of mood and thought from beginning to end. But at the same time all readers would agree that within each Part, in the slow process of reading as poetry ought to be read, it is often impossible to see a genuine poetic unity. Especially in Bradley's Part III, that is sections LXXVIII to CIII,† the movement is often wayward and inconsequential.

* B.B.C. Third Programme, 15 Oct 1950, in a series called "Poetry and Philosophy".

† [Section-numbers refer to the *Poetical Works* (Oxford, 1953). Bradley seems to have assumed that after 1872 (when the new Section XXXIX, *Old warder of*

The poem then was never planned as a whole, and its composition was spread over a long period; and also its theme was never properly *apprehended* as a whole. I say its theme; but part of the problem is to be sure whether there was a single theme. Is the theme the personal sorrow for Arthur Hallam's death? Is the theme the whole question of human immortality? Is the theme the interplay of the personal sorrow with the general doubt about survival?

I think we should agree now that, if we are to talk in terms of a single theme at all, then the theme is the interplay of the personal sorrow with the general doubting and debating. But even when so much is said, the matter is not finally defined; for the interplay is complex; and a part of what I have to say will be an attempt to unravel it.

The attempt can only be made with the facts about the friendship with Arthur Hallam and about his death in mind. Tennyson first came to know Hallam well in 1829 when they were both undergraduates at Trinity, and both members of the famous group of young men called the "Apostles":

> we held debate, a band
> Of youthful friends, on mind and art,
> And labour, and the changing mart,
> And all the framework of the land;

They were serious young men, in fact, who talked about psychology, aesthetics, economics and politics—unlike the later

> boys
> That crash'd the glass and beat the floor.

They shared each others' hopes and ideals; they went abroad together; Hallam stayed with the Tennyson family at Somersby; and a more special kind of link was formed when he got engaged to Tennyson's sister Emily. This friendship grew in intimacy and in mutual admiration for rather more than four years. In the summer

---

these buried bones, was added, and the succeeding sections were renumbered accordingly) all subsequent editions followed suit, but this was not so. For instance the Oxford edition of 1910 (ed. T. H. Warren) retained the pre-1872 text and numbering.]

of 1833 Arthur Hallam went abroad with his father, Henry Hallam the historian; on 15 September he died with complete suddenness of a burst blood-vessel in Vienna. His body was brought to England by sea, and was buried on the 3rd January 1834 at Clevedon, on the Bristol Channel:

> The Danube to the Severn gave
> The darken'd heart that beat no more;
> They laid him by the pleasant shore,
> And in the hearing of the wave.

To try to estimate the quality of Tennyson's first sorrow at this appalling loss, is the first step in trying to appreciate the relationship between the elegiac and the philosophical elements in the final poem.

There is little doubt, especially from the evidence in the new biography by Sir Charles Tennyson published last year, that not only Alfred but the whole family had come to look on Arthur Hallam as a centre of stability. Emily, of course, had lost a lover; but, as Sir Charles writes,

> the melancholy state of the whole family made a deep impression on their cousins. . . . Even Frederick's spirit was broken. He felt that the family had lost its sheet anchor. "Never", he wrote, "was there a human being better calculated to sympathise with and make allowances for those peculiarities of temperament and those feelings to which we are liable."

This is valuable in redressing the common view that the grief expressed in *In Memoriam* is grossly exaggerated. For if Frederick and other members of the family felt like this, they must have further tended to increase a sorrow in Alfred which we may fairly suppose to have been already greater than theirs. It is curious to find them also sharing a sense of loss which became almost a feeling of desertion, a feeling which has been noted as underlying a number of Tennyson's best poems. It does not seem possible to doubt that his first grief was immediate, genuine and overwhelming. Its first poetic expression was in *Break, break, break* and in *The Two Voices*.

> A still small voice spake unto me,
> "Thou art so full of misery,
> Were it not better not to be?"

The Two Voices is a poem about the temptation to suicide, the possible valuelessness of human life, and the doubt of immortality. Much of the matter of *In Memoriam* is already there; it was written under the first impact of grief; but it is no elegy and Hallam is not mentioned. The question then is, did Hallam's death bring on doubt for the first time, or did it intensify in new and terrible forms an already existing doubt about the whole status and future of human personality?

There is scarcely time to develop all the reasons for thinking that the doubt was already there; but, broadly, they are of two kinds— first, Tennyson's own preoccupation from childhood with questions about his own identity, and, second, the general, current speculations in the early thirties about the nature of the world and of man. In particular, the publication of Lyell's *Principles of Geology* coincided with the last years of Arthur Hallam's life. In a poem called *Parnassus*, written very many years later, Tennyson called Astronomy and Geology "terrible Muses"; the word "terrible" has its full force; they were causes of terror. They overthrew the traditional cosmology and the traditional time-scheme of history; they made impossible the literal acceptance of the account of creation given in the book of *Genesis*; and they forced the imagination to dwell, both in time and in space, on vistas of unprecedented vastness. I have argued elsewhere that the early Victorians in general, in the face of these new terrors, turned for comfort and reassurance to an intensification of their personal relationships; Matthew Arnold's poem *Dover Beach* is a clear expression of this development. And in Tennyson's case there is explicit evidence that he regarded his friendship as a safeguard against fear; he wrote in an early sonnet:

> If I were loved, as I desire to be,
> What is there in the great sphere of the earth,
> And range of evil between death and birth,
> That I should fear,—if I were loved by thee?

and

> 'Twere joy, not fear, claspt hand-in-hand with thee,
> To wait for death.

Thus the intensity of affection for Hallam, even in his lifetime, was linked to the terrors of speculation. I think that we can even go further and suggest that the affection increased posthumously, in proportion as his death increased the doubts and fears about human life. For *In Memoriam* most plainly shows the *fostering* of an affection after the loved person was lost; what has been called the exaggeration of the sorrow and the exaggeration of the love can be better explained, I believe, as the building up of a progressively more and more idealised friendship in retrospect, as a rallying-point when so much else was uncertain. Thus the memorial purpose of the poem and the speculative purpose each worked on the other from the beginning, because the friendship itself had so much of its peculiar value only in the context of the speculation.

How deeply Tennyson's feelings for Hallam were tinged with fear even after his death can be seen from the ending to *In Memoriam* section XLI; the dread of desertion persists even into an imagined immortality:

> For tho' my nature rarely yields
>   To that vague fear implied in death;
>   Nor shudders at the gulfs beneath,
> The howlings from forgotten fields;
>
> Yet oft when sundown skirts the moor
>   An inner trouble I behold,
>   A spectral doubt which makes me cold,
> That I shall be thy mate no more,
>
> Tho' following with an upward mind
>   The wonders that have come to thee,
>   Thro' all the secular to-be,
> But evermore a life behind.

It is, you see, an elaboration of the desertion theme; even though both friends should enjoy personal immortality, yet there would still be an eternal separation; for Hallam would have by then advanced too far in the "grades" of the future life for Tennyson to overtake him.

I have purposely so far stressed the fears and terrors of the speculative parts of *In Memoriam*, because I think most modern readers agree in finding that it is exactly those parts which come from the deepest experience and have achieved the most satisfying poetic expression. The corollary of this view is that the optimistic, progressive view of the world and of life, that in the poem ultimately triumphs, is correspondingly shallow, even emotionally dishonest, and so produces inferior poetry.

There is no doubt that for his contemporaries Tennyson's salvation of hope was his greatest achievement; this was a great poem of spiritual and emotional victory. Bradley, writing at the turn of the century, said that parts of the poem

> come home to readers who never cared for a poem before, and were never conscious of feeling poetically till sorrow opened their souls. . . "This", they say to themselves as they read, "is what I dumbly feel. This man, so much greater than I, has suffered like me and has told me how he won his way to peace. Like me, he has been forced by his own disaster to meditate on 'the riddle of the painful earth,' and to ask whether the world can really be governed by a law of love, and is not rather the work of blind forces, indifferent to the value of all that they produce and destroy."

Only a few weeks ago I was talking about this to an American poet and teacher, a man now in later middle age, who said he thought that younger readers now disliked *In Memoriam* because they thought that a mood of "honest doubt", tinged with a strong hope, was an untenable or disreputable position; whereas he himself thought it was both tenable and quite honourable. I answered him then that I thought the real objection lay, not in the tenableness or not of the ultimate residuary doctrine, but in the poetic presentation of it. An expansion of that answer is what I now want to attempt.

If you boil out the ultimate residuary doctrine of *In Memoriam* in some such phrase as "Love conquers Death", the result is of no more interest than the wording of a Wayside Pulpit or a poem by Wilhelmina Stitch or Patience Strong; and it makes no difference if you say the ultimate doctrine ought rather to be "On the whole I hope Love conquers Death". The trouble with the last part of

In Memoriam is that at times Tennyson himself seems to be under
the illusion that he can in some such way as this present his case in
a nutshell. The "honest doubt" passage—section XCVI—is a case in
point:

> one indeed I knew
> In many a subtle question versed,
> Who touch'd a jarring lyre at first,
> But ever strove to make it true:
>
> Perplext in faith, but pure in deeds,
> At last he beat his music out.
> There lives more faith in honest doubt,
> Believe me, than in half the creeds.
>
> He fought his doubts and gather'd strength,
> He would not make his judgment blind,
> He faced the spectres of the mind
> And laid them: thus he came at length
>
> To find a stronger faith his own;
> And Power was with him in the night.

I could go on for a whole twenty-five minutes saying nothing else
but why I think that passage fails as poetry; the specious wording
of the central paradox, based on equivocations, is the main objection;
and it is made worse by the button-holing "Believe me"; which is
as good as saying "Don't really believe me." But beyond this there
is a coarseness in the metaphors used to describe what should appear
as a highly complex and delicate process—I mean such phrases as
"a jarring lyre", "beat his music out" and "fought his doubts"; they
are crude and inexpressive.

Another example of this tendency to rely on a too slick near-
epigram or a catch-phrase at a critical moment is to be seen in
section CXXIV: it also is concerned with the vital question of the
resolution of doubt:

> If e'er when faith had fall'n asleep,
> I heard a voice "believe no more"
> And heard an ever-breaking shore
> That tumbled in the Godless deep;

A warmth within the breast would melt
The freezing reason's colder part,
And like a man in wrath the heart
Stood up and answer'd "I have felt".

The matter cannot, least of all for poetic purposes, be so drastically simplified. Such over-simplification is one of the forms of bathos, least of all tolerable at such a crucial point. It is, I think, literary faults of this kind that have led so many readers to think that all Tennyson's recovered faith is factitious and shallow.

One great strength of *In Memoriam* as a quasi-philosophical poem is in the images of the various stages of evolution. In this Tennyson not only caught the mind of his time, but even anticipated it; his knowledge of the details of Astronomy and Geology combined here with his descriptive skill to produce physical images of a kind that had scarcely been possible in an earlier age. Consider this, of geological change:

There rolls the deep where grew the tree.
Oh earth, what changes hast thou seen!
There where the long street roars, hath been
The stillness of the central sea.

and

The moanings of the homeless sea,
The sound of streams that swift or slow
Draw down Aeonian hills, and sow
The dust of continents to be.

Sections LIV to LVI are the central passages dealing with biological evolution, where a sanguine belief that *somehow* all will ultimately turn to good is wrung out of the despondent contemplation of Nature's wastefulness. But I think that the use of the scientific and evolutionary images—though very effective there— is not most effective in those passages which are explicitly dealing with questions of belief about man and the universe; they have their greatest force when used not for exposition, but as part of the matter apprehended in the emotional moments on which the development of the poem most truly depends. Such a moment is that presented in section xcv, when Tennyson had a kind of trance one evening while re-reading Hallam's letters:

> A hunger seized my heart; I read
> Of that glad year which once had been,
> In those fall'n leaves which kept their green,
> The noble letters of the dead:
>
> And strangely on the silence broke
> The silent-speaking words, and strange
> Was love's dumb cry defying change
> To test his worth; and strangely spoke
>
> The faith, the vigour, bold to dwell
> On doubts that drive the coward back,
> And keen thro' wordy snares to track
> Suggestion to her inmost cell.
>
> So word by word, and line by line,
> The dead man touch'd me from the past,
> And all at once it seem'd at last
> His living soul was flash'd on mine,
>
> And mine in his was wound, and whirl'd
> About empyreal heights of thought,
> And came on that which is, and caught
> The deep pulsations of the world,
>
> Aeonian music measuring out
> The steps of Time—the shocks of Chance—
> The blows of Death.

Here the imagery which he commonly uses for the vastness of astronomical and geological time, and still belonging properly to that, gives a peculiar greatness to this momentary spiritual touch with Hallam.

I think the true development in the later part of *In Memoriam* lies less in the *explicit* conquests of doubt; less in the assertions of the power of love; less in the sentinel

> Who moves about from place to place,
> And whispers to the worlds of space,
> In the deep night, that all is well.

less in the statement that

> all is well, tho' faith and form
> Be sunder'd in the night of fear.

The true development of the poem lies less in these passages, than in those moments of achieved happiness and hope, in which the optimistic evolutionary philosophy is not described, but simply taken for granted, as providing the setting and the mode of thought. There is no doubt that the poem does contain the record of a deep and genuine transposition of mood from despair to acceptance and hope. We can let all the over-simplified argument go, and the facile political optimism, and all the sillinesses and mannerisms with which the poem certainly abounds, and hold to such passages as the ending of section CXII:

> For what wert thou? some novel power
> Sprang up for ever at a touch,
> And hope could never hope too much,
> In watching thee from hour to hour,
>
> Large elements in order brought,
> And tracts of calm from tempest made,
> And world-wide fluctuation sway'd
> In vassal tides that follow'd thought.

or in the last part of the Epithalamium for Cecilia Tennyson, in the epilogue in which the bridal night and the conception of a child are seen in all their local beauty against the vastness of star and system rolling past.

MAN AND NATURE:
SOME ARTISTS' VIEWS*

I WAS trying to write the script of this talk over Easter. I looked out of my windows at the plum blossom fully out, and the pear not far behind and the first green showing on the apple trees; rooks carried twigs across my rectangles of clear sky; the sun has been shining on the table. I have not wanted to think specially about the Victorians, still less make up a talk about them; but the very things seen from the window brought scraps of their poems to mind; and it is a love of fact, like the Victorians', that has made me think what a ridiculous season this is, when all the poems belonging to April and May seem to belong simultaneously to the end of March. The blossomed pear tree, the wise thrush; the glassy pear-tree leaves and blooms, they brush the descending blue; that blue is all in a rush with richness.

> In Springtime when the leaves are young,
> Clear dewdrops gleam like jewels, hung
> On boughs the fair birds roost among.

Scraps of their descriptive poetry—what the Victorians called the poetry of "word-painting"—have been coming into my mind; and it has been a shock to remember that "In the Spring a young man's fancy lightly turns to thoughts of love" is a line out of *Locksley Hall*. For a good deal to do with Man and Nature is implicit in that line; and the word "lightly" is so curious.

And then my mind has wandered off to Darwin in the Galapagos Islands, where the volcanic landscape reminded him of the furnaces of Staffordshire; to Diana Warwick walking on the Surrey hills; to the Queen's life in the Highlands; to Millais's *Scotch Firs*, and *The Deserted Garden* and *The North-West Passage*. And it was this picture in the end—*The North-West Passage*—that gave me a clue

* B.B.C. Third Programme, 31 March 1948.

140

about where this talk might, with all the bewildering stuff that could go into it, begin.

The love of fact is the clue. You will remember that the sub-title of the picture is "It might be done, and England ought to do it". If there is a single fact about the geography of the globe still undiscovered, then something should be done to find it out, and it should be done by an Englishman. It is important that Darwin's work began on a naval survey voyage.

It was by means of the patient accumulation of fact that the Victorians domesticated mystery, made Romanticism respectable. From that point two attitudes developed; one was the purely scientific, for which the facts were all—as they were for Darwin— facts loved with a lingering passion. The other was a sentimental love of fact, for the sake of what could be easily attached to it in the way of belief and feeling. Both attitudes started from a common literalness of mind. Victorian sentimentality is largely the imposition of feeling as an afterthought upon literalness.

The *Penny Magazine* and *Chambers's Miscellany* and many other publications like them—some produced by the Society for the Diffusion of Useful Knowledge, and some by private enterprise— were designed to show that knowledge of fact about Nature and about History was of practical advantage. It was believed in the early-Victorian age that the common man could keep pace with science and that the more he knew about botany and the rest, the better and the more useful man he would be. There was a spate of popular informative factual literature in the thirties and forties. The Exhibition of 1851 was the climax of this phase, the visible triumph of Useful Knowledge. From that time things tended to become less popular and more specialised. It was realised that the facts were too complicated for popular exposition in detail; but the love of fact for its sentimental attachments remained. The love of literalism and the love of exaggerated sentiment are two essential points for understanding Victorian art. The problem was either to avoid literalism and an extreme of sentiment, or to reach a point of stability between them.

Nothing is more remarkable than the decay of the great Romantic tradition, the stifling of its grandeur; Romanticism, as I have said, was made respectable. This was brought about partly by the narrow practical business manners of a rising bourgeoisie, partly by the pre-eminent intellectual insistence on the importance of fact. The cosmic visions of Blake or Shelley were brought to trial against the cosmic facts of astronomy and historical geology. Man was dwarfed by the new conception of time and had to exaggerate his morality and his sentiment in order to restore his self-esteem.

The abnormal consciousness of time is very apparent in all Victorian painting—not merely in the obvious love of historical themes and antiquarian detail, nor in the anecdotal genre pictures and the countless illustrations to eighteenth-century novels, but also in pictures with a minimum of obvious anecdotal content. The world of their pictures is a world in which you expect things to happen. The pictures seem to refer to what has gone before or what will come after. This is achieved sometimes by the treatment of human figures who look as if they are going to walk out of the canvas in a moment; sometimes by animals, sometimes by wind or sea that blows and splashes in your eyes, sometimes by an object like a sundial, or a mossy stone, or a falling leaf. Even plain natural objects look like Tennyson's "Talking Oak" or his brook that babbles "Men may come and men may go, but I go on for ever". If there is a picture of a rainy afternoon you start wondering what there will be for tea.

This is partly because the style of vision is the vision of ordinary life. The world of Victorian art is the world of the plain, practical man, in which things happen and are done. It is an art to suit a practical age and be bought by practical patrons. This also helps to explain the appearance in the pictures of a "limitless" Nature: every effort is made to put everything in, as if the whole practical external world could be crowded onto a canvas. The desire for this limitless effect was so strong that the painter Henry Holliday actually made a special kind of huge stereoscope to increase his field of vision as widely as possible—a device with an exactly opposite purpose to that of the eighteenth-century landscape mirror, which was designed to reduce the field of vision to a manageable composition.

The invention of photography did not, I believe, produce visual habits which the painters had not already begun to develop. One might almost argue that photography was invented to meet an existing demand for records of visual fact, rather than the other way round. There is little evidence that in its early days photography seriously influenced painting one way or another. Both camera and painter's eye were alike used to make all-inclusive visual records; and in a sense the painter had an advantage because he could cheat: the photographers then chiefly cheated by trying to make their pictures look like paintings—a softened version of real life. Frith, who is often called a photographic painter, managed to get more clear detail into his pictures than any camera could achieve. He once tried to paint a portrait from a photograph, and gave it up as a failure. But Frith is the plainest example of all, of a painter with the practical domestic vision.

In the attitude to Nature shown in Victorian art there is a lack of individual physical vision and also a lack of what one might call spiritual insight. Constable's highly personal vision of light almost died with him, at any rate in England; he seemed to teach few others anything. Turner had a few imitators, but a glance at a landscape by, say, Pyne, is enough to show that all the essential qualities are missing. With Samuel Palmer the loss of vision and insight occurred in the life and work of the one man; in the Victoria and Albert Museum today one can see his glorious cherry-tree in the garden at Shoreham, side by side with one of his later landscapes: the two pictures seem to belong to different worlds. In poetry, the imitators of Wordsworth either catch only the superficial aspects of his themes, or else they express their desire for a spiritual experience in the face of Nature, which they confess they do not directly achieve.

One finds too that Wordsworth was often praised for the wrong reasons, especially for the minute fidelity of his natural description; yet he was not particularly good at this nor much interested in it. The examples that Ruskin quotes in *Modern Painters* are only such as would strike the eye of a man who was himself concerned about such things. The details that were so much loved in Tennyson were of a different kind, and Mrs Gaskell put her finger on the spot when she made the man in *Cranford* go and look at some ash-buds because Tennyson had said they were black. But they are black only to a literal vision in a particular kind of light. You will remember, too, all the controversy about whether the "sea-blue bird of March" was or was not a kingfisher. Chestnuts pattering to the ground, heavily hanging hollyhocks, rooks blown about the skies—these are the poetry of the period of literalism; and "the elm-tree bole in tiny leaf", of course.

Ruskin's *Modern Painters* is a valiant struggle—and one which has not even now lost its value—to reconcile the scientific consciousness, the fidelity to constant external fact, with the belief that art was somehow concerned with individual vision and with mystery. It is more than an ephemeral tract against current academic conventions and the art criticism of John Eagles; its concern with Locke's theory of primary and secondary qualities, with the theory of light, with the structure of clouds and so on, marks an attempt to incorporate, within the world of Nature with which the artist deals, the world of Nature with which the scientist deals. It is a plea that artists should *know*. To us the most surprising feature of the book is that of all modern painters the one constantly praised for his "pure straightforward rendering of fact" should be Turner; the example is so wide of what we would expect either from the theory or from the other painters given faint praise.

"Details alone", said Ruskin in the preface to the second edition, "and unreferred to a final purpose, are the sign of a tyro's work". "In landscape", he said, "botanical or geological details are not to be given as matter of curiosity or subject of search, but as the ultimate elements of every species of expression and order of loveliness." These last words are very obscure; but they show a common underlying problem for both painters and poets. Because the Romantic tradition said that Nature was somehow the source of important spiritual experience, and because the habit of mind of the following generation (with an empirical scientific philosophy) was to dwell so lovingly on factual detail, a suspicion came about that perhaps the cause of the spiritual experience lay in the detail. I think this is how Ruskin read, or misread, Wordsworth. It also helps to explain the sentimentality which I have called the imposition of feeling as an afterthought upon literalness.

I can best illustrate this from a description of the methods employed by Frederick Walker in his landscape painting given by a friend of his called North: "Walker painted direct from nature, not from sketches. His ideal appeared to be to have suggestiveness in his work; not by leaving out, but by painting in, detail, and then partly erasing it. This was especially noticeable in his water colour landscape work, which frequently passed through a stage of extreme elaboration of drawing, to be afterwards carefully worn away, so that a suggestiveness and softness resulted—not emptiness, but veiled detail . . . there is scarcely an inch of his work that has not been at one time a careful, loving study of fact." Lower down he writes of a possible reaction in Walker "from the somewhat un-natural clearness of definition in the early pictures of the Pre-Raphaelite Brotherhood".

A still more remarkable example of this mixture of sentiment and literalism occurs in a series of lectures *On Poetic Interpretation of Nature* which Principal Shairp gave in 1877. He says that the aim of a poet in observing the details of flowers "is to see and express the loveliness that is in the flower, not only the beauty of colour and of form, but the sentiment which, so to speak, looks out from it, and which is meant to awaken in us an answering emotion. For this end he must observe accurately, since the form and hues of the flower discerned by the eye are a large part of what gives it relation and meaning to the soul." He says the poet must see the "outward facts of the wild-flowers" as they stand related "to the whole world, of which they are a part, and to the human heart, to which they tenderly appeal".

To us these are very curious remarks. It is specially curious to find Shairp saying there is sentiment in the flower which *is meant* to awaken answering emotion in us. For his words do indeed seem to imply that this sentiment is verily in the flower, and is there for the poet to see. William Henry Hunt—bird's nest Hunt, that is—said, "I feel frightened whenever I sit down to paint a flower."

There was a popular little book, reprinted by the thousand, called

The Language of Flowers, and I bought the other day a far more elaborate work which showed how the visible natural world is really packed with all the details of ethics. The best work of the Pre-Raphaelites treats flowers with great particularity of detail in bright, clean colours: sentiment is not imputed to them; the flowers are treated primarily for their own sake; there may then also be an additional emblematic or symbolic meaning, but it does not distort the original directness. Holman Hunt always kept the emblematic purpose but unfortunately lost the directness of method. A whole series of sermons was preached on the botanical symbolism of *The Light of the World.* But if the flowers had been effectively symbolical the sermons ought not to have been necessary. There was no current convention in the matter. It has often been pointed out that it doesn't make two pins of difference poetically or ethically whether you say "The lilies and languors of virtue, the roses and raptures of vice" or "The roses and raptures of virtue, the lilies and languors of vice." I don't think that these curiosities can be simply explained in terms of either Anthropomorphism or the Pathetic Fallacy.

One of Millais's most effective and satisfying Pre-Raphaelite pictures, before his style went bad, is the drowning Ophelia; and in it there is a conscious reference to the symbolic use of flowers by Ophelia herself in the mad scene. Among many revealing critiques of Landseer's lions when they were added to the Nelson column was an article in *Art and Nature* which complained in one paragraph that they were not treated symbolically and heraldically enough, and in the next that they were not in detail naturalistic enough. The writer was evidently, like Holman Hunt, trying to have the best of both worlds.

The treatment of animals is, of course, another notable instance of the mixture of literalness and sentiment. Landseer was painting animals long before the Victorian age: but if you look, for instance, at his equestrian portrait of the Queen done in 1839, which now hangs in Wyatt's huge Gothic hall at Ashridge, you will find still lingering traces of detached eighteenth-century treatment in the pony and dogs. Stubbs and others painted plenty of emotional animals, but they had animal emotions. Landseer in his later manner painted dogs, as John Piper has said, "with human eyes". The habit of anthropomorphising animals spread outwards from dogs to horses and then to cattle. There is a picture by T. Sidney Cooper showing a number of cows at one side of a field, and at the other side, some distance from them, a single enormous bull. The title of the picture is *Separated but not Divorced*. The remarkable thing is that nobody seemed to think this funny.

In Landseer the process worked both ways. He made his dogs human: but he himself was quite prepared to go doggy. "He was a brilliant talker, and could imitate to perfection the cry of any animal with which he was familiar. Being asked one day at Lord Rivers' to go and see a very savage dog that was tied up in the yard, he crawled up to the animal on his hands and knees, and snarled so alarmingly that the dog, overcome with terror, suddenly snapped his chain, jumped over the wall, and was never seen again."

All the anthropomorphism and the sentimental treatment of animals (as also the sentimental treatment of human beings themselves, especially children) was a means of infusing into what was otherwise a purely materialistic "scientific" representation of the external world some kind of "spirit". It was, as I have already suggested, an afterthought. The effect which we call sentimentality —that is flabby and exaggerated sentiment—comes about partly because it is an afterthought, an added embellishment, extraneous to the first conception, and partly because the social and moral circumstances of the time required in art as well as in life the over-assertion of certain modes of feeling. The entirely novel stress on factual, measurable, statistical values and the expectation life offered of material gain—this called up in opposition an equally novel and self-indulgent stress on all those aspects of life which so obviously suffered from industrialism. Not all tenderness is sentimental, not even all Victorian tenderness. Mulready's picture *The Sonnet*, Madox Brown's *Autumn Afternoon*, and some of Arthur Hughes's paintings, especially those of lovers meeting, are admirably tender. But such things as *Bubbles*, *The Mistletoe Gatherer*, *Hope* by Watts, illustrate the false tenderness of excess. No other art in the world, however bad, has ever been bad in quite this sort of way: for its social context was unique. Both Nature and Art were being used as instruments for countering the obtrusive hardness of life. In this process Art and natural scenery were thought of as partners whom the artist was to bring closer and closer together.

The countless landscapes which hung in the mansions of magnates who had made their fortunes in the hideous towns were a sort of propitiatory offering to make up for the squalor; they were also in the evenings thought of as sources of refreshment, light and peace. This had its counterpart in the cult of the actual country and the seaside. The railways made travel possible for thousands who could otherwise never have afforded to go so far: the family summer holiday became an institution which was thought of as providing not merely rest from work but a spiritual regeneration through the sight of trees and fields and waves, and an education through collecting ferns and flowers and fossils and all the strangely curled and coloured creatures of the shore. Here is the beginning of Tennyson's *Sea Dreams*:

> A city clerk, but gently born and bred;
> His wife, an unknown artist's orphan child—
> One babe was theirs, a Margaret, three years old:
> They, thinking that her clear germander eye
> Droopt in the giant-factoried city-gloom,
> Came, with a month's leave given them, to the sea:
> For which his gains were dock'd, however small:
> Small were his gains, and hard his work.

But there was something rather arid in all this uplift and in the belief that Nature by some sort of automatic alchemy could heal and restore both soul and body. Flowers might be capable of sentiment and dogs of tears; but man's place in Nature could not solely be that of a parasite on their virtues. He was, after all, a part of Nature in his own right: he was modifying Nature far more quickly than Nature was capable of modifying him: and besides, the biological link between man and dogs and sea urchins became at once more apparent after the publication of *The Origin of Species*. By the sixties the poets and novelists, though not the painters, were waking up to the essential link between man's sexuality and the productive vitality of Nature, to the fact that when in spring a young man's fancy turned to thoughts of love, it did so not lightly but with a solemn swing in time with beast and bird. Though Blake, Keats and Shelley fully understood this, it is curious that Wordsworth's intense consciousness of closeness between Man and Nature was so little sexual, or at least that he does not seem to be aware of the fact; Tennyson was only faintly so; it is with Swinburne and Meredith that we again find clearly both the explicit recognition of sexual affinities and also the use of sexual imagery in other places. They both give a new importance and a new quality to the idea of Earth as the Mother of man as well as of all other living things, and in them, too, appears for the first time among the Victorians, openly confessed and worked out, the idea of sexual reproduction as the common principle of all Life—the idea which had been so magnificently stated by Lucretius. In Meredith it is most fully developed in the poems; but in the novels, too, it is a main factor in the development of characters and also in the connection between the characters and their landscape: the following passage exemplifies this sexual quality in *Diana of the Crossways*:

> She gave him comprehension of the meaning of love: a word in many mouths, not often explained. With her, wound in his idea of her, he perceived it to signify a new start in our existence, a finer shoot of the tree stoutly planted in good gross earth; the senses running their live sap, and the minds companioned, and the spirits made one by the whole-natured conjunction. In sooth, a happy prospect for the sons and daughters of Earth, divinely indicating more than happiness: the speeding of us, compact of what we are, between the ascetic rocks and the sensual whirlpools, to the creation of certain nobler races, now very dimly imagined.

This is something that George Eliot, for all her alertness to life and all her knowledge of contemporary thought, never expressed in her books. Emily Brontë had known it instinctively. Rossetti had inklings of it which came out in some of his pictures. But it was with Meredith, Hardy, and Jefferies that it became a primary theme.

The detailed method of description, whether in literature or painting, made it difficult to show passion for fear of being indecent; and the very trees seemed to stand without sap and without growth. Even in such a picture as Holman Hunt's *The Hireling Shepherd*, of which, in spite of all its symbolism, the subject is nothing but pastoral lust, all passion is not spent but absent. It was only when the kind of selection used by the great Romantics came in again that the vital principle of Man and Nature could again become a theme of art. By the end of the century, not only were the arts affected, but life as well. In *Love's Coming-of-Age* (1896) Edward Carpenter was quoting Meredith in support of his campaign for sexual frankness, and wrote of human love as belonging to the open air.

Sexual embraces themselves seldom receive the benison of Dame Nature, in whose presence alone, under the burning sun or the high canopy of the stars and surrounded by the fragrant atmosphere, their meaning can be fully understood: but take place in stuffy dens of dirty upholstery and are associated with all unbeautiful things.

At the beginning of this talk I mentioned the problem of avoiding altogether, or striking a point of stability between, literalness and sentiment. I should like to suggest that the virtues of—to take a few examples—Emily Brontë, Dickens at his greatest, Rossetti sometimes and Gerard Manley Hopkins almost always, lay either in this avoidance or this stability.

PRE-RAPHAELITE POETRY*

I THINK many listeners may have been a good deal surprised by the earlier talks in this series—surprised at their very stringently limited application of the term "Pre-Raphaelite" to a few artistic purposes and a few ideas. They have been concerned to stress the leading motives of a return to a direct view of Nature and the treatment of "modern" subjects, and to ignore or minimise the importance of the medieval and properly religious elements in Pre-Raphaelite work. This means in effect that Holman Hunt's view of Pre-Raphaelitism has triumphed, and that Dante Gabriel Rossetti is hardly allowed to be a Pre-Raphaelite at all. I agree that one must consider the movement as a whole, and that the fellow-travellers have to be taken into account as much as the leaders and the admitted "brethren"; and a similar principle should be applied to the themes and motives of their art. The fact we have to start with is that the medieval interests appeared very early, alongside the purpose of looking direct at Nature and treating "modern" subjects; the medieval and churchy elements did not come into the story only with the later group of men centred on Morris and Burne-Jones.

When *The Germ* appeared in January 1850, there was printed on its cover a sonnet by William Michael Rossetti intended to declare the purpose of the paper; he later said the sonnet meant that

> A writer ought to think out his subject honestly and personally, not imitatively, and ought to express it with directness and precision; if he does this, we should respect his performance as truthful, even though it may not be important.

And he added that this was meant to indicate for writers much the same principle which the PRB professed for painters. But it *is*

* B.B.C. Third Programme, 1 Nov 1948.

startling to see that the whole of this sonnet professing the need for personal honesty, directness, precision, etc., together with the title of the paper and the sub-title including the words "Thoughts towards Nature", should all be printed in heavy black Gothic type, so that the cover looks like that of a Puseyite parish magazine.

This sense of duality, even of incongruity, in artistic idiom is perpetuated in much of the contents of all the four numbers of *The Germ*. For instance, there is a poem in the first number by John Tupper, called *A Sketch from Nature*: its main theme is a description, in what was later called "word-painting", of sunset over the landscape seen from Sydenham Wood in 1849; it opens with a piece of blatant ballad-mongering:

> The air blows pure, for twenty miles,
>   Over this vast countrie:
> Over hill and wood and vale, it goeth,
>   Over steeple, and stack, and tree.

It then appears that the Surrey birds of 1849 included species called corbies and merles. This sort of archaism was a product of literary medievalising which already had a long history in several different modes.

In the past fifty years English poetry had developed more strongly and variously and had changed more radically than English painting. The academic painting against which the Pre-Raphaelites revolted was a long-delayed hang-over from the eighteenth century, a tradition which had failed to assimilate Blake, Constable, Turner, Palmer, and others. To have attempted an exactly parallel revolt in literature would have meant attacking very little more than University Prize poems. It has already been pointed out that the Pre-Raphaelites' painting was very literary painting; in fact they deliberately went to literature for their themes, and their treatment and style of vision were deeply influenced by the poets— especially by Keats and Tennyson. It is thus not surprising that much minor poetry written by Pre-Raphaelites or fellow-travellers shows an exaggeration of Tennyson's mannerisms. Woolner's *My Beautiful Lady*, for instance, is full of such echoes:

I see a lurid sunlight throw its last
Wild gleam athwart the land whose shadows lengthen fast.

One could well illustrate from Tennyson all the Pre-Raphaelite principles as they were explicitly put forward; and this has led people to say over and over again this year that Tennyson was a Pre-Raphaelite poet. If one has to use these labels it makes more sense to call the Pre-Raphaelites Tennysonian painters; but I want to suggest that the most important Pre-Raphaelite poetry was not Tennysonian, and that it attempted something which was never quite explicitly put forward as a Pre-Raphaelite purpose.

In its simplest form Pre-Raphaelite medievalism was merely one aspect of Pre-Raphaelite naturalism. This is made very plain in the second number of *The Germ* in an article by F. G. Stephens, under the pseudonym "John Seward": its title is "The Purpose and Tendency of Early Italian Art". Its whole argument is that the early Italian painters *were* naturalistic, that they showed "the simple chastity of nature" before "the introduction of false and meretricious ornament". Stephens understood them to be motivated by a desire for "truth in every particular", and he argued that nineteenth-century science had given a new stimulus to just this same motive. This is the purest and simplest pre-Raphaelite doctrine.

But it at once raises two questions:

(1) Was medieval freshness and naturalism really governed by similar motives and backed by similar mental processes to those of nineteenth-century science?

(2) Was the cultivation of nineteenth-century scientific naturalism an adequate or interesting formula for the production of works of art?

The most important Pre-Raphaelite poetry implied an emphatic answer "No" to both these questions. It was searching through the mixture of modernism and medievalism after deeper purposes.

When a medieval artist painted a religious or scriptural theme he dressed the figures in the normal clothes of his own time.

153

James Smetham, a painter on the edge of the Pre-Raphaelite circle, recorded a conversation with Ruskin about this in 1855. Ruskin admitted that on his principles in nineteenth-century religious pictures the people should be in modern dress, adding that "if it would not look well, the times are wrong and their modes must be altered".

> J. S. "It would be a very great deal easier (it is a backward, lame action of the mind to fish up costume and forms we never saw), but I could not do it for laughing."
> J. R. "Ha! but we *must* do it nevertheless."

"I could not do it for laughing." There is a main clue to what I am trying to discuss.

One of the big problems for the Pre-Raphaelites and for all their generation was to try to see the daily life of Victorian England—complete with all its keepings of dress and furniture and social habits—as having an equivalent spiritual and human significance to that which medieval life had in all its details for medieval poets and painters. One method was to use modern themes to bring out the moral and social tensions which underlay the surface of slick prosperity; but there were also personal, psychological, sexual and religious tensions which became more apparent in the life and literature of the later fifties and the sixties.

The series of poems which best illustrates this dilemma in the poetry of the mid-century is Coventry Patmore's long work *The Angel in the House*; and it is significant that Patmore at once found sympathy for the Pre-Raphaelites and contributed to *The Germ*. Now, *The Angel in the House* is an attempt to invest an ordinary Victorian courtship and marriage in the prosperous educated classes with as deep a spiritual and psychological significance as was felt to attach to the great poetic loves of the past; the main narrative stresses all the details of modern dress, archery parties, passing the port after dinner, etc. etc., while the running comment in the Preludes and lyrical parts attaches to these details a highly wrought passion more delicate and sustained than the gusty discontent in *Maud*. The trouble was that people laughed; they felt as Smethan¡ did about Lord John Russell portrayed paying homage to the Infant Saviour with his top hat standing by on a pedestal. There seemed to be an irreparable cleavage between the facts of modern society and the depths it was recognised poetry ought to touch. This cleavage is not yet healed; all our living poets have been conscious of it; so were the Pre-Raphaelites.

The medieval world attracted them not from a mere love of archaic patterns and forms or by a nostalgia for more colourful ways of life (though these things entered into it) but because medieval art did not betray any such cleavage between daily visible fact and accepted truth and values. They saw that medieval modes of apprehending reality were productive of great and satisfying works of art, as the modern modes of mixed science and sentimentality were not. They attempted, by exploring the possibilities of allegory and symbolism, to restore a harmony they thought modern life had lost.

A proper discussion of this attempt would involve many complex problems of metaphysics and theology that I am not competent to tackle: I can only just suggest certain untechnical lines of thought. We have to consider the status of symbols, allegories and emblems; by status, I mean the kind of significance they were supposed to have, and the means by which they were supposed to have any significance at all. This discussion is closely linked to the revival of sacramental doctrine in the Oxford Movement.

The Sacrament of the Eucharist provides the clearest example of what I mean, and best illustrates what I mean by status: there was (and is) a "High" and a "Low" view of this sacrament. The High view maintains that after consecration there is some kind of identity between the elements and the body and blood of Christ, and because of this, extreme reverence and care are shown for the physical elements; this is almost exaggeratedly stressed, with medieval quotations, in the Anglo-Catholic books of ceremonial and devotion of the 1850's. The elements are much more than mere symbols, mere reminders of Christ's sacrifice; they do in some way embody it.

In medieval life this sacramental view of things was not confined

155

to the theological sacraments; the mere making of the sign of the Cross could be potent in exorcism; holy water had special powers; miraculous power inhered in physical relics and holy places; every detail of Nature was in some sense a sacramental embodiment of spiritual reality. Language itself, in the words of consecration, forgiving, blessing, and cursing had theological power, and magical power in spells. The words of Scripture were interpreted in various ways, ranging from the literal-historical to the mystical. Thus both painting and literature were charged with significance at many different levels. Most of this wealth of implication was slowly destroyed in the sixteenth and seventeenth centuries. The Anglo-Catholic and Roman Catholic revivals of the nineteenth involved in various ways the recovery of some part of it. But science and history had utterly transformed the ways in which men could be said to "believe in" sacraments, in the sacramental view of Nature, symbols, and myths. The Catholic countries failed no less than the Protestant to produce any great religious art.

For the members of the Rossetti family this whole question of symbolism was conditioned by the intensive study of Dante in which they were brought up by their father. In Dante was to be found the fullest development of medieval symbolism, of every kind of status, from the theologically sacramental, through the cosmological to the conventions of courtly love and their private development in the Beatrice theme. All the children knew Dante better than they knew any English poet. William Bell Scott wrote of Dante Gabriel Rossetti:

> He had never thought of pietistic matters except as a sentiment, theology being altogether ignored by him. . . . He had no idea of the changed position of historical forms or cosmogony of religion by geological and other discoveries; and, indeed, was himself not sure that the earth really moved round the sun! "Our senses did not tell us so at any rate, and what then did it matter whether it did move or not?" What Dante knew was enough for him. He then remembered Galileo, another Italian, and gave in! It might matter in a scientific way, oh yes!

This is an interesting story, but not for Scott's reasons. Rossetti was not apparently in any accepted nineteenth-century sense a believing or practising Christian; but to say he thought of "pietistic matters" as a "sentiment" gives just the wrong turn to his unscientific views of the universe; this may be partly a matter of the changed force of words—even Pater said that with Rossetti common things are full of "sentiment"; but Pater also acknowledged the force of the likeness to Dante; and "sentiment" is one of the last words to apply to Dante. It is more important to say of Rossetti that he had some power of making spiritual things and the details of religious myth concrete, than that he had an etherealised apprehension of the physical. It is this latter method that leads to an aestheticism for which poppies and lilies are nothing but gestures. But Rossetti lived in a society in which little of the Dante symbolism was generally accepted; in which his own sense of identity between symbol and thing symbolised was little understood. This sense was not continuous or absolute even in himself: he darted from one level to another, sometimes appealing to a knowledge in his readers which might not be there, sometimes using with tremendous effectiveness a symbolic image which carried its own interpretation in itself. Thus in *The Blessed Damozel* it is rather ineffectual and merely decorative to say that she had seven stars in her hair; but it is quite another matter to say she looked down from "the fixed place of Heaven", or to describe the souls rising up as being like "thin flames". These phrases both stand by themselves and become richer by association and knowledge. In *Jenny* the roses and lilies are brought in with awkward explanations of their purpose; but here is Victorian London at night-time, charged with meaning by a single symbol:

> you stare
> Along the streets alone, and there,
> Round the long park, across the bridge,
> The cold lamps at the pavement's edge
> Wind on together and apart,
> A fiery serpent for your heart.

Dante Gabriel became a father of aestheticism through others' misunderstanding of the poetic problem with which he was trying to deal.

His sister Christina solved the problem within her own compass almost to perfection. She had no strong predilection for Dante references or for historical themes; but she seems to have assimilated in her youth something of the essential quality of the medieval method and to have adapted it without strain or affectation to contemporary feelings; in her religious poems she avoids the problem of modern or medieval dress and keepings by emphasising neither; but still her persons and situations and scenes have a clarity and sharpness which belong with the Pre-Raphaelite aims. Two of her longest poems—*Goblin Market* and *The Prince's Progress*—are allegories which have the greatest virtues of all allegory, that they can be apprehended at a number of different levels and demand no gloss. Because Christina was a devout Anglo-Catholic of utterly unquestioning faith she was able to use Catholic symbolism with complete internal conviction; there is no uncertainty about her levels. It is no accident that Gerard Manley Hopkins was devoted to her poems in his youth; for it was he, not the aesthetes, who truly developed Pre-Raphaelite aims. It is notable too in Patmore's poetry of his later Catholic life that the strain is less, and he abandons the laughable anxiety over modern keepings. The pictorial allegories of Holman Hunt seem to me essentially Protestant and post-medieval in mood; there is no fusion, and none of his pictures could be understood without enormous explanations in the catalogue.

I feel I have attempted too much and too difficult an argument for my space; but I am sure that further thought along these lines is essential if a centenary of the Pre-Raphaelites is to be worth celebrating.

GERARD MANLEY HOPKINS I*

IN 1918 a small book called *Poems of Gerard Manley Hopkins* was published, edited by Robert Bridges. To most people the author's very name was unknown. He was a Victorian Jesuit priest who had died young in 1889; he was born a hundred years ago, in 1844. To those of us who were young in the twenties the voice and idiom of these poems seemed to belong to a young contemporary. The rush of words, patterned closely together; the compact elliptical syntax; the new words coined; old words laid against each other in startling compounds and phrases; the assonances; the variety and occasional roughness of the rhythms—qualities of style like these revealed in new, strong flexible forms what Hopkins himself called "the naked thew and sinew of the English language".

Hopkins was a slight, even frail man. At Highgate School they called him "Skin". But in his face strength of character was seen strangely combined with extreme sensitiveness and extreme precision: it was a face that nobody who saw it ever forgot. In 1863 he went up to Balliol. At Oxford he bloomed and flourished. He was an extremely good scholar, and his ordinary work in Latin and Greek trained his style in a confidence and niceness of structure which appeared even when he wrote a postcard to a friend. Words already fascinated him; at that time philology was one of the fashionable sciences, and he seized on it for what it could give. He delved for the origins and meanings of words in five or six languages. He noted the innovations of poets like Sophocles and Aeschylus. Without this early and continued inquisitiveness, he would never have had the confidence for his later work; for example, when he described boys bathing in a river, and used the word "downdolphinry", or wrote of candlelight seen coming from a window:

* B.B.C. Home Service, June 1944, celebrating the centenary of Hopkins's birth. Printed in the *Listener*, 22 June.

"To-fro tender trambeams truckle at the eye". He read English poetry very widely, including a lot of Shakespeare; and Tennyson's *Enoch Arden* volume, which appeared in 1864, stirred him to some astonishingly mature and valuable criticism.

Hopkins's friendships with Robert Bridges and others began in the setting of *The Scholar Gipsy*. He walked to Elsfield, where he noted the "great elliptic-curved oaks" and "the bloomy green of larches"; he walked along the Isis, where he saw the fans and globes and bosses of water coming through the locks. He walked to Binsey, where the poplars

> dandled a sandalled
> Shadow that swam or sank.

He was a close and wonderful observer of the smallest intricacies of form and colour in objects—the grain of stones, the veins of leaves, the fretting and lacing and wimpling of clouds, water, plumage and trees. From these sharp details he saw what he called the "inscape" of things, the essential form to which each minutest part contributed. Both the detail and the inscape he aimed to show in the most beautiful little drawings in pencil. As he saw the variety of shapes in stillness, and their transformation and changes of colour in movement, his mind thronged instantly with likenesses and comparisons which he often used to build part of a final image in a poem ten or even twenty years later. Such an image is this, of the waning moon: "dwindled and thinned to the fringe of a finger-nail held to the candle". For a time he even thought of becoming a professional painter. But another vocation prevented it; at Oxford his life was governed, as it was ever afterwards, by his religion. His whole view of the world and all his thoughts came to be conditioned by Christian symbols and the Catholic interpretation of life. He now saw, in the laced and fretted shapes of Nature, parts of the whole beauty of God's being. A few years later he wrote: "I do not think I have ever seen anything more beautiful than the blue-bell I have been looking at. I know the beauty of our Lord by it."

His intellectual development was deliberately confined within the classical and Catholic tradition: he began to leave other books aside as irrelevant to his purposes; and this very limitation—call it narrowness if you will—added sharpness and precision to his thought. The overbearing stress of religion when so young might well have made him a monster or a prig or have led him into fanatical eccentricity. There was a lot of playing at monkhood and fanciful churchiness in the sixties, but he steered clear of it all; he had a certain candour and greatness and prudence even as a young man, which his fancies never overrode; and his wit seemed to add to his dignity. He became a Roman Catholic while he was still an undergraduate and was received by Newman personally at Birmingham. Two years later he entered the Novitiate of the Society of Jesus. For seven years then he gave up writing all but trivial occasional poetry. He thought it was not consistent with his profession; but wherever he went he peeped, and botanised, and entered in his Journal, hoarding images for poems. He was walking in the garden one day at Stonyhurst when one of the old Fathers pointed him out to the gardener as a great scholar. "That's impossible," the gardener said; "I saw him the other day in the garden turning round and round and looking at a piece of glass in the path. I took him for a natural."

Then one day in 1875, on a hint from one of his superiors, he wrote *The Wreck of the "Deutschland"*, his longest and in many ways his finest poem. The first ten stanzas are a great meditation on the ways of God's dealings with man, built round his own spiritual experience. I will quote one stanza, which illustrates well his wording, his love of strange colours, his sense of God found through Nature:

> I kiss my hand
> To the stars, lovely-asunder
> Starlight, wafting him out of it; and
> Glow, glory in thunder;
> Kiss my hand to the dappled-with-damson west:
> Since, tho' he is under the world's splendour and wonder,
> His mystery must be instressed, stressed;
> For I greet him the days I meet him, and bless when I understand.

This poem was offered to the Jesuit paper *The Month*, but the editor dared not publish it. None of his greatest work was printed in his lifetime or even read by more than half a dozen friends. Yet for his friends' publications and fame he had a cherishing care. The poems of Bridges and the later work of Coventry Patmore were discussed in letters almost line by line, and out of these details grew his magnificent pages of general criticism, which are among the most interesting things written by any English poet about poetry. His own artistic power and rightness he never doubted for a moment, provided conditions were right. But the conditions for his poetry were not always right. He never once wavered in his religious vocation, but it was not easy to find the right work for him as a Jesuit priest. After ordination in 1877 he was for two years a preacher in churches in London, Chesterfield and Liverpool. This work put him in closer touch with ordinary people, and in Lancashire particularly they warmed his heart. But horror of man without grace, of the world "soured with sinning"; hatred of the industrial Midland landscape where, as he said in a poem, "all is seared with trade; bleared, smeared with toil"; fears for the future of England when he described the unemployed as "by Despair, bred Hangdog dull"—all these things gave many of his poems a terrible bitterness. The striking of opposites between this bitter tension and the relief found only in Christ is the emotional crux, is the true subject of many of his poems.

For all the last part of his life he was teaching classics, first at Stonyhurst and then as Professor of Greek in University College, Dublin. In Ireland his colleagues and pupils hardly appreciated or understood him. One day, an old pupil of his told me, when he had been explaining at great length, but with no clear success, the precise shade of meaning of a word in Homer's *Iliad*, he made a student lie down on the floor and hauled him along the lecture-room to demonstrate the exact way the corpse of Hector was dragged round the walls of Troy.

In Dublin Hopkins felt isolated; his health and his laborious rather elementary work thwarted him. His spiritual life was at a crisis such as few spiritual writers have attempted to describe. Yet, at this very time, when he felt himself a eunuch, not breeding "one work that wakes", he wrote a series of sonnets which most of all make this centenary the commemoration of a man who, though he wrote so little, should be remembered with the greatest of our poets. Hardly a poet who began writing between the wars was not directly influenced by Gerard Hopkins. His elaborate metres and highly-wrought control helped restore to English verse both a firmness and a freedom of movement it was in danger of losing. He showed perhaps more clearly than any poet since the seventeenth century that the passion and music of verse can belong with highly conscious and informed intellectual activity. But when we read Hopkins now, it is not his subtlety and quaintness which most come home. It is the very things he sometimes thought himself to lack— "the roll, the rise, the carol, the creation" of his verse; the terrible pathos of his feeling for man and for the ultimate being of things; the solemn construction of his poems, built with careful thought like a piece of music by Purcell, whom he loved, through all the intricacy of numbers, to the greater glory of the God in whose service he lived and died.

GERARD MANLEY HOPKINS II*

THE policy which Robert Bridges adopted in publishing at first only selections from Hopkins's poetry and delaying the greater part of it for thirty years has at least ensured it a full recognition in our own time. But many critics have inferred, from the fact that we are able to appreciate him in ways in which some of his contemporaries were not, that there is a special affinity between his poetic character and that of writers who live long after him and are in fact essentially different. He has been wrenched out of his context and distorted by ephemeral and propagandist judgment.

Miss Phare, whose book is the first detailed study of his poetry to be published, has felt the pressure of such criticism, and partly associates herself with it by calling Hopkins a "Modernist-Victorian"; but she does not make clear her reasons for choosing this title. She recognises that Hopkins's work is unlike much contemporary poetry in that it is not allusive, and that it does not employ what have been called "private symbols"; but she does not press on to the conclusion, for which there is much evidence in her book, that in the whole structure of his thought and imagery Hopkins does not belong to our generation at all, and that his adoption into it is excessively misleading. He would not have understood what was meant by a "poetic logic" or a "logic of imagery"; for him the connection between images was controlled by the same logic as he applied in a lecture on Homer or a sermon on the Passion. This is not the method of contemporary poetry nor the cause of its occasional obscurity. Hopkins wrote in ever-more-detailed refinement on a theme, not to suggest the subtle connections between one theme and another in a system of images related only in the scheme of the poem itself. If, therefore, as Miss Phare suggests, "the publication of his poetry in 1918 has left English

* The Poetry of Gerard Manley Hopkins, by E. E. Phare (Cambridge). Reviewed, Times Literary Supplement, 25 Jan 1934.

164

poetry in a condition which seems to have many new possibilities", it would seem that when once the superficial likenesses between his poetic vocabulary and the poetic vocabulary of the present time have been fully understood, his most powerful effect will be to check the development of many prevailing poetic habits. But it is more likely that he, like Milton, will be found to have made so fine a language for himself and brought it within its limits to such perfection that his influence will be widest in pale imitation and most valuable in plagiarism. Hopkins's own attitude to great work was "to admire and do otherwise".

The first five sections of Miss Phare's book are loosely built round comparisons of Hopkins with other poets, and from these comparisons her own opinions develop. The longest and most fruitful for her purposes is an unexpected comparison with Wordsworth. She finds first a common pantheism, but nowhere in the poems or prose does Hopkins fail to make the wide, and for him portentous, difference between creature and Creator. The relationship is made clear in the sonnet *Spring*, in the octet of which is described the beauty of created things that in the sestet are shown in their present divergence from the first purity of creation. Knowledge of this double removal from Deity saves Hopkins always from pantheism. The work which is next compared to Wordsworth's is "the little group of poems in which he tried to enter sympathetically into the hearts of other human beings, to trace the primary laws of human nature working in incidents chosen from his everyday experience"—*The Bugler's First Communion, Felix Randal, Brothers, The Handsome Heart, Spring and Fall,* and *On the Portrait of Two Beautiful Young People.* She finds in all these poems except the last two some kind of emotional failure. In *Felix Randal* Hopkins is "encouraging his emotions to take more sway over him than they would normally"; in *The Bugler's First Communion* he affects the reader with a "forced heartiness", and "his attempt at simplicity and directness fails". Miss Phare herself notices that her "rather peevish fault-finding" does not explain the "failure" of these poems. The explanation of them is in Hopkins himself.

He knew very little about other people except as they fitted into the context of his own thoughts or became by chance the object of his affections. As a priest he had little mission experience, and perhaps could hardly have borne more; in his friendships, valuable as they were to him, there seems to have been a curious lack of real personal intimacy, and his family affections were not immediate:

> To seem the stranger lies my lot, my life
> Among strangers. Father and mother dear,
> Brothers and sisters are in Christ not near.

He could win and give affections of a kind, but not such as to satisfy him:

> I am in Ireland now; now I am at a third
> Remove. Not but in all removes I can
> Kind love both give and get.

These feelings were not due merely to his living in Ireland nor to the particular mood of frustration in which this sonnet was written. All his most intense experience was solitary. He wrote that in looking at beautiful things even one companion spoiled his ecstasy. This solitude was extremely sensitive to every invasion from outside and was perhaps intensified by the knowledge that his affections, once moved, were almost overpowering in their effects on him; for he suffered the maximum feeling from the slightest incident, and drew the fullest inference from a single word. One small occasion filled him "brim, in a flash full". Men were to him a source of wonder and physical delight, as in *Harry Ploughman*, when he articulated all the members of their beauty; or else were a sudden stimulus, in their moral life, to most complex states of intense feeling. It is possible to see that real intimacy might have been too much to bear. He marks the novelty of the special affection roused in him by the dying blacksmith:

> This seeing the sick endears them to us, us too it endears.

His emotions here certainly "take more sway over him than they would normally", but they do not have to be encouraged. This occasion, as that of the bugler, rushes on him with power, and the complex thoughts, fears and comments with the images that attend them are inevitably caused by it. The feeling is no more forced and exaggerated than his involuntary tears at the accounts of the Agony in the Garden and the conversion of de Rancé.

Two similar charges are brought against *The Wreck of the "Deutschland"*. "Hopkins is not sure enough of himself, not certain enough that the traits which he is expressing are those of his own individuality", and here also he has artificially intensified his feelings. It is not clear which parts of the poem are included in the first of these censures: the second is explicitly applied to the twentieth and twenty-second stanzas. Hopkins's own account of the origin of the poem makes it clear that it was the fact that he was himself affected by the wreck which led his Rector to make the suggestion of a poem. He had written nothing of importance for over seven years, and it would seem that the first ten stanzas, in which there is no mention of the shipwreck, though they use a few images which belong to it, work in a concentrated way upon a vein of experience from those seven years as painfully personal as that of the "terrible sonnets" themselves. The straining and oddity which one must recognise are parallel to the straining and oddity of the experience: there is no gap between the thought and the expression. To reject the first ten stanzas of the poem is to reject the whole state of mind which produced them. Miss Phare then turns to the curious emphasis which Hopkins lays on the facts that the drowned nuns numbered five and that they came from Protestant Germany; but both these facts are prominent in the newspaper accounts from which Hopkins derived his knowledge of the wreck. The magnificent narrative passages in the poem which Miss Phare praises so rightly follow these accounts with astonishing fidelity—at the crisis of the poem almost word for word. If these points had impressed themselves on the journalists, why should not Hopkins interpret them symbolically without being insincere?

In an interesting part of her book Miss Phare explains Hopkins's love of wildness, unaccountableness and pied things as a kind of revulsion from "the tidy, cut-and-dried mental world of the Jesuit", "an antidote to the dullness and flatness which one imagines would characterise a world which had been made entirely comprehensible", as, for instance, it is made comprehensible by Duns Scotus, whom he loved. She posits an alarmingly divided mind. But surely the reason why he was so fond of changing and irregular things was not that he wanted to retain their confusion fully confounded, but that it was exactly such things as these which exerted his intellectual passion for minute distinctions to the utmost, and many of his finest poems are poems of this passion. The being of everything is to be found exactly in its dappling. It is to this that his reading of Scotus is most relevant. The peculiar individuality which Scotus called *haecceitas*, and the *distinctio formalis a parte rei* are to be directly connected with his love of objects between which minute distinctions can be made. And Scotus further allows that the concrete individuality of each object can be known in at least a confused way intuitively. In a later part of her book Miss Phare gives a quotation from Gilson on the Scotist theory of individuation, and quotes one of the sonnets in which it is most explicit: it is therefore curious that she should have interpreted the love of what is dappled and pied as an *escape* from the mental habit implied by a concurrent love of Scotism. Again, when she says that Hopkins's imagery is almost entirely motile or dynamic, Miss Phare wisely adds: "There is little to be said, I think, in favour of attempting to classify poets according to the motile or static nature of the imagery which they use." Hopkins's love of actual movement (which is a very different thing from "motile imagery") is to be found in nearly all his finest poems: "Meaning motion fans fresh our wits with wonder," he says in the sonnet on Purcell. It is to be noted that in the Scotist philosophy of Nature every body has not merely a material form, but also a vital form. A special element of its being is its activity and movement. Scotism made articulate to him in its own language many things which had been life-long preoccupations from the unaided bent of his mind.

GERARD MANLEY HOPKINS III *

THESE letters cover twenty-four years in the life of a man devoted to the Society of Jesus and to poetry. The turning-point in a Jesuit's life is the Tertianship, ten months of "second noviceship" before taking his last vows. Gerard Hopkins began his Tertianship on October 10, 1881, thirteen years after joining the Society, and six years after he had again begun to write poetry. At this critical time in his life he and Canon Dixon, each a poet and each in his own communion a priest, exchanged a series of letters in which they discussed with earnest care the place of poetry in a religious life. These letters are the centre of the whole correspondence. It is now possible to see the full importance of Hopkins's seven years' silence and his considered attitude to composition and to publishing. He distinguished between the writing of poetry and the possible fame resulting from its being known. Publication should be left to obedience, for St Ignatius looked upon individual fame as the "most dangerous and dazzling of all attractions": "there is more peace and it is the holier lot to be unknown than to be known". Against this Dixon, fearing that his friend might give over composition altogether, pleads passionately that "one vocation cannot destroy another". It is one of his most moving letters, and Hopkins received it just at the beginning of a month's retreat.

During this time Hopkins had given up actual composition that he might, as in his noviceship proper, *vacare Deo*; but it is clear that in the intensive revision of his life from November to December 1881 he aimed at reaching a final conclusion about his work. Towards the end of the retreat, on the tercentenary of the death of

* *The Letters of Gerard Manley Hopkins to Robert Bridges;* and *The Correspondence of Gerard Manley Hopkins and Richard Watson Dixon.* 2 vols. Edited by Claude Colleer Abbott (Oxford). Reviewed, *Times Literary Supplement*, 31 Jan 1935.

Edmund Campion, he began to answer Dixon's letter. His essential position is unchanged, but it is invigorated by a tremendous confidence. Composition is not to be forgone, because poetry in itself has a value in the sight of God: "Now if you value what I write, if I do myself, much more does our Lord. And if he chooses to avail himself of what I leave at his disposal he can do so with a felicity and with a success which I could never command." Publication is therefore in God's hands. But for a Jesuit the necessary guidance is conveyed partly by his appointed superiors, and history has shown that poetry is seldom a serviceable means to the Society's end; "there have been very few Jesuit poets and, where they have been, I believe it would be found on examination that there was something exceptional in their circumstances or, so to say, counterbalancing in their career"—and the letter continues as a remarkable essay on Jesuits famous in various arts.

It is impossible not to find in this letter a suspicion that there was something exceptional in his own circumstances, or counterbalancing in his career, and that the confident justification of his poetry was the result of reviewing the last thirteen years. The facts bear this out. "Après son ordination," says M. André Brémond, "Hopkins fut appliqué a divers ministères. Ses changements fréquents de résidence sont l'indice d'un succès incertain." Before taking his last vows he was able to mitigate the pain of this ill-success and his frequent unhappiness by the knowledge that his poetry, bringing no fame in his lifetime, was a proper service of God even within the Society.

> Only what word
> Wisest my heart breeds dark heaven's baffling ban
> Bars or hell's spell thwarts

was written not by a man whose whole life was a denial of his nature, but by one whose nature in whatever life would have turned a great part of his experience into a cause of pain.

As a Jesuit his experience was necessarily limited. In October 1879, when he was beginning work on his tragedy of St Winefred, he wrote to Bridges, almost complaining: "I have for one thing so little varied experience." But this limitation was in several ways valuable. In the first place he was able to exploit to its fullest what experience he had, and, "working on a concentrated vein", produced his finest poetry. Then, his limitation also saved him from the emotional, social and political muddle which vitiated the writing of so many great Victorians, while his detachment made him all the more an acute critic. His political sympathies cut across all the "secular" politics of his time: he was despondent, almost fatalistic about the future: and there is a direct connection between this despair of civilisation and the gloomy forebodings in many of the poems, where youth and innocence will surely be "soured with sinning". Political fatalism is joined to the doctrine of the Fall.

> Enough: corruption was the world's first woe.
> What need I strain my heart beyond my ken?
> O but I bear my burning witness though
> Against the wild and wanton work of men.

His personal independence of opinion in many things, and most of all in literature, was guaranteed by his being a Jesuit. The Society at the time contained very few men who could share anything of his passion for poetry, indeed very few of them knew or cared whether he was a poet at all. If he had had friends available for conversation in the Society, or if he had been able to meet Bridges or Dixon more often, these letters might never have been written. As it is they are an almost complete record of his life as a poet and critic. They cover and explain the texts of his own poems; they criticise in detail the poems of Bridges and Dixon as they were sent to him; and they contain some of the finest general criticism in the language. Towards the end of his life Hopkins wrote to Bridges: "I have the passion for explanation and you have not"; and there is little doubt after reading the earlier letters that it was Hopkins's lasting passion for explaining the structure of verse which originated Bridges's own experiments and his studies of metre. But his way was both slower and less sure. On first receiving *The Wreck of the "Deutschland"* he refused to read it more than once: he tried to adapt Hopkins's sprung rhythm to his own use, but only to be told "*The Passer By* in particular reads not so much like sprung rhythm as that Logaoedic dignified-doggerel one Tennyson has employed in *Maud* and since." And after a particularly passionate explanatory criticism of the "Hector" sonnet he wrote to ask whether Hopkins thought there was really any good in his going on writing poetry. He was a pupil in a strict but loving school. He was more cautious than his master because he lacked Hopkins's immense vitality and inventiveness: he wisely rejected many emendations to his own poems because they showed too clearly another idiom. For example:

> Her fall of fold is daylight in my view

is in itself a better line than

> 'Tis joy the foldings of her dress to view,

but it is part of another poem. On other points Hopkins's explanations were successful. In the first edition of 1883 the first line of *Prometheus the Firegiver* reads:

> From high Olympus and the domeless courts.

In 1882 Hopkins had attacked "domeless" tooth and nail:

> Courts can seldom be domed in any case, so that it is needless to tell us that those on Olympus are domeless. No: better to say the kamptuli-conless courts or Minton's-encaustic-tileless courts or vulcanised-india-rubberless courts. This would strike a keynote at once and bespeak attention. And if the critics said those things did not belong to the period you would have (as you have now with *domeless*) the overwhelming answer, that you never said they did but the contrary, and that Prometheus, who was at once a prophet and as a mechanician more than equal to Edison and the Jablochkoff candle and the Moc-main Patent Lever Truss with self-adjusting duplex gear and attachments, meant to say that emphatically they had *not* got those improvements on Olympus and he did not intend that they should.

In the 1905 edition "aetherial" is substituted for "domeless".

By destroying his own side of the correspondence Bridges weakened his own defences to such attack; nor is it easy without his letters to estimate his real opinion of Hopkins's poetry. With Dixon, however, we can feel the impact of each new batch of manuscripts—his astonishment and admiration billowing out with kindly sympathy mixed among them. He hardly ventures on detailed criticism, but from the first he is far nearer to Hopkins in spirit than Bridges ever was. For Bridges detested Catholicism, and the Jesuits still more: he even went so far as to suspect Hopkins of insincerity. Yet even so some of Hopkins's most beautiful letters to him are about religion; he explains the special significance of the feast of Corpus Christi and expounds a difficult passage in *Galatians*; but it is a pity, he says, that Bridges would not talk about important things, but only about literature.

And the letters had to be about it too. Hopkins had not much time to read widely after 1868. His specialist studies, his self-restrictions, and, later, parish work, teaching and often the lack of books gave him long regrets, but what he read he read with extraordinary insight. His criterion of "seriousness", of being "in earnest" in literature was defended largely by moral analysis, but it was accompanied by and helped to sharpen his immediate judgments of taste. His criticisms of Carlyle and Kingsley and his delighted recognition of Stevenson's genius show the two methods of approach working closely together. His admiration of Dryden resounds against depreciation now by Bridges, now by Aubrey de Vere:

> I can scarcely think of you not admiring Dryden without, I may say, exasperation. And my style tends always more towards Dryden. What is there in Dryden? Much, but above all this: he is the most masculine of our poets; his style and his rhythms lay the strongest stress of all our literature on the naked thew and sinew of the English language.

It is small wonder that he assailed Swinburne. His love for Milton is not confined to Milton's art—though the letters contain more of his valuable analysis of the Choruses of *Samson* and parts of *Paradise Regained* than has yet been published—Milton had above all things the quality of "seriousness". Yet his life may have no praise. Letter after letter, whether given to the minute details of a single line in one of his friend's poems, or to a wide division of the schools of English verse, is enlivened by Hopkins's ubiquitous originality: he can touch nothing without leaving his mark on it. But even when he is in a "griggish mood" this originality flows in a pattern on the page. Everything is designed and comes to a foreseen end.

Professor Abbott's edition is magnificently complete and informative. There are only two points for criticism: too many unimportant notes distract the eye to biographical details at the bottom of the page; and the introductions do not introduce what they precede. Introductions to these letters should have been designed to help the reader on his way through them: in place of such help we have general essays on the poetry of Hopkins and Dixon which add very little to an understanding of it.

THE EIGHTEEN-EIGHTIES*

On the evening of April 8, 1888, an old man came into the Warden's drawing-room at Keble College, Oxford, carrying a lighted candle. He put the candle out and went up most cordially and quickly to a young woman who was waiting there. He asked after herself and her father. "Then he sat down on a small uncomfortable chair, where he fidgeted greatly"; and they plunged into talk. He said how Oxford in the past two generations had been torn and rent, what a " 'long agony of thought' she had gone through! How different from Cambridge!" They went on to talk about the country as a whole; he said it had been a *wonderful* half-century; and he agreed that though there had been a slackening of State religion there had "unquestionably come about a quickening of the State conscience". Then about religion he said he didn't believe in any new system, but in the great traditions, in a degeneracy of man, in the Fall—in *sin*—in the intensity and virulence of sin. They spoke about evil being caused by removable physical and social conditions; and about miracles, and the evidence of the Christian character in history. . . . Then the Warden's supper bell rang; Mr Gladstone said he must not put the household out, and Mrs Humphry Ward arranged to come again at half-past nine in the morning.

The occasion of their talk was Mrs Ward's new novel *Robert Elsmere*, which Mr Gladstone—how strange it seems!—was going to review: he had in fact been writing to Lord Acton about it for learned support in his argument. When his article came out, the *Pall Mall* congratulated the Liberal Party on Mr Gladstone's new preoccupation; for two and a half years he had been able to think about nothing but Home Rule and Ireland. "But Mrs Ward has changed all that." A lady fighting her way into an omnibus was overheard to say: "Oh, my dear, *have* you read Weg on Bobbie?"

* B.B.C. Third Programme, 3 Dec 1946, reviewing *England in the Eighteen Eighties* by Helen Merrell Lynd.

A single novel has rarely caught so much of the essential mood and temper of a decade, and touched in passing so many of its tastes, quirks, earnestnesses and doubts as *Robert Elsmere* caught and touched those of the eighties. Elsmere's struggles with religious doubt now live less for their earnestness than for their contexts. His first phase ran parallel with the early lives of such men as Charles Gore and Henry Scott Holland, incorporating the surer findings, but repudiating the spirit, of the *Septem Contra Christum*; concentrating on the Church's corporate social responsibilities. Even in this phase, as in fact on Scott Holland, the influence of T. H. Green was strong. In his second phase, reached under the influence of a saturnine version of Mark Pattison, Elsmere throws the Incarnation and the Resurrection overboard; but—invigorated and reassured by Green, thinly disguised as Mr Grey—he retains a strong sense of social consciousness and conscience, such as Gladstone admitted to Mrs Ward was a great feature of the time.

And indeed it was, salted with some anxiety and fear. The old classical, individualistic Liberalism was everywhere breaking down: pure *laissez-faire* had done its negative work, had become a mere fatalistic do-nothing Conservatism: Gladstone's world was ended. His Government of 1880–5 had been in uneasy alliance with semi-socialists and with the new Chamberlain radicals; the break-up of the Liberal Party in '86—though occasioned by Ireland—expressed the deeper fact that the philosophy which had prevailed since 1832 was quite inadequate to the modern facts. In '87 Gladstone was writing of "the leaning of both parties to socialism, which I radically disapprove".

The eighties were in fact the period in which the conflict which still controls our politics first became clearly apparent and generally understood—the conflict between the desire for freedom and the blatant need for planning. This aspect of the decade has been the subject of an American book, by Mrs Helen Merrell Lynd, *England in the Eighteen Eighties*: and she gives it a sub-title, "Toward a Social Basis for Freedom". She was writing mainly for Americans in the belief that "contemporary American life might gain from a study of this critical period in England". This aim may help to excuse certain errors and even some ignorance of English institutions and tastes; yet the book should not be neglected here, because it ranges so thoroughly through such various evidence, over a few chosen aspects of one decade. Mrs Lynd points out that certain favouring factors—mainly the long lead which England had over all other countries in industrial development, with the freedom of the world's markets and the expanding economy which this implied—long obscured the discrepancy between social facts and social theory, and that "the recognition of this discrepancy, when it did come, came relatively swiftly and abruptly". In the eighties it was first fully recognised that there were in practice many limitations on economic individualism, and that what there were were not enough. She then makes a very good analysis of the current idea that freedom and planning were irreconcilable alternatives, and properly brings T. H. Green's Hegelianism to her aid. The main body of the book then expounds in great detail what the theorists, the practical parliamentary politicians, the leaders of organised labour and the Churches said and did, as they became aware of the stubbornness and complexity of their problems.

Yet when this great detailed survey has been made—in 500 pages—one is left with a dry mouth and a head full of doubts and questions. Even remembering that this is sociological history, and not social history, a different thing, one wonders why the boundaries have been drawn just where they have. Three omissions, even within Mrs Lynd's limited subject, seem particularly startling: there is nothing about family life, nothing about the relations of the sexes, nothing about the position of women. Yet how much, psychologically and economically, of any individual's attitude to society—even politics—is conditioned by these three things.

In the eighties a fundamental change of attitude to women, a shift in the balance of power between the sexes, began to find public and even legal expression. The Married Woman's Property Act was passed in 1882; in 1884 that forgotten heroine Miss Miller of the London School Board refused to pay her taxes on the very principle that had founded the United States. In '83 the name of Miss Perrin of Girton appeared among the Wranglers, and Miss Ramsey was Senior Classic in 1887. It has been said by an expert in such matters that the fashions of the early eighties "suggested a bevy of celibate Police-women". *Princess Ida* belongs to '84.

In *Robert Elsmere* the struggle of Rose Leyburn to win her right to be seriously trained as a musician expresses both the change of attitude towards women's professions, and also the decay of patriarchal despotism which marked the family life of the decade: even a deathbed wish of her father had hung over Rose's head for years. The Modern Girl of the eighties was prepared to talk openly, with hideous daring, of "The Governor".

I think Mrs Ward would have observed a deep psychological link between the decline of *paterfamilias* and the failure of *laissez-faire* capitalism; it is disturbing and a little inexplicable that Mrs Lynd should not even touch upon it; that in a chapter of thirty pages on Education she attempts no discussion whatever of the children's homes or parents, whether they went to Eton or the new Board School round the corner.

One puts down her book, full as it is of learning and acuteness, depressed and rather exhausted. For though it is all about human life and hopes of freedom and the conditions under which freedom can be won in an organised society, she is so abstract, so concerned to make her points, that the human purpose of it all slips out of sight. She is Olympianly aloof. Scientific socialism, sentimental socialism, Fabianism, Chamberlain's Radical Programme, Morris's alliance with Hyndman, slip like prepared specimens under her microscope and are put away in their grooved boxes for future use. Underlying her words there seems to be a sort of subdued deference to Marxism in its austere and tragic forms, and something like a fear that the freedom she is concerned to win may turn out to be a bourgeois thing. The result is that in her book personality seems to count for nothing. All the great people of the time are freely mentioned and quoted—Gladstone himself, Manning, Morris, John Burns, Chamberlain—in fact the index is alarming; but they have exactly as much vivid human life as *Reynolds' Newspaper* or the *Annual Register*.

The distinctive qualities of different lives do not concern her; not what people eat, drink, wear; how they make love; how they decorate their houses and spend their leisure. It would even seem as if a great deal of their reading was reading about the difficulties of freedom and planning. Yet she goes out of her way to mention *Robert Elsmere* several times, and explains its enormous sales as a consequence of the Education Act of 1870. But she does not explain why this new reading public and this public's father, "the intelligent artisan", should have been so interested in the protracted spiritual struggles of an enthusiastic young clergyman, with a wife from the Lake District. One reason, at least, for this popularity was that the belief in the reality and value of each individual soul was still a living belief, and the problems concerning its destiny were still living interests. You may take this to mean no more than that a large part of the British proletariat was bourgeoisified; and in a sense it was: but many alert individuals in all classes were then still, in their reflective moments, capable of being irradiated, trans- figured by this idea of personal freedom and personal responsibility.

If you persistently doubted the value of the individual; if in your reflective moments you found yourself stubbornly incapable of being irradiated or transfigured by anything at all; if the Lakes and Surrey bored you equally, except for a few nostalgic reminiscences; if you were too good at music to bother with it much, and too well informed to be capable of entertaining conversation; if you looked at your books and said:

> Here's Carlyle shrieking "woe on woe"
> (The first edition, this, he wailed in);
> I once believed in him—but oh,
> The many things I've tried and failed in!

then you were another very typical eighties figure—a figure Mrs Ward sketched in her character of Mr Langham. He nearly fell in love in Surrey, but did just escape transfiguration and lived to win melancholy pleasure in watching well-meaning people take feeble precautions "against the encroaching, devastating labour- troubles of the future".

For the universities, and Mrs Ward's uncle Matthew Arnold, and her friend Walter Pater, had produced a crop of what William Morris harshly called cultivated parasites. And in the eighties some of these parasites were saying something like this: "We have talked, thought and pondered; we have become reconciled to the descent of man; we have treated the Bible 'like any other book'; we have tried to worship; we have clung to faith beyond the forms of faith; we have yearned for the Unknowable, and the Eternal not ourselves; we have searched even our own souls; we have rediscovered the Renaissance, and Greece at a third remove; we have striven after culture, and cultivated feeling; we have fortified ourselves against death by thoughts of its beauty:—now, is there anything we can *do*?"

A small group said suddenly in sepulchral chorus: "Try sin: Mr Gladstone believes in the intensity and virulence of sin." But Morris, who had been "doing" all his life, said: "No; not that: there's no joy of creation in it. Weave cloth, print beautiful books, make furniture, paint pictures or write epics if you're a good hand at a grind: but none of your stuff'll be any good unless you're a Socialist: so the first thing to do is to come along to Trafalgar Square."

The section of Beatrice Webb's autobiography, *My Apprenticeship*, which deals with the seventies is called "In Search of a Creed": the section beginning with the early eighties is called "The Choice of a Craft".

No decade can be properly understood without understanding its personalities, its personal problems, its attitudes toward the idea of personality itself. Both freedom and planning begin at home, are continued in solitude and expand into politics in the third place. In the eighties Mrs Ward and Beatrice Potter seemed to know this instinctively; but Mrs Lynd, fearing to make "a false dichotomy between the individual and Society", has written a long and interesting book in which the individual is hardly given a chance to put his nose round the door. So it is not unfair to suggest that *England in the Eighteen Eighties* should be supplemented by *Robert Elsmere*, *My Apprenticeship* and perhaps, if there's time, "Weg on Bobbie".

PART THREE

DICKENS

THE MACABRE DICKENS*

THE present lively interest in Dickens has in it an element never before prominent in all his hundred years of popularity—an interest in his mastery of the macabre and terrible in scene and character. His understanding of and power of describing evil and cruelty, fear and mania and guilt; his overburdening sense, in the crises, of the ultimate loneliness of human life—things like these are now seen to be among the causes of his enigmatic hold on people's hearts. He has worked as much beneath the surface as above it; and he was possibly not himself fully conscious of what he was putting into his books. The floor of consciousness has been lowered. The awful area of human experience in which small cruelty and meanness and stupidity may swell and topple over into murder, insane revenge, sadistic, bloody violence and riot; the area where dream and reality are confused or swiftly alternating—these are now seen to be closer to ourselves and to common life than our grandfathers suspected. They thought that Dickens on his violent and evil side—when he wrote about Sikes and Jonas Chuzzlewit and Bradley Headstone—was writing about a special, separate class called criminals; that Miss Havisham, Mr Dick and Miss Flite belonged to another separate class called lunatics—at most social problems; at least, wild exaggerated flights of fancy. We now see more plainly that John Jasper may be any one of us; that the murderer is not far beneath the skin; that the thickness of a sheet of paper may divide the proud successful man of the world from the suicide or the lunatic. We have also lived again into what used to be dismissed as melodrama.

Lord Acton once wrote in a letter that Dickens "knows nothing of sin when it is not crime". Within the narrow limits of theological pigeon-holes this is true; the word "sin" hardly occurs in the novels; wickedness is not regarded as an offence against a personal

* B.B.C. Third Programme, 3 June 1947.

God. But if the judgment is that Dickens knows nothing of evil unless it is recognised and punishable by the law, it is quite false. The great black, ghastly gallows hanging over all, of which Dickens writes in the Preface to *Oliver Twist*, is not just the official retribution of society against those who break its rules; it is a symbol of the internal knowledge of guilt, the knowledge that makes Sikes wander back and forth in the country north of London, dogged not by fear of the police but by the phantom of Nancy, the knowledge that produces the last vision of her eyes which is the immediate cause of his death. Acton, with the logic of Catholicism, thought it a fault in Dickens that he "loved his neighbour for his neighbour's sake"; but, within the range of moral action that this allows, Dickens is continually dealing with the forms of evil which the absence or failure of love may breed, and with the more terrible effects of emotional greed, the exploitation of one person by another, which often overflows into cruelty and violence. His methods of dealing with these moral problems and the conflicts they involve are various, but they are always peculiar and oblique; they are rarely brought out openly on the main surface of the story; they are never analysed as the story goes along. They are sometimes displayed through a grotesque character in such a way that they become so sharp and hideous that it is hard to recognise their seriousness and truth. Such, for example, is Quilp's cruelty towards his wife, which seems a fantastic travesty of human action if one overlooks Mrs Quilp's one phrase:

> Quilp has such a way with him when he likes, that the best-looking woman here couldn't refuse him if I was dead.

That one sentence goes to the core of Quilp: for all his grotesque exterior he has in him a secret and serious human *power*: he is no figure of fun.

Except in such sudden phrases as these, Dickens's imagination usually concentrates through all the greater part of a story now on the black, now on the white, exclusively: the two don't interpenetrate. It is only in the portraits of boyhood and adolescence, such as those of Pip and the early Copperfield, that the medley of moral direction is really convincing. The adult characters for most of their course drive headstrong forward, virtuously or villainously or in some grotesque neutral zone where moral decisions do not have to be made. It is as if Dickens was afraid of attempting to portray the full complexity of an adult. Then, quite suddenly, a portentous thing happens. It is worth noticing first what does *not* happen. I cannot think of a single instance in which one of the good characters suddenly reveals a streak of evil: the Jarndyces and Cheerybles and Brownlows persevere infallible and unsullied to the end. The startling thing that *does* happen is that the villains suddenly reveal, if not a streak of good, a streak of vivid power, and then an immense depth of intricate, confused and pitiable humanity. Suddenly their awakened sense of guilt, their fears, remorse, regrets, and above all their terrible loneliness strike out like lightning from the complex plot. As death comes upon them they are transformed, not by any crude magic of reformation such as works wonders with Scrooge, but by an understanding and sympathy, a knowledge of their fears and weakness, far more heart-rending than the moral judgments which convention and the plot pass against them. Examples of this are Fagin, Sikes, Jonas Chuzzlewit, even Quilp: but for the moment let us look closely at Mr Carker in *Dombey and Son*.

Carker has most often been regarded as a typical villain out of melodrama. One critic at least has called his drive across France from Dijon to the coast a "masterpiece of melodrama". So persistent has this way of regarding it been that this same critic himself heightens the scene by speaking of Carker's "last journey through the *stormy* night". But Dickens makes no mention of any storm whatever; in fact he writes in quite a different mood of "a sigh of mountain air from the distant Jura, fading along the plain". It is nearer the truth to say that in this scene Carker shakes off the last suggestion of melodrama and becomes a figure of immense significance. I will quote a few paragraphs—not continuous—from the description of the later part of this drive:

> Gathered up moodily in a corner of the carriage, and only intent on going fast—except when he stood up, for a mile together, and looked

back; which he would do whenever there was a piece of open country—
he went on, still postponing thought indefinitely, and still always
tormented with thinking to no purpose.

Shame, disappointment, and discomfiture gnawed at his heart; a constant apprehension of being overtaken, or met—for he was groundlessly
afraid even of travellers, who came towards him by the way he was
going—oppressed him heavily. The same intolerable awe and dread
that had come upon him in the night, returned unweakened in the day.
The monotonous ringing of the bells and tramping of the horses; the
monotony of his anxiety, and useless rage; the monotonous wheel of
fear, regret, and passion, he kept turning round and round; made the
journey like a vision, in which nothing was quite real but his own
torment.

It was a fevered vision of things past and present all confounded
together; of his life and journey blended into one. Of being madly
hurried somewhere, whither he must go. Of old scenes starting up
among the novelties through which he travelled. Of musing and brood-
ing over what was past and distant, and seeming to take no notice of the
actual objects he encountered, but with a wearisome exhausting consciousness of being bewildered by them, and having their images all
crowded in his hot brain after they were gone.

Whatever language this is, it is not the language of melodrama;
it is a tremendous analysis of the psychological effects of guilt,
shame and thwarted vanity. It is only in the light of these great
final scenes that Carker's character as shown earlier in the book
becomes intelligible; it is then seen that he is not the motivelessly
malignant villain of melodrama: he is a man of intellect, of great
ambition and great sexual vitality; his worse flaws are self-centredness and vanity. It is exactly this sort of man who would be
afflicted with a total blindness about what Edith Dombey, in a
position, as he thinks, to satisfy both his ambition and his sexual
desires, was really thinking and feeling. The final disclosure would
have been bitter to Carker for many reasons, but bitterest perhaps
because it showed him that he had been abysmally blind and *stupid*;
yet he was too self-centred, intricate and cunning to allow reflection
on his own stupidity to come uppermost in his tortured thoughts.
There is much of Dickens himself in Mr Carker: and it is startling

to see the hopelessness of his wheels within wheels of thought: there is no solution but death.

One of the problems that face the critic of Dickens is to explain how this intimate understanding of morbid and near-morbid psychology links on to his apparent optimism, and above all to his humour. I think we can safely say that the countless scenes of gregarious and hearty happiness, which seem to us so unconvincing, seem so because they represent a revulsion from the abysses of evil, a strenuous and ardent *wish* to achieve happiness, rather than the realisation of it. But what of the great grotesque and humorous characters—Mrs Gamp, Pecksniff, Mr Turveydrop and the rest? One very fruitful suggestion was made by George Henry Lewes, only two years after Dickens's death:

> In no other perfectly sane mind (Blake I believe was not perfectly sane) have I observed vividness of imagination approaching so closely to hallucination. . . . Dickens once declared to me that every word said by his characters was distinctly *heard* by him; I was at first not a little puzzled to account for the fact that he could hear language so utterly unlike the language of real feeling; but the surprise vanished when I thought of the phenomena of hallucination.

Lewes applied this idea both to the speaking of certain characters and also to the visual descriptions of persons and scenes. In each case it was the definiteness and insistence of the image or the sound which were abnormal. This idea is, I think, extremely useful in helping to explain the impression one gets from the books of isolated spells of intense imagination which then stop; it also helps to explain the feeling of isolation about the characters: one almost hallucinatory experience succeeded by another, the two being mutually exclusive. There was no comprehensive, constructive, master imagination which held the diverse experiences together, except in very rare instances, mostly to do with memories of childhood. The great grotesque comic characters—Mrs Gamp is the purest of the type—are the best examples of this exclusive, one-track intense development and could not have their unique stature without it. In other instances the form of hallucination was not that of something seen or heard externally, but an internal illusion by which

Dickens himself virtually assumed the character of which he was writing. His daughter Mamie described how she saw him grimacing in a glass, talking aloud the speeches of a character, completely unaware of his actual surroundings, not even noticing that she was in the room.

If one starts by thinking of Dickens as a man with an imagination of this quality and intensity and exclusiveness, it helps to explain not only the recurrent treatment in the novels of various forms of mania and illusion, but also the preoccupation with evil. Similar processes of concentration, exclusion and distortion must have occurred in the mental part of his own life, as distinct from his written work. Edmund Wilson, in his essay *The Two Scrooges*, argued that Dickens was "the victim of a manic-depressive cycle, and a very uncomfortable person". His own life was, in a sense, far beyond what could be said of most men, acting out, or attempting to act out, his own imaginings. His passion for theatricals was only a symptom of the trouble, or an effort to work it off without serious consequences. In real living the concomitant of blindness, especially to the thoughts and feelings of other people, may be resentment and hatred, even to the point of imagining murder, against those who fail to conform to the policy or come up to the idea of themselves that it entails. But there will also be moments of terrible awakening when the illusion and the self-deceit it involved are ended, and there will be a great wave of remorse and guilt and shame for the evils imagined or other evils actually done. There is evidence enough to show that Dickens's personality was strong enough, especially over women, to project his own imagined policies upon others so that in general they conformed; at certain crises the attempt failed and a hideous major conflict came out into the open. Lewes said he saw no traces of insanity in Dickens's life; nor would he; for Dickens normally had a very strong conscious control, and was able to work out many of his conflicts through his novels. But his daughter Kate, Mrs Perugini, did significantly say to a friend that after his wife left their home Dickens behaved towards the children "like a madman", that all the worst in him came out; and she added that her father was "a very wicked man".

This is a very different matter from saying that he was a common-place bounder; there is no need for Dickens's descendants to defend him against charges of being a dishonest drunken libertine: neither the charges nor the defence are relevant to a man of his size and complexity and importance. It is clear from the evidence of the novels alone that Dickens's acquaintance with evil was not just acquired *ab extra*, by reading the police-court reports (much as he loved them) and wandering about Seven Dials and the Waterside by night; it was acquired also by introspection. His own tempta-tions and imaginings, isolated and heightened by the peculiar, narrowing, intense quality of his imagination, fed daily by the immense power which he felt himself to possess over others' per-sonalities—these were the authentic sources of his great criminal characters. Their ultimate trembling loneliness, or hunted wander-ings, or self-haunted hallucinations, or endless, destroying self-analysis, came also from himself. Our generation has come to recognise this by introspection, too.

AN INTRODUCTION TO
*OLIVER TWIST**

DICKENS began *Oliver Twist* as a serial in *Bentley's Miscellany*, of
which he had just become editor, in February 1837. He was a
young man of twenty-five, full of confidence and energy, who had
suddenly found himself famous and was very pleased about it.
Pickwick was not yet even finished; but, so far from trying to repeat
his success as a popular humorist, he began "The Parish Boy's
Progress". Some of his public, wanting more Pickwicks, protested;
but they still read. Dickens, trained as a journalist, responded most
readily to an outside stimulus; he breathed the air and smelt what
was wanted. The declared subject was intensely topical and, by
chance, the course of events made it more so as the publication pro-
ceeded. The controversies, alarms, hardships, and bitternesses
which attended the introduction of the new Poor Law in 1834
may now seem remote; but *Oliver Twist* cannot be fully understood without remembering that it was planned and begun in an
atmosphere of heightened public interest and of anxiety which
deepened as the story ran.

It was Dickens's first attempt at a novel proper. The sequence
of the external events which befall Oliver and form the framework
of the book, though improbable, is at least straightforward, organised, and fairly well proportioned; but all the subordinate matter
designed to explain and account for these events is at once complicated and careless. It has often been remarked that many features
of the plot have a strong likeness to the melodrama of the time.

* The Oxford Illustrated Dickens, 1949. [To his Introduction House
appended this note. "This Introduction owes a great deal to the essay of
Edmund Wilson called 'Dickens: the Two Scrooges' in *The Wound and the
Bow*, and to George Orwell's 'Charles Dickens', reprinted in *Inside the Whale*.
A fuller discussion of Dickens's attitude to the Poor Law and the 'philosophers'
will be found in my book *The Dickens World*."]

Many conundrums are solved "off", and are then expounded to the audience in hurried, uneasy dialogue. The coincidence by which Oliver is made to break into the home of his unknown aunt Rose is not more startling than that, for instance, by which Jane Eyre, exhausted and starving, collapses on the doorstep of her cousins. Such things were then part of the idiom of storytelling. But in *Oliver* the disproportion and lack of continuity or development, in many subordinate parts of the story, are not even in that way idiomatic. The past history of the Leefords and their connection with Mr Brownlow and the Maylies is treated almost contemptuously. Monks is at first a most promising villain and appears in an air of genuine mystery and terror; but he collapses in ridiculous ruin, as if his creator had lost interest or not given himself time to do better —there may be something in both these explanations.

Dickens was in fact doing more work than even he could altogether cope with. The last number of *Pickwick* did not come out till November 1837, when *Oliver* had already been running for ten months: the first monthly part of *Nicholas Nickleby* appeared in April 1838 when *Oliver* was still a long way from being finished. Simultaneously, Dickens was editing the *Miscellany* and contributing occasional papers of his own. On top of this he took on the editing of Egerton Wilks's *Memoirs of Grimaldi* which needed much rearrangement and a good deal of rewriting. Such furious work was characteristic of his temperament. He plainly could give himself little leisure for thought; and cool thinking was no part of his method. Under pressure he speeded things up rather than postponed them. The story of *Oliver* was in fact finished and published in three volumes in November 1838, before the serial publication was complete.

He was then living at 48 Doughty Street, and his brother-in-law, Henry Burnett, described an evening there:

> One night in Doughty Street, Mrs Charles Dickens, my wife and myself were sitting round the fire, cosily enjoying a chat, when Dickens, for some purpose, came suddenly from his study into the room. "What, you here!" he exclaimed; "I'll bring down my work." It was his monthly portion of *Oliver Twist* for *Bentley's*. In a few minutes he

returned, manuscript in hand, and while he was pleasantly discoursing he employed himself in carrying to a corner of the room a little table, at which he seated himself and recommenced his writing. We, at his bidding, went on talking our "little nothings",—he, every now and then (the feather of his pen still moving rapidly from side to side), put in a cheerful interlude. It was interesting to watch, upon the sly, the mind and the muscles working (or, if you please, *playing*) in company, as new thoughts were being dropped upon the paper. And to note the working brow, the set of mouth, with the tongue tightly pressed against the closed lips, as was his habit.*

And Forster records that he "never knew him to work so frequently after dinner, or to such late hours (a practice he afterwards abhorred), as during the final months of this task".

On top of this appalling pressure of work the book was interrupted by the sudden death of Dickens's sister-in-law, Mary Hogarth, a girl of seventeen who lived with him and his wife. Dickens had for her an intense romantic affection; she died in his arms. He was so prostrate with grief that he could not work, and missed one monthly instalment of *Pickwick* and one of *Oliver Twist*. The character of Rose Maylie became an idealised portrait of Mary, and Dickens externalised his sorrow in Rose's otherwise irrelevant illness, only at the last minute reprieving her from death.

The unity of the book derives from impulse and from the energy of its imagination, not from its construction.

Superficially the impulse would appear mainly didactic and moral; and it was this aspect of the story that Dickens himself emphasised in the Preface which he first wrote for the edition of 1841. In that Preface he concentrated on his portraiture of thieves and murderers and prostitutes "as they really are, for ever skulking uneasily through the dirtiest paths of life, with the great, black, ghastly gallows closing up their prospect". He suggested that such realism in itself would perform a "service to society". He was then answering critics, like Richard Ford in the *Quarterly Review*;†

* Quoted by F. G. Kitton, *The Novels of Charles Dickens*, pp. 29–30, and in his *Dickens by Pen and Pencil*. The description was written at Kitton's request.
† Vol. lxiv, p. 97.

who said "we object *in toto* to the staple of *Oliver Twist*—a series of representations which must familiarize the rising generation with the haunts, deeds, language, and characters of the very dregs of the community. . . . It is a hazardous experiment to exhibit to the young these enormities, even on the Helot principle of inspiring disgust."

Dickens's answer was, in effect, a plea for broadening the whole scope of prose fiction, for the abandonment of false attitudes. Low life and criminal life exist, he argues, and nothing but a healthier frame of mind can follow from the knowledge of them. The technique and tone of what came to be called realism vary from generation to generation; speech tabus are inconstant; even the forms in which moral purpose is expressed are largely a matter of fashion. Allowing for such changes in custom, we must recognise in *Oliver*, besides its own inherent qualities, a novel which permanently affected the range, status, and potentialities of fiction. Even Ford admitted as much when he wrote:

> Life in London, as revealed in the pages of Boz, opens a new world to thousands bred and born in the same city, whose palaces overshadow their cellars—for the one half of mankind lives without knowing how the other half dies: in fact, the regions about Saffron Hill are less known to our great world than the Oxford Tracts; the inhabitants are still less.*

The "revelations" in the novel were not in themselves by any means new: Dickens was not in that way a pioneer: he used material that was fairly well known, and ready to hand. The Saffron Hill district was notorious, among those who were inquisitive or needed to know, as the haunt of pickpockets and thieves: the two eldest Trollope boys, for instance, went there and found that

> Saffron Hill was a world of pocket-handkerchiefs. From every window and on lines stretched across the narrow street they fluttered in all the colours of the rainbow, and of all sizes and qualities. The whole lane was a long vista of pennon-like pocket-handkerchiefs!†

The appalling filth of the slums in that area had been familiar in

* *Quarterly Review*, lxiv, pp. 87–8.
† T. A. Trollope, *What I Remember*, vol. i, p. 11.

the cholera epidemic of 1832. The Jew fence was not merely a
London character: he was known all over the country:

> A Jew seldom thieves, but is worse than a thief; he encourages others
> to thieve. In every town there is a Jew, either resident or tramping; sure
> to be a Jew within forty-eight hours in the town, somehow or other. If
> a robbery is effected, the property is hid till a Jew is found, and a bar-
> gain is then made.*

It was also common knowledge that young recruits for gangs of
thieves were most commonly enticed by girls of the Nancy type,
who haunted lodging-houses and pubs like The Three Cripples.
In his knowledge of such things Dickens was by no means unique;
but using it in a novel, with all the heightened interest of a vivid
story, he brought it home to the drawing-rooms and studies and
boudoirs where ignorance, blissful and delicate, might be touched.
In *The Newcomes* Thackeray made Lady Walham take *Oliver
Twist* secretively to her bedroom.

Some vague stirring in the intelligence or conscience was indeed
all that the novel could be expected to achieve; for a serious, considered moral lesson is very hard to find. If the purpose were to
show that the starvation and cruel ill-treatment of children in baby-
farms and workhouses produced ghastly effects on their characters
and in society, then Oliver should have turned out a monster or a
wretch, a boy who did very well at Fagin's school. Instead of this
he remained always a paragon of sweet gratitude and the tenderest
right feeling: at school he was distinguished for invincible green-
ness and showed no skill or even promise in bringing back fogles
and tickers. When it has finally been disclosed that Oliver's
parents were an unhappy gentleman of means and the daughter of
a naval officer, are we to conclude that Dickens's main lesson was
that a good heredity can overcome anything, and that in some cases
environment counts for nothing at all? He probably never even
asked himself the question in that form; from his other work—
more perhaps from his journalism and speeches than from his novels

* Quoted from a *Report of the Society for the Suppression of Mendicity*, in
Quarterly Review, lxiv, p. 360.

—we know that all his emphasis was on the physical environment generally; but Oliver and Nancy teach the opposite; it was a dilemma he never fully faced and certainly never solved.

But Dickens's most revealing comment on *Oliver* was not in his Preface. For four years in the prime of his life he practically abandoned writing, gave rein to his exhibitionism, his histrionic and mesmeric powers, and poured his prodigious energies into public readings from his own works. The effect was that of a complete, competent, highly emotional, theatrical performance. As time went on he developed an increasing desire to read "The Murder of Nancy" from *Oliver Twist*. "I have no doubt", he wrote, "that I could perfectly petrify an audience by carrying out the notion I have of the way of rendering it." He had known for thirty years that the whole episode was charged with emotional dynamite; for he had reported to Forster just after he had finished writing it: "Hard at work still. Nancy is no more. I showed what I have done to Kate last night, who was in an unspeakable '*state*': from which and my own impression I augur well."

He overrode all objections and began the public readings of the "Murder" early in 1869. At Clifton in January he gave "by far the best murder yet done", and wrote of the performance: "We had a contagion of fainting. And yet the place was not hot. I should think we had from a dozen to twenty ladies borne out, stiff and rigid, at various times!" At Cheltenham old Macready said the murder was "two Macbeths". Milling crowds, more or less hysterical, were common. The performance got such a hold on Dickens that he gave the murder at three readings out of four, and sometimes four nights in a single week. His doctors noticed that, though his pulse rose with all the public readings, it rose far higher—dangerously high—when he read the "Murder". This was in fact a main cause of his death, and during the period of obsessive passion for this reading he said he walked the streets as if he himself were wanted by the police.

How utterly remote are these scenes and this state of mind from the earnest moralities of the Preface! To understand the conjunction of such different moods and qualities in a single man is the beginning of serious criticism of Dickens. The theme of murder, and still more of the murderer being hunted and haunted after his crime, treated not as a detective story, but as a statement of human behaviour, recurs several times in his major work. Both Sikes and Jonas Chuzzlewit are transfigured by the act of murder.

The psychological condition of a rebel-reformer is in many ways similar to that of a criminal, and may have the same origins. A feeling of being outside the ordinary organisation of group life; a feeling of being an outcast, a misfit or a victim of circumstance; a feeling of bitter loneliness, isolation, ostracism or irrevocable disgrace—any one or any combination of such feelings may turn a man against organised society, and his opposition may express itself in what is technically crime or what is technically politics: treason, sedition, and armed rebellion manage to be both. Dickens's childhood had been such that all these feelings, at different times in different degrees, had been his: he knew no security and no tenderness: the family home was for a time the Marshalsea prison, and for six months Dickens himself was a wretched drudge in a blacking-factory. These two experiences, and others similar, lie behind the loneliness, disgrace and outlawry which pervade all his novels. These were always his leading psychological themes. *Oliver Twist* reveals them in an early stage, not fully developed, certainly not analysed, but very clear. Oliver himself is so much the mere embodiment of the idea of a lonely ill-used child that he is scarcely granted character enough to be anything else. Noah Claypole is a second, and far more convincing, example of what may happen to a boy branded by society. The workhouse is merely the extreme form of the debtors' prison. The Fagin-Sikes group are both outlaws and social outcasts: it is curious to find even Swinburne, whose panegyric on Dickens is not generally remarkable for social or psychological insight, calling Fagin and Sikes "victims of circumstance and society".

It is not merely true that Fagin, Sikes, Nancy, and even the Dodger, are treated with more intelligence and interest in the novel than any other characters; they are also treated, in the deepest sense, with more sympathy. Dickens is prepared to take infinite pains to follow the working of their minds, to clarify their policies and motives, to give their personalities scope in the descriptions of all that they do or suffer. The absence of this sort of sympathy in the treatment of Monks, whose melodramatic and inefficient malignity is contemptuously devised to supply the mechanism of the tale, brings out the point by contrast. Fagin and Sikes are never despised, even though what they do is despicable. The cringing meanness of the one and the unmitigated coarse brutality of the other are treated with immense and serious respect: Dickens lives into these characters as they grow. At the crisis in the life of each there is no question of moralising or preaching: Dickens identifies himself with them; he himself is the lonely outcast capable of crime. Fagin in the dock, when "the court was paved, from floor to roof, with human faces", when "in no one face—not even among the women, of whom there were many there—could be read the faintest sympathy with himself", is a figure of the most terrifying loneliness; and the jumping of his mind from detail to detail—one man's clothes, another man's dinner, the broken spike —is the psychological counterpart of Sikes's haunted wandering in the country north of London. In Sikes the criminal impulse is cruder and more violent: but Dickens's understanding is not less. The atmosphere of horror is achieved just because of his fear that he might do exactly such a murder as Sikes did. During the famous readings he used to speak jokingly of giving way to his "murderous instincts"; but it was no joke.

The lasting impression left by this novel is one of macabre horror. For us there appears to be little connection between the mood and incidents of the later chapters, and those of the earlier. We begin to wonder whether perhaps, as the Fagin-Sikes themes took hold upon him, Dickens was liable to forget his sub-title, "The Parish Boy's Progress". But to an alert reader in 1837–9 the factual and emotional connection between the beginning and the end would have seemed far stronger: the mood of the book was topical.

The "philosophers", with blood of ice and hearts of iron, on whom Dickens pours his sarcasm in the early chapters, were the Malthusians and economists, whose theory of population underlay the new Poor Law of 1834. Their doctrine briefly was that, however much the general wealth of the country grew, there would always be a section of the population below subsistence level, because of an inevitable natural tendency of population to increase faster than the means of subsistence. Vice and misery were the two first checks on the multiplication of unwanted mouths; the only third possible check was moral or prudential restraint, which meant the prevention, by one means or another, of breeding in the poorest classes. All forms of dole, charity or relief to a man unable to maintain himself or his family were suspect, because they were a direct inducement to breed in idleness, and thus aided the dismal course of nature. If the preaching of thrift and continence failed, the only acceptable policy was to give relief in the most unattractive form, under conditions which made breeding impossible.

By the Act of 1834 the Parish remained the primary unit of administration, and relief depended on a parish "settlement". For Poor Law purposes parishes were formed into "Unions"; each Union had its Workhouse, and a Board of Guardians to administer relief. But, as far as possible, relief was to be given only in the "house". Conditions there were deliberately made hard: the diet was sparse; husbands were separated from wives; a special uniform was worn, and so on. The "Workhouse-test" was intended as a deterrent. Dickens does not discuss the rightness or wrongness of the basic theory, nor the evils of subsidising wages from the rates which its application was largely designed to cure. He directs his angry sarcasm only to some of the human consequences of what was done.

The original Poor Law Commissioners, on whose findings the Act was drafted, had quite rightly urged that different classes of pauper needed different treatment. The old, the infirm, the insane, the diseased, unable to earn their own living, were a charge upon the community of a different kind from the able-bodied unemployed or the "sturdy beggar". Children in particular, and orphan children most of all, were plainly in a separate category, and no workhouse-test could be held to apply to them. But, through inefficiencies and difficulties in the practical application of the Act, these proper distinctions did not generally lead to differences of treatment. The workhouse tended to remain the "general-mixed" institution which had been such a scandal in the earlier days; people of both sexes, of all ages, all physical and moral conditions, were herded indiscriminately together, and treated like recalcitrant idlers, all equally kept on low diet: the deterrent system, meant only for the able-bodied, in practice put the screw on all alike. The children obviously suffered worst.

Oliver was born in a workhouse of the old law; when he came back from Mrs Mann's, the new law had just come in and "the Board" had just been set up. Dickens seems to have imagined the actual workhouse building unaltered, for the new "Bastilles" were not built in a hurry; Bumble was probably meant to be a "parochial officer" taken over from the old system: in these respects Dickens was attacking abuses allowed to continue. But the low diet was the one outstanding typical feature of the new system. Dickens's "three meals of thin gruel a day, with an onion twice a week, and half a roll on Sundays" was a telling caricature of the Commissioners' recommended dietaries. To a modern reader, after the rationing of two wars, these dietaries do not, on paper, seem quite so terrible: but it is hard to say how they worked out in practice. Certainly they were very ill-balanced and dull. In the No. 1 Dietary for an able-bodied man, published in 1836, there was meat on only three days of a week, and $1\frac{1}{2}$ pints of gruel every day. Women were to have less, and children over nine the same as women; children under nine were to be dieted "at discretion". Contemporary opinion can be judged by the fact that in March 1838 the Guardians of the Dudley Union presented a petition to the House of Lords complaining that the diets recommended by the Commissioners were not enough to feed the paupers: and then already half the country was laughing or weeping over Oliver, who "asked for more". It also happened that in the third year of the new law there was a very severe winter; in the fourth a trade depression; and that the fifth was a year of scarce food and high prices. With these causes of hardship the unpopularity of the law grew, and *Oliver Twist* appeared to be not merely topical but prophetic.

Through administrative muddles and false economy, through conflicts between the central and local authorities, through jealousy of the central power, and most of all through the impotent fears engendered by Malthusian orthodoxy, the condition of pauper children remained appalling for many years after *Oliver Twist* was written. Dickens did not forget the image of the Good Samaritan on Bumble's buttons. As a journalist and editor he published many articles on the subject, the gist of which was summed up in *Household Words* in 1850:

> Ought the misdeeds of the parents to be visited on their innocent children? Should pauper and outcast infants be neglected so as to become pests to Society . . .? Common sense asks, does the State desire good citizens or bad?

Oliver Twist had been written in a period when the possibility of armed revolution was constantly before men's minds—there was in fact an abortive rising in 1839; and in that atmosphere the problems of the Poor Law had an urgency and horror which they lost in the relative security and peace of the mid-Victorian age. When Dickens came back to the book and gave the readings of the "Murder", he had thirty years of burning life and imagination behind him: the obsessive interest in violent crime, registered on his pulse, was linked in memory both to the early Chartists and the lynchings by Rebecca and her Daughters, and also to the terrors and rebelliousness of a lonely outcast child, of whom the wretched Oliver himself was but a very pale and ineffectual reflection.

G.B.S. ON *GREAT EXPECTATIONS**

I

THE publication for the first time in England of an essay by Mr Shaw on Dickens is not an event to let slip with just a casual notice. His Introduction to *Great Expectations* was first printed in the U.S.A. in 1937, preceding an elaborate edition of the novel illustrated by Gordon Ross, published by the Limited Editions Club of New York; it is thus almost unknown in the United States and scarcely heard of here. It is not mentioned by William Miller in *The Dickens Student and Collector*, for which much of the work was done at Harvard: yet its sixteen pages are worth more than many groups of sixteen volumes that could be arranged from the portentous mass of Dickensiana listed by Mr Miller. It has, of course, a clear, vigorous text with some punch in every sentence: and this lifts it at once above the drivelling and trivial verbosity that passes so often for criticism of Dickens; and I am told from two sources that the English text is the same as the American but for a few very small changes.

First, it is a delight to find Mr Shaw expressing the opinion that *Great Expectations* is Dickens's "most compactly perfect book". He justifies this by stressing its freedom from "episodes of wild extravagance" and the fact that it is "all-of-one piece and consistently truthful as none of the other books are": "the story is built round a single and simple catastrophe". Dickens knew and cared to know little about "The Art of the Novel". Readers and critics even in his later days were reaching with difficulty the admission of such an art; and Dickens would have been almost the last novelist

* *Great Expectations* by Charles Dickens. With an Introduction by Bernard Shaw. The Novel Library (Hamish Hamilton). Reviewed, *Dickensian*, Spring and Autumn Numbers 1948.

to qualify as an artist. Nor would he have wanted to qualify. Mr Shaw is excellent on "Dickens's position as a member of the educated and cultured classes who had neither education nor culture". "When Dickens", he says, "introduced in his stories a character whom he intensely disliked he chose an artistic profession for him. . . . There is real hatred in his treatment of them." Many of his comments on the visual arts were "those of a complete Philistine". All this is very well borne out by the careers of the two Dickens heroes who are closest to Dickens—David and Pip. David actually ends as a novelist, but we have no description whatever of the kind of novels he wrote or the problems he tackled in writing them; we are left to assume that he took them in his stride, as Dickens took his. Pip the blacksmith's apprentice becomes a "gentleman", and "reading" is often mentioned as one of his great accomplishments in gentility; but nothing is revealed about what he read or his taste, or what good he thought he got out of it. Music and painting have no part in his life. He acquired a liking for the theatre (again, one assumes, like Dickens); but the only detailed account of his theatre-going is that of the visit to see Mr Wopsle as Hamlet; and at the end the reader is left with more awareness of the problems of the dresser in fitting the heroic actor's stockings than of the tragic dilemmas of the hero.

"The cultural side of art", says Mr Shaw with complete justice, "was as little known to Dickens as it is possible for a thing so public to remain to a man so apprehensive"; yet *Great Expectations*, for all the failure of its ending, is a great work of art, fine in form and style; it is quite unique among Dickens's books: it is, paradoxically, the artistic expression of that otherwise artless and cultureless society which it describes and exposes. It has a unity of tone and purpose, a reality and seriousness found in none other of the novels.

Mr Shaw says that in *Great Expectations* Dickens "let himself go". The critical importance of these words varies with the emphasis: they are more important if the emphasis is on "himself" than if it is on "go". For in countless other parts of his work he "let go" his other self, the impersonator, the actor who grimaced and spoke the words of his characters aloud as he wrote about them, forgetting all the details of ordinary life. His great grotesques are all "lettings-go" in this sense. And his great criminal, distorted, evil characters are "lettings-go" of a secret inner strain of his. But in *Great Expectations* it was his more open, social, autobiographical self he let go; it is the pendant to the first part of *David Copperfield*, the more mature revision of the progress of a young man in the world.

II

It is, of course, a snob's progress; and the novel's greatest achievement is to make it sympathetic. When Pip plays Beggar-my-Neighbour and, later on, sophisticated French games of cards with Estella; when he has just heard of his fortune, and the cattle on the marshes seem "in their dull manner, to wear a more respectful air now"; when he first dines with Herbert Pocket; when he visits the town in the Havisham-Pocket context without calling on Joe at the forge, and then, on getting back to London, sends him some fish and a barrel of oysters to salve his conscience; above all, when Magwitch comes to his rooms in the Temple—on these and countless other such occasions Dickens is touching the very quick of that delicate, insinuating, pervasive class-consciousness which achieved in England a subtle variegation and force to which other countries, with fewer gradations between the feudal and the "low", have scarcely aspired. Many of our novels have played on class themes, but none with such lingering, succulent tenderness. Mr Shaw says that "as our social conscience expands and makes the intense class snobbery of the nineteenth century seem less natural to us, the tragedy of *Great Expectations* will lose some of its appeal". It may need a little more effort to understand—and the novel is indeed already a historical document of the first importance; but its permanent appeal derives from its adaptation of an age-old theme to a particular complex modern society.

Many critics have seen in it an allegory or at least a symbolism. The disappointment of Pip's expectations, following upon the discovery of their source, is taken to be an expression of disgust at the groundless optimism and "progressive" hope of mid-Victorian society. What Mr Shaw calls the bitterness of Dickens's "exposure of the futility of Pip's parasitism" is often taken to be a bitterness in the knowledge that all the material wealth and boasted progress of that age were parasitic on the drudgery of an exploited working-class, a hideous underworld of labour. Mr Shaw does not push his social interpretation quite so far. But he does take the novel to be a "tragedy", and he says: "Its beginning is unhappy; its middle is unhappy; and the conventional happy ending is an outrage on it." "Pip's world is a very melancholy place, and his conduct, good or bad, always helpless." And he says of all Dickens's later work:

> When he lost his belief in bourgeois society and with it his lightness of heart he had neither an economic Utopia nor a credible religion to hitch on to. His world becomes a world of great expectations cruelly disappointed.

All this is very important. It is plain that in the later novels—*Little Dorrit, Great Expectations,* and *Our Mutual Friend* above all—Dickens's attitude to money and to the power of money in life has undergone a drastic revision, and that this reflects the development of capitalism in mid-century: the joint-stock company and investment have taken the place of the old-fashioned honest "counting-house" businessmen of the Fezziwig-Cheeryble-Garland type, who plainly worked for their living and often lived over the office. The new power of money is vaster, anonymous and secret; and those who make the big fortunes do not work for them, but juggle with paper. Merdle, Veneering, and Lammle are the new businessmen. The clearest expression of Dickens's opinion about the effect of this upon society is in the rhythmical satiric exhortation to "Have Shares" and be mighty, in *Our Mutual Friend.* The plots of all these three novels turn on Big Money; and in each a main point is that the money bears no intelligible relation to the amount and quality of the work put into earning it. Pip's is an extreme case: he does not even know where the money comes from. When he learns he is appalled: his fortune turns to dust and ashes.

III

But is the melancholy contemplation of dust and ashes the final scene and mood of the novel? Are utter despair and unrelieved disgust at the whole scheme of society into which he has "risen" Pip's final state? Even leaving out the botched-up ending with Estella, it is not; and it is clear from trains of action laid earlier in the story that Dickens never meant it to be. Pip is not utterly corrupted and brought low either in feeling or in fortune. He does two actions which bring benefit to his middle-class friends; both concern money. He secretly arranges the funds to set up Herbert in a partnership, and he praises Matthew Pocket to Miss Havisham, so that she leaves him "a cool four thousand". Furthermore, it is his provision for Herbert which saves his own fortune after the Magwitch bubble bursts. Dickens must have planned this reward for good-heartedness early on; it was not part of the tacked-on happy ending. Pip is enabled to keep his acquired class character; he goes off to the East as a member of a firm of which he says: "We were not in a grand way of business, but we had a good name, and worked for our profits and did very well." Are we to conclude, as the tragic interpreters conclude, that this part of the ending, though not tacked on, was yet planned as a concession by Dickens to his readers, because he had set himself, as Mr Shaw insists, to earn enough to bring up a large family in high style, because he could not financially afford to leave Pip to what in his inner heart he believed to be his proper fate? I don't believe it. If that was the motive, why be so explicit? When Dickens wrote so clearly that Pip's firm worked for their profits, he went out of his way to restate what he still believed to be the proper basis of the wealth of a "respectable" middle class. Even in the later fifties and the sixties he was still clinging, though rather desperately, to his ideal of the businessman in the small private firm. His hatred for the gross and illegitimate wealth of such as Merdle did not extend to all middle-class standards and values.

It is important to the understanding of the novel that Pip has aspirations before he has expectations; these are developed in the scene with Biddy in Chapter xvii.

"Biddy," said I, after binding her to secrecy, "I want to be a gentleman."

"Oh, I wouldn't, if I was you!" she returned. "I don't think it would answer."

"Biddy," said I, with some severity, "I have particular reasons for wanting to be a gentleman."

The particular reasons are, of course, to do with his passion for Estella; and when his fortune comes, the wretched Pip sees his expectations through Estella-coloured glasses; he thinks of his fortune as a means of realising the longing hopes and day-dreams which concentrate on her. The emotional tension of the book up to the time of Magwitch's return derives from this sexual situation, not from the money situation alone: in fact Pip takes his money very calmly for granted; he doesn't take Estella calmly at all. Mr Shaw says that she "is a curious addition to the gallery of unamiable women painted by Dickens", and that the notion "that anyone could ever have been happy with Estella is positively unpleasant". He suggests that the portrait of her is an elaborate and recent study from life: the clue to understanding her is that "Estella is a born tormentor". This is not quite the whole story; for the interest of Estella as an individual is to see the impact of Miss Havisham's reiterated bitter teaching on a ditch-born orphan. Dickens was rarely quite clear in his expressions of the relation between heredity and environment, though the themes preoccupied him. Oliver Twist is one notable anomaly; Estella is another, rather more complex. He hints rather than states that with her parentage you could hardly expect the girl to turn out otherwise. But the explicit emphasis is all on Miss Havisham's upbringing:

"With my praises, and with my jewels, and with my teachings, and with this figure of myself always before her, a warning to back and point my lessons, I stole her heart away and put ice in its place."

She has been trained to be a tormentor and has learned the lesson gladly.

IV

The critique of snobbery is so full, so convincing and so sympathetic because Dickens has woven the snobbery so skilfully and even unobtrusively with the sexual passion. Estella does not appear often in the book; but she is always there in the back of Pip's mind. The collapse of Pip's expectations about Estella should have been every bit as much the matter of the title as the collapse of his expectations about money. His snobbery had its root in his desire; and all the irony of the book turns on the fact that both the money and the girl derive from Magwitch; this is very bitter indeed. There is a significance in it far beyond the particular case, a far deeper and more universal significance, I think, than in any supposed political allegory. The sexual element in snobbery is one which social critics and historians have not always emphasised enough. The day-dreams of a genteel life include day-dreams of a woman who is a "lady", a creature of great beauty, brilliance, delicacy, fineness, able in idleness to keep her beauty fresh, to be unsullied by work either in the house or as an earner; the desire to possess, maintain and cherish such a creature, with all the fascinating attributes of a mistress that a fervid adolescent imagination can invent, is one of the impulses that make men want to "better themselves". Pip's dreams of Estella are sharpened by the other women in the book. His sister, Joe's first wife, is the soured working-class woman, old before her time, always in her apron, always self-pitying about her chores, always scolding, a woman in whom all the fascinations of femininity either never flowered or withered soon. Contrasted with her is the fatuous, pure "lady", Mrs Pocket, who spends all her time reading the *Peerage*, helpless to look after even herself, letting her husband, household, and children fecklessly slide: she too is a complainer. At one end of the scale is Mrs Joe, the extreme from which Pip hopes to "rise"; at the other is Mrs Pocket, the *reductio ad absurdum* of being "up in the world". Between them is Biddy, who is of the world of Agnes, though her class is different. Wise, generous, loving, attractive, mild but strong—she is the good living woman who waits in reserve in many Dickens books; but they never have very much personality, and that is the trouble. Pip knows Biddy's worth all right, but, with his big ideas, he can't take her quite seriously; he slights her when he merely tries to be nice. Estella has all the vigour and obvious vividness and glamour—something to aspire to—that Biddy lacks. Biddy is something to accept; Estella is something to build on. And building is Pip's special weakness. A distinguished French critic has here recently touched the spot:

> Ce qui caractérise le parvenu, c'est qu'il espère trop, c'est qu'il a de la chance dans ses espérances, et c'est ainsi qu'il aime. Il sait bien qu'il n'est pas aimé; mais il garde son espérance et revient avec un courage obstiné.*

V

The special unity of the book, which Mr Shaw and all its admirers particularly stress, is brought out by the ingenuity of plot through which both the amorous and social expectations are ultimately seen to derive from the same source. When Pip has made that discovery he reveals to Magwitch on his deathbed a secret of his own heart. It was partly Estella's being a "lady" that had fed his passion for her from boyhood, when he believed she was the real article by birth. The aim of all Magwitch's transport life had been to make Pip a "gentleman". At the deathbed, despite the horror that he feels for Magwitch, Pip reveals to him the story of Estella:

> "Dear Magwitch, I must tell you, now at last. You understand what I say?"
> A gentle pressure on my hand.
> "You had a child once, whom you loved and lost."
> A stronger pressure on my hand.
> "She lived and found powerful friends. She is living now. She is a lady and very beautiful. And I love her!"

Having just heard and understood, Magwitch then immediately dies. In that scene everything has come full circle; every word of it

---

* Alain: *En Lisant Dickens*, p. 158.

tells. It had been his own coarseness as a blacksmith's apprentice that had made Estella seem so remotely far above him, and he had been ashamed; it had been Magwitch who gave him the means to lose the coarseness and almost overcome the shame; he had scarcely assimilated the knowledge that this was the low and terrifying convict's doing, when he discovered that this man was indeed the father of the very girl who in her beauty and ladyhood had seemed so wildly and desperately remote. That deathbed scene is the confession from Pip that ultimately he and Magwitch had been actuated by the same sort of motive. Mr Shaw does not quite give full weight to this scene:

> But Pip—and I am afraid Pip must be to this extent identified with Dickens—could not see Magwitch as an animal of the same species as himself or Miss Havisham. His feeling is true to the nature of snobbery; but his creator says no word in criticism of that ephemeral limitation.

Surely this last scene is criticism enough without any labouring of the point. "Dear Magwitch," says Pip; at the moment of death he can use the word of love, can recognise the kinship, can even admit community of ultimate thought. This is indeed too terribly true to the nature of snobbery; Pip could never have maintained such a mood with Magwitch alive, and if he had thought he would recover he would never have told him about Estella. It was a sort of viaticum. And surely Dickens knew what he was doing.

Mr Shaw rather complains that Dickens

> never raises the question why Pip should refuse Magwitch's endowment and shrink from him with such inhuman loathing. . . . Inspired by an altogether noble fixed idea, he had lifted himself out of his rut of crime and honestly made a fortune for the child who had fed him when he was starving. If Pip had no objection to be a parasite instead of an honest blacksmith, at least he had a better claim to be a parasite on Magwitch's earnings than, as he imagined, on Miss Havisham's property. It is curious that this should not have occurred to Dickens.

The novel is not an essay in ethics; this may have occurred to Dickens, but the important point is that it did not occur to Pip;

and that is in general keeping with the truth to life which Mr Shaw praises. The horror of Magwitch which Pip had as a child in the churchyard and during the fight with Compeyson in the ditch on the marshes would have stayed with him for life; he had indelible memories of terror linked to Magwitch; the beginning of the book is so fine, so well in keeping with all that follows, because it gives the full weight and proportion to those childish fears; and those very fears are caught up again into the mood of apparently crude snobbery in the Temple. This is one of Dickens's greatest novels just because the moral problems are not seen too simply. Pip is not a young philosopher acting and feeling on argued moral principle. The childish fears hitched on to social snobbery by a complex, unconscious process in which the sexual love for Estella had the strongest play. It is just because Pip could not have rationally defended his loathing of the Warmint that it is so strong and awful. And indeed it does seem to be going a little far to say that Magwitch's fixed idea is "altogether noble"; for he was not concerned so much about Pip's true well-being as about his own capacity to make a "gentleman" of him; Pip was to be Magwitch's means of self-expression, just as Estella was to be Miss Havisham's; they each wanted to use a child to redress the balance of a world gone wrong, to do vicariously what they had failed to do direct. In the Temple Magwitch is not really concerned much about the grateful return for Pip's help on the marshes; he is concerned to view, assess, appraise the "dear boy" as his own creation. For Magwitch is a snob too. It is curious that this should not have occurred to Mr Shaw. A main theme of the book, running in two parallel strands of the plot, is that the attempt through money and power to exploit a child will lead to ingratitude and even more bitterness. Pip's presence both at the death of Magwitch and at the awful scene of Miss Havisham's repentance is meant to show him as the channel through which they purge themselves of their errors too.

Thus, emotionally as well as socially and financially, Pip appears as "helpless". He directs nothing; things happen to him; everybody except Joe and Biddy uses him for purposes of their own. They let him go his own way and help him out of scrapes. But there is never any question of his return to the village for good, with an effective, working reconciliation with them. His new class character—amounting to very little more than voice and table manners and range of friends—is firmly established and he is left to continue in it. Dickens was not going to say that all his gains were negligible. Of the two children used for experiment Estella suffers in the long run more than Pip; she is not of the receptive kind.

Dickens did not himself anywhere, I think, call the book a "tragedy"; but he did say from the very beginning when he was planning it that a "grotesque tragi-comic conception" first encouraged him.* And in view of later criticism it is almost harsh to find him saying of Joe and Pip: "I have put a child and a good-natured foolish man, in relations that seems to me very funny."† And Pumblechook is there all along to prick Pip's tragic element; it is as if Polonius were allowed all through to gloss Hamlet's soliloquies; but it is significant that not even Pumblechook twits Pip about Estella. The fact is that all Dickens's stories published in parts or in serial—and *Great Expectations* was a serial in *All the Year Round*—grew in the writing beyond their first conception. But the growth of this novel never became rank; it never got out of hand. Though Pumblechook and Wopsle are grotesque characters, and belong to the histrionic method of "letting-go", they never get out of hand and spoil the proportion of things. A great feature of the book is the way in which minor characters, like Orlick and Wemmick, grow as it proceeds; each of them has, in his own way, a dream, and each is a comment on Pip. Wemmick's castle is not a castle in the air, but a castle at Walworth with a deaf old man inside. The acknowledgement of the lasting difference between Walworth and Little Britain is just the acknowledgement that in his life Pip could not yet make. Orlick's mad resentment against Mrs Gargery is a release of what Pip bottled up.

* Forster: Bk. ix, Ch. iii.   † Ibid.

VI

The book is every bit as rich as any other Dickens novel; but not with a squandered and disordered richness. The grotesques are under control and all fit directly into the external narrative and also into the main psychological theme. This applies even to Miss Havisham. She is not in the ordinary realistic sense of the word an utterly impossible person. It has to be remembered too, that in this, as in most of Dickens's novels, the imaginary date of the action is considerably earlier than the date of writing. I have not worked out an exact internal chronology from the hints given up and down *Great Expectations*—and indeed it might not be possible to do so; but it is clear at any rate from the mere span of Pip's life that the beginning of the book cannot have been later than the 1830's. In other words Miss Havisham belongs to an age in which great eccentrics were a more normal part of the English social scene; the greater uniformity of manners, the muting and levelling of style, the suppression of feeling by what was called taste, had not yet clouded our life. But though these things had not made Miss Havisham "impossible", they have coloured Dickens's treatment of her, writing as he was in the early sixties. She is a private, secret grotesque, unknown to the world: she does not storm outrageously through the action of the book like a Mrs Gamp or a Quilp. As usual, various suggestions have been made about "originals" for Miss Havisham and for items in her life. Some such old recluse was burned to death in her house near Hyde Park; a wedding-breakfast room, with cake and all, had been sealed up in the tavern called "Dirty Dick's" in Bishopsgate Street Without.* On 29th January 1850 an inquest was held on Martha Joachim, who had died at the age of sixty-two at York Buildings, Marylebone:

> In 1825 a suitor of the deceased, whom her mother rejected, shot himself while sitting on the sofa with her, and she was covered with his brains. From that instant she lost her reason. Since her mother's death, eighteen years ago, she had led the life of a recluse, dressed in white, and

---

* See F. G. Kitton: *The Novels of Charles Dickens*, p. 193.

never going out. A char-woman occasionally brought her what supplied her wants. Her only companions were the bull-dog, which she nursed like a child, and two cats.

This report Dickens certainly read, as it is taken from the *Household Narrative* (1850, p. 10) of which he was the editor. It seems clear that Miss Havisham is another example of Dickens's regular habit of fusing together items from a number of different sources, remembered over a considerable time. In the details of the spiders and so on he let his imagination run, just as he did over such things as the workhouse diet at the beginning of *Oliver Twist*. But Miss Havisham's peculiar greatness is that she is built so convincingly into the main structure of the book, linked to Compeyson, Magwitch, Pip, Jaggers and the Pockets with such a clever combination of converging possibilities, that she presides over the plot like a convincing Fate. "In *Great Expectations*", writes Mr Shaw,

> we have Wopsle and Trabb's boy; but they have their part and purpose in the story and do not overstep the immodesty of nature. It is hardly decent to compare Mr F.'s aunt with Miss Havisham; but as contrasted studies of madwomen they make you shudder at the thought of what Dickens might have made of Miss Havisham if he had seen her as a comic personage. For life is no laughing matter in *Great Expectations*.

VII

Since the first instalment of this article was written I have had the pleasure and advantage of reading an essay by Professor John Butt in the *Durham University Journal* for June 1948. It is called "Dickens at Work" and it studies the effect on the construction of the novels of their publication in monthly parts or as magazine serials. *Great Expectations* was a serial in *All the Year Round*, and appeared in thirty-six weekly instalments from 1st December 1860 to 3rd August 1861. Professor Butt calls attention to the fact that at the end of the thirty-ninth chapter, that is two-thirds of the way through the novel, Dickens wrote: "This is the end

of the Second Stage of Pip's Expectations"; and he draws the inference that at this point Dickens "seems to have paused to decide
what he should do next", implying that he had got so far without
knowing how the story was to continue and finish. His evidence
for this inference is in two places:

(1) The letter from Dickens to Forster (*Life*, Bk. IX, Ch. iii),
which was sent with the opening chapters of the third division of
the story, conveys, according to Professor Butt, "something of the
triumph of discovery":

> It is a pity that the third portion cannot be read all at once, because
> its purpose would be much more apparent; and the pity is the greater,
> because the general turn and tone of the working out and winding up,
> will be away from all such things as they conventionally go. But what
> must be, must be. As to the planning out from week to week, nobody
> can imagine what the difficulty is, without trying.

(2) The master plan for the third part of the novel still survives in
Dickens's handwriting, attached to the manuscript in the Wisbech
Museum, and is printed in full by Professor Butt. The whole of
this plan need not be repeated here, for it is followed out fairly
faithfully in the finished novel. But Professor Butt's inference from
it is of great interest, and has much bearing on what I wrote in the
earlier instalment of this essay. Professor Butt states that "internal
evidence" shows that the Wisbech plan was drawn up shortly after
the letter to Forster was written. He does not say exactly what this
"internal evidence" is; but, assuming that it is conclusive, the
further question remains: are we justified in inferring that, even if
none of the Wisbech plan had been written down till then, no items
in it had occurred to Dickens until after the whole of the First and
Second Stages of the book had been finished? Was there really an
utter break at the end of Stage Two, in which Dickens had no idea
at all about how the plot was to develop? The matter is of interest if
we are right in praising *Great Expectations* for being "compactly
perfect" and "all-of-one piece". I made a good deal in the earlier
part of this article of the unifying ingenuity and importance to the
whole theme of the novel of the fact that Estella is ultimately

shown to be Magwitch's daughter. We now find that "Estella, Magwitch's daughter" appears near the beginning of the Wisbech plan for Part Three. I find it rather hard to believe that this entry records the first occasion on which this idea occurred to Dickens. If it was so, how had he intended to develop the significance of the treatment of Jaggers's housekeeper in Chapter xxvi, Stage Two? It is obvious that this woman with the powerful wrists was mysteriously built up for some purpose; but was the purpose doubtful even in Dickens's own mind? Or was Estella to have been her daughter by another father? Or what? We cannot know, on the evidence as it exists. Nor, on this evidence, are we justified in concluding that Dickens did not all along intend to make Estella the housekeeper's daughter by Magwitch.

It is worth stressing this point, because Professor Butt builds a good deal on the Wisbech plan, not only for the method of composition of *Great Expectations*, but also for all the later novels. He argues that Dickens *tended* not to plan the details ahead for each novel as a whole. But it seems to me to be going too far to argue that, because a plan was not written down, or has not survived, there never was a plan even in the author's head. I think it could be shown that *some* details, even some moves in the story of a novel, were almost improvised (e.g. the sending of the Peggottys and Micawbers to Australia); but it is quite another thing to suggest that in a number of cases the greater part of the endings of the novels were left open until much of the writing had been done.

The Wisbech plan does, however, reveal several other interesting points. It shows that Dickens's intention to make Pip go abroad and join Herbert in Clarriker's business was explicit at least by the time Stage Two was finished; this, as I pointed out, was Pip's salvation; it was this that redeemed his life of prosperity from utter and total failure. The plan shows clearly that from fairly early on Dickens meant him to retain his new friendships and his new class character. The final note in the Wisbech plan is this: "The one good thing he did in his prosperity, the only thing that endures and bears good fruit." It bears good fruit not only to Herbert but to Pip himself. The very emphasis that Dickens gives this note, by placing it as his last comment on the whole plan, gives it almost the status of a leading "moral", and it should put an end to the idea that the novel is altogether tragic and that every atom of Pip's expectations was to be blasted. It is entirely consistent with Dickens's mainly individualistic and sentimental ethic that Pip's one good deed should have its reward, even for himself.

It is also noteworthy that the Wisbech plan contains no mention of any final meeting with Estella. The only mention of Estella is in the note about her being Magwitch's daughter. The plan does plainly say that Pip's main reason for going down to the marsh village again after recovering from his illness was "to propose to Biddy". After "Finds Biddy married to Joe" there is no mention of Pip's love affairs. All this fits the rounded, careful plot that Pip was to lose both the fortune and the girl, and that both were to derive from Magwitch. I find it hard to believe that this firm symmetry was achieved only in the last stage of writing; and it seems unlikely that proof can now be given that it was so.

VIII

It is in keeping with Mr Shaw's methods and character that a large part of his Introduction to *Great Expectations* should be about *Little Dorrit*. It all grows out of the discussion of Dickens's culture. Mr Shaw writes:

> You may read the stories of Dickens from beginning to end without ever learning that he lived through a period of fierce revivals and revolutionary movements in art, in philosophy, in sociology, in religion: in short, in culture. Dean Inge's remark that "the number of great subjects in which Dickens took no interest whatever is amazing" hits the nail exactly on the head. As to finding such a person as Karl Marx among his characters, one would as soon look for a nautilus in a nursery.

And the very next paragraph begins with the sentence: "Yet *Little Dorrit* is a more seditious book than *Das Kapital*." This judgment is based on the attack on the Civil Service and on the attacks on Parliament in *Little Dorrit*, *Bleak House* and elsewhere.

Of course Shaw has to admit that Dickens "never saw himself as a revolutionist"; and he gives the following summary of Dickens's political position:

> He was an independent Dickensian, a sort of unphilosophic Radical, with a complete disbelief in government by the people and an equally complete hostility to government in any other interest than theirs. He exposed many abuses and called passionately on the rulers of the people to remedy them; but he never called on the people themselves. He would as soon have thought of calling on them to write their own novels.

Far too much that has been written and said about Dickens's politics has been written and said with the misguided expectation of finding something definite and almost systematic. He certainly was an unphilosophic radical; *The Chimes* and *Hard Times*, to mention nothing else, show how violently he was *anti* the current form of Philosophical Radicalism; he was even an unsystematic radical, and was suspicious of both theoretical systems and practical systems because he thought of the individual human element as more important, and ultimately more powerful, than they. But this individualistic humanism was qualified in two respects. It was qualified first by experience; as time went on Dickens began to see its weakness. The more bitter and less sanguine mood of his later books can be missed only by a reader who has been befogged by the earlier. The old expansive Christmas ethic is almost dead. It recurs in Mr Boffin almost as a caricature of its former self. Magwitch is no benevolent idealist whose goodness may regenerate society; he is a power-lover and a snob, whose specious generosity all but corrupts Pip and brings about his good almost by chance. The old Christmas ethic is represented by Joe, in whom it is humble, narrow and cautious. Joe's relations with Old Orlick could be quoted to illustrate the break-down of the kind of employer-employed relationship which Dickens had earlier loved to idealise. Orlick never seems to be intrinsically evil in himself as Compeyson is shown to be evil; he is jealous, revengeful, full of hate; but he seems all the time to have been thwarted by something outside himself, something it is beyond Joe's range to understand.

He is indeed a baffling figure to a modern reader, and seems to me to represent an unresolved (perhaps only half-conscious) problem in Dickens's own mind.

Mr Shaw writes that Dickens never "called on the people themselves". This is not wholly true of his journalism; there was, for instance, his article *To Working Men* about Public Health in *Household Words* for 7th October 1854; there were other particular articles, such as *A Poor Man's Tale of a Patent*. But in general I think it is true that he was suspicious of the people in the mass. The curious passage in *The Old Curiosity Shop* showing the dread of physical-force Chartism has its counterparts in the description of the popular riots in *A Tale of Two Cities* and in *Barnaby Rudge*. Old Orlick seems in his own individual self to echo this dread of the mass in action. He is less a criminal than a turbulent, discontented underdog, and I think many readers of *Great Expectations*, if they look into their minds carefully about the matter, will find that they have been all along according him a sort of uneasy sympathy touched with fear. Orlick represents the element in English society with which Dickens never came to terms. He could assimilate the pitiable underdog; but the rash, independent, strong, turbulent, losing underdog, who became criminal more by accident than by choice, always disturbed him. Orlick is far more interesting than Compeyson or Magwitch, because his author did not put him flat and fair in the criminal department. There was an underlying fear that "the people" in the mass might turn out to be Orlicks.

IX

Dickens's individualistic humanism was also qualified by an authoritarian strain. He saw all the worst effects of uncontrolled *laissez-faire*. It is worth repeating what has often been said before —that he had a great admiration for compulsory centralised powers as the best means of solving certain particular administrative-political problems. His Benthamism was not purely negative, and he could follow the new Benthamite formula for reform—Report,

Legislation, Inspection—when circumstances seemed to him to demand it; he judged each question independently on its own merits. His opposition to so many features of the Poor Law of 1834 has diverted attention from the new measures of government and administration that he supported. He had no love whatever (except that he had a delight in describing all muddles) for the muddle of petty local authorities, Vestries and Boards that found themselves faced with a task for which they were never designed—that of administering a modern industrialised state. Even his satire of Bumble in *Oliver Twist* can be taken as a criticism of unsuitable parish officers taken over from the regime of the Old Poor Law as if they were competent to work the New. But it was in other directions that his advocacy of efficient central government is plainest.

Before *Little Dorrit* the chief focus of attack had been Public Health. Not so much in his novels, but in speeches, in articles and in other ways, Dickens had argued that the control of the physical conditions of the new labouring population needed an over-riding power that lifted it out of the hands of individual property-owners and even out of the hands of small local authorities. He supported the first Board of Health (of which the centenary falls this year) with all the means at his disposal. He supported the 1851 Act for the compulsory licensing and inspection of Lodging Houses. His article *A Monument of French Folly* (1850) was a bitterly sarcastic plea against the Court of Common Council of the City of London for the centralised control and police inspection of Cattle Markets and Slaughter Houses, ramming home the superiority of the French example. His enthusiastic articles in praise of the C.I.D. in their centralised campaign against crime are too well known to need mentioning again.

It seems to me that especially after 1850 the focus of his political interest was on special powers related to special functions, and that he had no generalised theory or principle which unified his particular interests. *Little Dorrit* was, of course, subversive in that it was a frontal attack on all incompetence and all vested interests in the business of governing or not-governing; it was an attack on a

class and on a kind of person; reduced to general terms it became a
plea for an active and efficient bureaucracy. The book was topical
to the Northcote-Trevelyan reforms in the Civil Service. Vested
interests, idleness, sloth and stupidity remain the vices of bureaucracy still; but the social emphasis is now quite different; the point
of attack would have to be different; the educational problems involved are entirely different and, except perhaps in the Foreign
Office, the prevailing traditions are now different too. There are so
many various and subtle ways of being slow and incompetent that
the dynamite which Mr Shaw finds in *Little Dorrit* now seems a
little damp.

A NEW EDITION OF
DICKENS'S LETTERS*

In my house there is a little lop-sided room too high for its size, with a disproportionately big window and fireplace. It used to be the lodger's room, but now it is called sometimes Dickens Room, and sometimes just The Office. It has become an office in everything, except for a peculiar bogus divan-bed along one wall, in which unfortunate guests are put. For after eighteen months the mere machinery of editing Dickens's Letters became so big that we had to give up a room to it.

To the left of the fireplace, shelves hold thirty-nine box-files, mostly three inches deep and foolscap size.† From there along the mantelpiece runs the *Dictionary of National Biography*, an excellent fit; and at the Z end, after a few Supplements, the *Index and Epitome* props up a blue folder solemnly marked "Microfilm Guide". This is kept in place to the right by a glossy-green block of eight card-index drawers.‡ These act as an index to the whole work, and as a symbol of that ideal of managing paper which I began to learn not, I must say, in any university, but at the Staff College at Camberley.

I am sure that every bit as much pleasure can be got out of information when it is organised as when it is not. And the organisation has an appeal, a glamour, even a fantasy, of its own. An index can be almost as interesting and as wayward as a memory. This index now contains about 8,000 cards, one for each letter of Dickens known to us.§ We know there are more extant letters than this, but we have not yet chased and recorded them. The card ideally gives a record—and the index is wayward because of the

---

* B.B.C. Third Programme, 14 Oct 1951. Printed in the *Listener*, 18 Oct.
† [There are now some fifty.]
‡ [There are now ten.]
§ [The number has since risen to 9,690.]

varying degrees in which this ideal is approached—of a letter's past history in print, if it has any and we know it; the location of the manuscript, if we know it; an account of our handling of the letter; a reference to the file containing our text, if we have got beyond the printed sources; and sometimes a few short jottings and spatterings of notes on other points. The main jottings for notes are filed with the texts. The serious work of annotation must be done near the end; for we find, as the new letters stream in, that one often annotates another. That part of the edition, then, is now slowly accruing rather than being systematically constructed. The first thing is to make good texts.

Along the next wall of the room is a collection of books—cheap texts of Dickens's works, thumbed and scribbled on; sets of the three periodicals he edited, *Bentley's Miscellany*, *Household Words*, and *All the Year Round*; a complete run, from its beginning in 1905, of that remarkable periodical called *The Dickensian*, published by the Dickens Fellowship; many books, of very patchy quality, about Dickens and his works; and diaries and memoirs and biographies of his more important friends, many of which contain texts of letters or extracts from them. The collection is by no means complete or perfect; but the work would be impossible if we had to rely on libraries for things in constant use.

The chair is in the angle of two tables. A large writing-table is in front; a small narrow kitchen table runs up against it at right-angles on the left. This plan was made chiefly to suit our work from microfilm; for we are using microfilm as the first source of our texts of the many letters in the big collections in America; it is far cheaper and handier than photostat, and every bit as good. A film-strip projector (really just a modern, electric magic-lantern) stood back on the small table throws its image on a little screen of white card slightly forward on the large table, conveniently just ahead of the typewriter. The kit for this method costs less than half as much as a portable microfilm-reader made for the purpose, and gives just as good results. The shallow cutlery-drawer in the kitchen table takes the rolls of microfilm, in a tiny space for thousands of letters. Photostats would occupy yards of files.

But this layout of tables has other advantages. On a shallow shelf built in under the kitchen table all the typing-paper is to hand; and a deep shelf below takes the books most often needed for reference. Here are three different editions of Forster's *Life*; Hatton and Cleaver's *Bibliography of the Periodical Works of Charles Dickens*; a *Dickens Concordance*; a copy of *Men of the Time*, and one of *Men of the Reign*; C. R. Cheney's *Handbook of Dates*—essential in dealing with imperfectly dated letters. These things can be reached without getting up from the chair, and, most important of all, here are the different editions of Dickens's letters that have been already published.

The first edition of all was edited by Dickens's sister-in-law, Georgina Hogarth, and his daughter Mamie—that was in two volumes in 1880, published by Chapman and Hall; they added a third volume to this in 1882; in the same year these three volumes were rearranged to form a new edition in two volumes. And the whole was altered and rearranged again in a one-volume edition published by Macmillan in 1893. From that time until 1938 no attempt was made to produce a collected edition of the letters; and then three fat volumes of *Letters*, edited by Walter Dexter, formed part of the beautiful limited edition of Dickens's works published by the Nonesuch Press—2,577 large pages altogether of letters alone. In the interval a number of separate collections—or at least selections from them—had been published independently, and many letters had dribbled out in pamphlets and periodicals; but all these were widely scattered, variously edited and often incomplete. The Nonesuch edition gathered up a great part of this material and included a great deal more from manuscript sources, and it is now the edition which any serious reader must consult. But the Letters could never be bought without a whole set of the Works, and the present market-price of the whole set—they come into the market very rarely—is £100 or so. The collected Letters are thus virtually inaccessible, and the ordinary interested reader (as distinct from the student who can go for long times together to one of the big libraries) has nothing available but one or other edition of the family selection which we nickname "Mamie-Georgie".

And it *is* a family selection, edited by family methods, showing all possible faults of editing in a bewildering variety of forms and countless instances. No blame is due to anyone; it is just a typical example of how such family jobs were then done. Wholesale, silent omission is here the mere child's-play of mishandling. Bits of two separate letters of different dates are fused together, without any warning being given, under a single date; and in shortening the edition for one volume in 1893, bits of no less than three letters were put together as belonging to one, even though they had been presented differently before. It was even odder to add words to the text which Dickens never wrote at all. In the Mamie-Georgie version of a letter describing Macready's daughter Butty occurs the phrase "with a face of great power and character", and there is no sign whatever of these words in a microfilm view of the manuscript.

Unfortunately the Nonesuch editor was so rushed that he perpetuated a number of these errors and did not have the opportunity or the time to see all the manuscripts; and many more letters have come to light since the thirties. So we are starting again from scratch and are relying on no printed text when we can go to the original. A sample may help to show how far we have so far (in just over two years) been able to go beyond the Nonesuch edition. If we take the letters to correspondents whose surnames begin with the letters A to C, the Nonesuch prints just over 1,200, including those of which only extracts are given, and those which are merely mentioned as existing, no part of the text being printed. In that same group we have so far got transcripts from original manuscripts of 478, and transcripts from facsimile (that is, from microfilm or photostat or from photo-facsimiles in printed books) of 451; this means first or second quality texts of 929 letters. We have microfilm waiting for transcription of (very roughly indeed) 650 more; and we have record of 540 of which we have not yet seen originals or facsimiles. That makes a total of about 2,100 for our edition, as against 1,200 in the fullest edition at present published. I doubt whether that proportion would be borne out all through; this sample is not altogether typical, in that it includes among the microfilm not yet transcribed the huge correspondence to Miss Burdett Coutts which was recently sold in New York and is now in the Pierpont Morgan Library. The arrangement about this is that Professor Edgar S. Johnson, one of the American members of our Advisory Board, is to edit first a selection,* and we then follow with the whole. Professor Johnson has estimated, quite independently of our records, that there are 3,500 extant letters of Dickens unpublished; and it would take too long to try to confirm or deny it!

Dickens was so famous so young; long before he was thirty, people were treasuring his letters and seeking his autograph. We have come across very few cases of recorded loss or destruction; in fact, off-hand, I can only think of John Forster and one innocent child.† On the other side there is the old man of seventy-four who in 1913 said Dickens had given him five letters to post when he was a lad of seventeen or eighteen, and he could still clearly remember the names and addresses on four of them. The things were looked on as important even in the fifties. Everybody tended to preserve, and then to treasure or to sell. The prices in the market are still high. Besides this, Dickens was a man of incredible energy with countless friends and a liking for keeping much of his work in his own hands. Even when he was an editor he would often write a full, polite letter of rejection to a contributor entirely in his own autograph. For these reasons the number of his extant letters is so prodigious that an office and all this machinery are needed to handle them.

I can imagine somebody asking or wondering whether it is really worth publishing the whole lot, down to the last letter of rejection and the note ordering new boots for the coachman. I think it can be justified. Dickens was a man of major importance for many reasons; it is a *sine qua non* of proper biography that the letters

---

* [Published in 1953. See p. 234.]

† [Other instances of destruction have since come to light: the daughters of R. H. Barham destroyed all Dickens's letters to their father, considering letters to be private things: H. K. Browne ("Phiz") "had a bonfire to lessen the lumber", on which most of his letters from Dickens were consumed: the letters to Augustus Egg were destroyed during the Blitz of the second war, as were some miscellaneous Dickens letters in the Central Library, Walworth: finally a consignment of Dickens letters was lost in the Prestwick air-crash of Christmas 1954, though luckily these had already been transcribed by Mr and Mrs House.]

should all be brought together in print, properly indexed and annotated; and the filling of the gaps will contribute also to the social history of the century. And even for the ordinary reader the view of Dickens's personality could never be complete without seeing day after day the streaming energy of his correspondence in bulk and detail; a mere selection disguises all that, and fails to show how even in an order to a wine merchant a character and a style are given to every syllable. With all the letters a day falls into shape under one's eyes. And in this actual work of the editing, one of the great rewards is to see how in a moment a gap in the filing-system is filled, and simultaneously the vision of the life expands and becomes clearer.

I can illustrate this by just trying the machinery where I sit. Take a date at random, say my own birthday 22 May, in a central year of Dickens's life, say 1850. He must have been at work on *David Copperfield* then; it came out in parts in 1849 and 1850. Look up in Hatton and Cleaver—No. XIII May, No. XIV June, No. XV July. Perhaps he was working then on the July Number, that is Chapters 44 to 46, including the housekeeping of Doady and Dora. But besides *Copperfield* he was then editing *Household Words*, which had started as a new venture only in March of that year. Look at the typed copy of the Contributors' Book. The key to the filing-system hangs framed over the mantelpiece; everything about *Household Words* is R.3.d (R.1 and R.3 live together in a single box, because R.2 is very special). Here is the thing, giving the names of all the contributors for each issue. The current number for 18 May had two contributions from Dickens himself, the well-known article called "The Begging-Letter Writer" and something called "Card from Mr Booley", which I can't remember at all. So I look it up in volume I. It's a short note on pages 175–6, all about "Mr Booley's remarks in addressing the Social Oysters" linked up to Mr Thomas Grieve and "the beautiful diorama of the route of the Overland Mail to India". There simply isn't time to look into this now. But the next number of *Household Words*, for 25 May, has an article of Dickens's own I know well and have quoted somewhere, called "A Walk in a Workhouse", a splendid social article looking back to Oliver and forward to old Nandy and Betty Higden, just an incidental part of a life's campaign against the administration of the law of 1834, but written with incredible gusto. That must have been in print by 22 May, possibly with final proofs still to correct. And besides, Dickens might even then have been thinking over or altering the article he did in collaboration with Wills for the number of 1 June—"A Popular Delusion", all about Billingsgate and the marketing of London fish, ending up with a huge fish meal including salmon and lobsters, followed by punch "in wicked tumblers of immense dimensions".

Nothing ties down to the day, May 22, but here all round it accrues an immense amount of work; one after another, and one on top of the other, typical Dickens themes pile up in thought or proof or manuscript, all along with the current instalment of *David Copperfield*. He may well have had no time to write any letters on 22 May at all. Which volume of the Nonesuch does 1850 come in? I can't ever be sure; they didn't put the year-dates on the spine —and that's a mistake we mustn't repeat. I think Vol. II; yes; May; p. 216; letters for May 12, 13, 18, 24. A short letter to John Leech on Saturday, May 18, from the office of *Household Words*:

> Book me for the Derby—but don't you think we ought to have four on 'em? As to a hamper from Fortnum & Mason's, *that* I consider indispensable.

Then there's nothing till the mere mention, with no text at all, of a letter to Talfourd of May 24, referring to *David Copperfield*. It is rather a long gap, even over a week-end. I will see if we have found any new ones: that means the F.1 series of files, the carbon copies of our own new texts, kept in chronological order to be the working supplement to the Nonesuch edition. F.1.b is 1841–50. We've got a new letter for 12 May, and no less than three new ones for May 22.

DEVONSHIRE TERRACE
Twenty Second May, 1850

Mr Charles Dickens presents his compliments to Mr Ellerman, and begs to acknowledge the safe receipt of Mr Ellerman's drama, and of his obliging note.

Same address and date:

Sir.

I beg you to assure the Members of the Newsvendors' benevolent and Provident Institution, that I am very much gratified by their generous remembrance of me on the occasion of their last Annual Meeting; and that any services I can render them, at any time, are freely and cordially at their command.

Your faithful Servant

CHARLES DICKENS

Mr Edward W. Cole.

The day begins to fill out; the stream of complimentary copies, of books the great man is asked to read, the unending demands on his time, the need to answer. Then a note about an old loyalty and affection—the Newsvendors' Association for whom he made some of his happiest speeches.

And then the third letter from Devonshire Terrace on 22 May 1850:

Sir.

In reply to your courteous letter, I beg to say, that my avocations would not admit of my responding to such a requisition as you describe, though I should be very sensible of the honor of its presentation to me.

I am Sir

Yours faithfully and obliged

CHARLES DICKENS

James G. Winn Esquire.

The jottings for the notes made by one of my associate editors there say: "A note from the donor of this letter says that it is an answer to one from Winn suggesting that CD allow himself to be nominated as a Candidate for Parliament." I do not know the value of that authority yet; but suppose it is sound, see how the calm refusal even of that just fits into the day's work. 22 May has come considerably to life.*

* [Since 1951 two further letters of 22 May 1850 have come to light. The first is to Edward Chapman and concerns a drawing of the packet-ship *Britannia* which was to be used as a frontispiece to the first cheap edition of *American Notes* (1850).

Dear Sir,

Mr. Stanfield wonders you didn't send him a paving-stone to draw upon,

You will have noticed all along that I talk of *us* and *our*. Of course a job of this size has to be done by a team. Besides myself there are two Associate Editors, former pupils of mine; my wife is Assistant Editor; and there is an Advisory Board of seven English and three American members. We have just sadly lost that great French Dickensian the Count de Suzannet, who before his death had helped us with extraordinary patience and generosity. Two years ago we made an appeal in the Press for knowledge of manuscripts, all over the world. The response was huge—answers from every continent except Asia, and the address-book has now the names of nearly 200 owners or helpers.* Such is the posthumous interest in Dickens and the power of his personality.

---

as send a block in this unprepared state. I send you his drawing to do the best you can with. It costs nothing, and I wish it to be kept very clean and returned to me.

Faithfully yours,
CHARLES DICKENS

The second letter is to Daniel Maclise. Hankey was a director of the Bank of England and Dickens was collecting material for an article called "The Old Lady in Threadneedle Street", which appeared in *Household Words* on 6 July 1850.

DEVONSHIRE TERRACE
Twenty Second May, 1850

My Dear Mac.

I called on you yesterday, but you were out. *They would prefer another day in town.* If you will let me know at what hour we shall meet for Ditton, I shall be (of course) punctual. Whereabouts in that Wilderness, the Bank, am I to ask for Mr Hankey?

Ever Faithfully
CD]

* [It now has more than 400.]

THE DICKENS STORY*

THERE occur in academic life, even in English studies, both in the United States and here, devoted, quiet characters who settle down to the study of one particular author, not in the way of rivalry, or making a name, or staking out claims in manuscripts like gold-prospectors, but more in the spirit of a medieval schoolman writing a "Commentary on the Sentences", or an old-fashioned scholar like Twining producing a slow, massive, entertaining edition of the *Poetics* of Aristotle. Professor Johnson is, I think, a man of this kind. A few years ago he was not at all widely known in the States; but I soon came to know by correspondence that he was quietly and modestly working away at a new full-scale life of Dickens, from the original sources. He would stand or fall mainly by one book: and the first thing to say is that he triumphantly stands.

For years the necessary biography of Dickens for serious work or reference has been the edition of Forster's *Life* with J. W. T. Ley's notes. Ley's notes were useful additions, but thin. Forster's book itself was, of course, the approved, almost the official, life; it had privileged, direct knowledge; it had vitality and sense; it belonged with the unchallenged biographies of major Victorian persons such as Trevelyan's life of Macaulay, and the huge work on Disraeli by Monypenny and Buckle. Forster's view of Dickens, and his handling of particular episodes, have been challenged and even overthrown since then: but his book as a whole has held its own till now.

Since Forster the task has been one of tracing, collecting, surveying and assessing new evidence. This has been done in curious ways; Dickens has attracted a number of amateur enthusiasts, often interested in byways and trivialities (where Pickwick slept and where David Copperfield drank beer) rather than in the main serious matters of either biography or criticism. Since Edmund Wilson's

* B.B.C. Third Programme, 16 Oct 1953. Printed in the *Listener*, 22 Oct.

essay called "The Two Scrooges" (and even before) it has been fashionable to snipe at these amateurs as duffers or idolaters. Some of them have certainly been both; but still it is a fact that the serious work of collecting new evidence about Dickens's life *in general* (apart from special subjects like the matter of Ellen Ternan) was carried on by them and by nobody else. Above all, the fullest collection of Dickens's letters yet published was organised and edited by one of them, the late Walter Dexter, whose three fat volumes in the Nonesuch edition have been the chief source of all recent biography till Professor Johnson came into print.*

It is interesting to wonder why the professional scholars kept off Dickens, as they certainly did. I can suggest only two plausible reasons. One is that Dickens has always been "news", as no other English writer ever has been; and academic people were possibly shy of what was always hot for journalists, or else bedevilled by facetious monomaniacs. The other reason in a sense develops from this, but has far more precise factual consequences. As a result of this newsy popularity, Dickens's autograph manuscripts have had an exceptional appeal to every sort of collector, great and small: they began to come piecemeal into the market soon after his death, and there has been a constant commercial traffic in them ever since. Not only have manuscripts constantly been changing hands, through the sale-rooms and dealers' shops, but there has also been a widespread belief (among some collectors, I think, and among some dealers certainly) that the fact of publication lowers the price of a manuscript in the market. This meant that it was difficult to trace Dickens's manuscripts in large quantities; and it also meant there was uncertainty about permission to publish, even when they were traced.

But nowadays things are rather different: many of the big collectors of the last generation have died, and given or bequeathed their materials to libraries. For social and financial reasons few big collectors have followed them in the field; and the chief buyers have themselves been, and still are, not private individuals who might sell again, but public collections and libraries. Thus there has been

* *Charles Dickens: his Tragedy and Triumph,* by Edgar Johnson. 2 vols (Gollancz).

going on for some years a process by which the materials for a new life of Dickens have been becoming more concentrated, more stationary, and more accessible. Furthermore, as the generation which knew Dickens himself has receded further into the past, more documents have come out of purely private family papers into the open.

I am suggesting that for these social and economic reasons (all growing ultimately from his newsy popularity) it has only recently become possible to attempt a life of Dickens based on a thorough survey of new material. Also, as so many of the big rich collectors were Americans, and as American libraries are more heavily endowed than ours, a great part of the material is in the United States. Professor Johnson was well placed in New York, because two of the biggest collections are in the Pierpont Morgan Library and the Berg Collection in the Public Library there.

These purely technical points are not widely known or understood, and it is plain that they are by no means trivial when one finds Professor Johnson's statement that, apart from the vast mass of printed evidence, he has consulted about 3,500 unpublished primary documents.

The first thing that has impressed me about his book (and it is a long book in two volumes of over 1,100 pages, without the notes and index) is the control with which he has mastered and ordered this huge mass of evidence. Knowing it and ordering it well into a scheme of mainly chronological narrative is one thing in writing this kind of biography; it is another thing to use the material in detail with grace and tact. Professor Johnson has succeeded here too. For a large part of the book he quotes, of course, Dickens's own words; they tell as nothing else can; they both relate and reveal. But a quotation too long continued can spoil proportion and hold up the movement (this was one of Forster's faults); Johnson has an excellent instinct for knowing when a quotation ought to stop; when he ought to rely on summary, or state a fact, or make an inference, or even refer to some other critic or biographer. He moves adroitly from one to another of these different methods without the result appearing a patchwork. His prose does not creak with the machinery of adjustment, and he never stops to pontificate about his sources or his task.

The book thus manages to combine vigour and speed of movement with richness of content. In consequence, one sees the dynamic force of Dickens's personality fully displayed in act as it has never been displayed before. The pressure and complexity of his life can be taken in and appreciated. Here he is rushing his newspaper reports in a wild race from Bristol to London; here he is simultaneously starting a family, editing a magazine, and writing two long novels at once; here he is quarrelling and arguing with publishers or going to court about copyright, in the middle of furious creative production; here he is converting a waterfall in the Isle of Wight into a shower-bath and then immediately dashing away to his favourite Broadstairs because the muggier climate does not suit his writing. Here he is rushing back from Italy to London solely to read *The Chimes* aloud to a group of his friends.

> Now, you know my punctiwality [he wrote to Forster]. Frost, ice, flooded rivers, steamers, horses, passports, and custom-houses may damage it. But my design is, to walk into Cuttris's coffee-room on Sunday the 1st of December, in good time for dinner. I shall look for you at the farther table by the fire—where we generally go.

These, I know, are familiar episodes; but through the freshness of Professor Johnson's presentation they have struck my mind again almost as if I had never read them before. One sees more clearly than ever the power of concentration, strangely combined with a furiously energetic restlessness.

The great quantity of this new material has not produced any startling or melodramatic changes in the main facts and events; rather, everything is amplified and sharpened. This is particularly clear in the quotation from letters of passages which were toned down or omitted by earlier transcribers of the text. Many of the letters in later life to Georgina Hogarth, for instance, now reveal an increasing preoccupation with money, and also a number of extremely funny and slightly malicious comments on his friends.

The most interesting major readjustments of emphasis seem to me the following: all Dickens's family background and childhood are treated far more fully and convincingly than before, and are also related in a brilliant chapter to the fictional adaptations in *David Copperfield*. The father, John Dickens, in spite of all the likenesses to Micawber and Dorrit, seems clearly to deserve the love, and ultimately loyalty, that Dickens always gave him. Next, the long, tangled, and highly technical story of Dickens's relations and quarrels with his various publishers is here told in more detail than in earlier biographies, but also skilfully interwoven with the narrative of personal life and the progress of the various books. His sharpness in business weaves in and out of the Christmas sentimentality and the haphazard radicalism. Next, the successive editorships, of *Bentley's Miscellany*, the *Daily News*, *Household Words*, and *All the Year Round*, are given the prominence they deserve. Lastly, the use of the huge correspondence with Miss Burdett-Coutts, along with other, less striking, new material, shows Dickens's indefatigable and efficient zest for practical good works.

The Coutts correspondence requires special mention because Professor Johnson has edited a separate volume of 280 of these letters, which has also just been published in England.* Though the texts of these letters are on the whole accurate, the annotation and other editorial matter shows signs of being hurried, as the biography does not. They are not among Dickens's most brilliant and interesting letters. Their importance rather is that they show at length (and the full Coutts correspondence of over 500 letters will show at much greater length) the administrative capacity and the minute patience in details, with which Dickens advised Miss Coutts in her charities over many years. In dealing with the famous home for fallen women at Urania Cottage, Dickens not only lays down the kind of religion required there, but the kind of furniture too. He tells the matron what to say to one obstreperous inmate; others he interviews himself. In a letter about the girls' clothing, he encloses two patterns of material and discourses at length on their merits. This kind of attention he gave to many other projects, in which

---

* *Letters from Charles Dickens to Angela Burdett-Coutts, 1841–1865*, selected and edited by Edgar Johnson (Cape).

Miss Coutts had no part; to all the amateur theatricals got up to help impoverished writers; to his charity readings; to the Royal Literary Fund; to the marriage of his brother; to the misfired Guild of Literature and Art. This grind of charitable business would be astounding in any man: it is scarcely credible in the greatest English creative genius of his time.

There is one main feature of this biography which is less satisfactory. Interspersed throughout it, at appropriate places in the main narrative, are critical chapters on the works that belong to that period of Dickens's life. I cannot help feeling that these may have been an afterthought, added perhaps even when a lot of the book had been written. They are very uneven in quality; I have already mentioned the excellence of the *Copperfield* chapter, but that is related in a special way to the design of the rest of the book. The other critical chapters do sometimes provide a useful summary of current critical views of the books they treat, but elsewhere they fall into current mistakes and do not bear many signs of careful thought. They are also marred by two pervasive faults. They all unremittingly dwell on the social and political propaganda in the novels, at quite disproportionate length; and these themes are treated with much repetition, with too little attempt to make clear the influences and guiding principles behind this part of Dickens's work, and with intermittent efforts to assimilate his political opinions to those of a modern democratic socialist.

Also in these critical chapters I find myself baffled by errors of judgment or failures to mark essential differences of literary mood and purpose. To take one glaring example of this: here is the ending (which is intended to reach an emotional climax) of the critical chapter on *Great Expectations*:

> As Pip and Estella, with linked hands, leave that misty and forlorn garden of their childhood they are reminiscent of the parents of humanity exiled, but not utterly without hope, from another Garden:
>
>> The world was all before them, where to choose
>> Their place of rest, and Providence their guide.
>> They hand in hand, with wandering steps and slow,
>> Through Eden took their solitary way.

To me, Pip and Estella are not reminiscent of Milton's Adam and Eve at all; and as soon as I try to apply in detail that parallel between the ending of the novel and the ending of *Paradise Lost*, it breaks down at every point. Milton has been pillaged to provide an extra atmosphere of vague grandeur which a moment's thought must dissipate.

On the pivot of this grandeur we turn to the next biographical chapter, headed "Intimations of Mortality"—a heading designed to warn us that, through strain and overwork, Dickens was threatened with paralysis of the left side. But this perversion of Wordsworth, coming immediately on top of the far more serious perversion of Milton, produces a cloying conglomeration of literary reference, which we fear can only reach its climax in adapting to Dickens Matthew Arnold's words about Keats: "He is; he is with Shakespeare": and, pat, this expected climax comes in the emotional ending of another chapter on page 1141.

The book, I think, would make its impact best if it were read first without these critical chapters at all. The biography would then be seen as a unity of the greatest merit. If I were asked to say, in a phrase, what view of Dickens it presents, I think I should answer at once that it presents Dickens's view of himself, and seems to have been intended in its whole design to do so. It does not tend to this end by the method of argumentative defence or the other method of outright panegyric; but more subtly, by using Dickens's words as the chief medium of conveying impressions, moods, and views of events. This becomes clearest in the treatment of the very difficult matter of his separation from his wife. Because Dickens himself believed, or came to persuade himself, that separation was in 1858 necessary and inevitable, gently and unobtrusively all the earlier comments on his marriage that might be seen as pointing to that end are brought to the fore, and others slightly underplayed.

I do not mean that Professor Johnson has tried to reconstruct an autobiography; far from it; he intervenes, describes, discusses, even sometimes debates, and makes judicious decisions. But in the end it is Dickens in his own voice and his own estimation that prevails. Perhaps this is the biography we most needed now. Dickens's view of himself has superseded Forster's view of him.

PART FOUR

MEN AND BOOKS

THE ART OF READING*

In my youth I used to look with strong feelings of distress and shame upon the books in the Everyman Library—the Everyman books, of course, as they used to be, in all the fuss and swirl of decorative design on spine and end-papers and title-page. The distress came just inside the cover: there was an allegorical woman on one side, standing among a pattern of leaves and tendrils and lotus-like flowers; the pattern spread away onto the opposite side, where the tendrils embraced and entwined a neatly torn, deftly disordered scroll, bearing these words:

> Everyman, I will go with thee and be thy guide,
> In thy most need to go by thy side.

These words on the scroll were the cause of my distress. I took them then to mean that the book, allegorical woman and all, was offering to be my intimate and constant friend, to dog me about with experience and advice, faithfully and inescapably, an ever-present help in trouble, and out of it.

But that was the very last thing I wanted a book to be or do. Better call a book a specially luxurious meal to eat, or an adventure to enter on, or a territory to discover and explore or even to invade —anything but a dogged, over-constant companion. For one felt proud and free: books were under one's own control.

The shame always occurred opposite the title-page. There was a GREAT QUOTATION, considered suitable to each kind of literature. Fiction had: "A tale which holdeth children from play and old men from the chimney corner." Poetry had: "Poets are the trumpets which sing to battle. . . . Poets are the unacknowledged legislators of the world." For all the young pride and freedom, these noble gobbets could shame and humble. Suppose one suddenly

* B.B.C. Third Programme, 14 Jan 1947, reviewing *The Reading of Books* by Holbrook Jackson (Faber).

got bored or disgusted by Divine Philosophy, said to be "how charming": suppose the tale which might be fit to keep old men from the chimney corner failed to keep a boy from swimming, or playing idle French cricket? For literature was an extension of life, one only of many ways to enjoy the splendour and wonder. One could not live up to the Everyman claim that literature was always something greater. It was appalling to be reminded in front of a very useful crib to Livy that "The sages of old live again in us." But the worst shame of all was caused by the awful extract: "A good book is the precious life-blood of a master spirit embalmed and treasured up on purpose to a life beyond life." What would it be, if one fell asleep and dropped this precious life-blood on the floor, safely embalmed though it was?

Because of the shame, one resented this heavily ornamented, factitious reverence for literature. It was impossible daily to live up to masterpieces; yet one could invade masterpieces with gladness.

That mood fairly represents the starting-point of a new book by Mr Holbrook Jackson called *The Reading of Books*, a provocative, packed, slightly mystifying, but very entertaining essay on the Art of Reading—that is, the art of reading *imaginative* literature. Mr Jackson does not claim to be a scholar or a critic; he modestly describes himself as a Bookman. But he is not a Bookman in the red leather, yellow leather style, with old logs and old wine. He is vivacious, experimental, restlessly inquisitive, open to impressions wherever they may come from. He is also rather undiscriminating, insinuating and evasive. He must live in a study lined with books, with a row of commonplace books full of extracts and references at his elbow: but I'm sure his study has more than one door, and a french window. This new book of his is a jumpy, exhausting thing. His method is to call clouds of distinguished witnesses before he makes his own point quite clear. He revels in quotation with sly glee; and his witnesses' evidence is so interesting in itself that one is liable to forget to ask how relevant it is, or what exactly it is intended to prove. And Mr Jackson himself has meanwhile disappeared for the moment, and comes back with a new section, and a new set of witnesses testifying to something rather different.

He states at once that the end of reading is "living, not reading", and that it is "a mode of life rather than a substitute for life". He next puts forward his main theory that reading is as much an art as writing, the reader an artist. In so many words this old paradox does not get us very far, because it turns on an equivocal use of the words "art" and "artist". Other sentences scattered through the book are needed to give clues to the sense in which Mr Jackson understands them. "Books are necessary", he says, "to authors and readers for much the same reasons. Whether we read them or write them they are means of expression. . . . We often, perhaps generally, read ourselves into the words, often unknowingly. . . . authors write as readers read. The one projects himself into an idea or an image, the other into the book in which the idea or the image is recorded." He elsewhere says his aim is to make out the case for the use of books by readers "*as a means of self-expression*".

He is so guarded, elusive and qualifying in his presentation of this theory that I must treat it here broadly in caricature, with some unfairness. But it is not unfair to say that from the point of view of both author and reader—and he spends much time on the authors—Mr Jackson is as thoroughly subjectivist as he can be. He thinks this is the great step forward made by modern criticism: the ego is everywhere. The work of literature, the poem or the novel, so far from being a fixed thing of any importance in itself, becomes for him merely a discourse between the personalities at the two poles, changing and fluctuating with every occasion and every reader.

He teaches the exact opposite of Martin Tupper, who said: "A good book is the best of friends, the same today and for ever." A book is not even "the same" to its own author. Mr Jackson quotes Coleridge to the effect that a poet who has had all the labour, hesitations and postponements of composition can never see his own poem as a whole in the same way as a reader can, "to whom the whole is new and simultaneous". And he gives the example of George Moore, who said about *A Mummer's Wife*: "As the public verdict continued to affirm itself . . . the book I knew of was changed, metamorphosed, disappeared, and another bearing no more than a distant family resemblance to my *Mummer's*

Wife was gradually forced upon me. I have since forgotten the old, and accepted and am content with the *Mummer's Wife* of critics and friends." If the book does not remain the same even for its author, how much less is a book the same for any two of its readers. For Mr Jackson a reader virtually recreates each book by imputing his own personality and experience to it.

This is, so far, an important part of the truth, a part which has deeply modified all serious literary criticism in our own time. But Mr Jackson is determined to carry the idea even further, to see where it leads him. "Books", he says in another place, "rarely if ever put anything into the mind of a reader which is not already there. The primary effect of reading is awakening not informing." And again: "The aim of the fit reader is the intensification, not the dilution, of what is peculiar to his own personality."

I think this is carrying the theory to a ridiculous, even a danger-ous extreme, false to the history of taste and style and also to the development of individuals. A poet, such as Wordsworth, whose work is at first almost entirely neglected or refused because it is not understood, can, in fifty or sixty years, so make his way with the public that his mood becomes part of the normal sensibility of educated people. Hopkins said of Wordsworth that he had "seen something" and put all human nature in a tremble. At first this was realised by very few people; but through a long succession of readers his new vision and mood became accessible. Much the same has now happened with Hopkins himself.

The personal influence of Wordsworth on John Stuart Mill— not called in evidence by Mr Jackson—illustrates exactly that point. The peculiar qualities of Mill's personality beforehand were an exaggerated intellectualism, a minimisation of the force and value of feeling in human life, a self-conscious analytical seek-ing for happiness, which destroyed the thing it sought. At the crisis he had reached the stage of

> A grief without a pang, void, dark and drear,
> A drowsy, stifled, unimpassioned grief,
> Which finds no natural outlet or relief
> In word, or sigh, or tear.

He said: "In vain I sought relief from my favourite books." The ever-constant, over-familiar friends since offered by the Everyman Library, though at his side in his most need, did not guide him. What was familiar completely let him down. That is, I think, a common experience—that at the height of any major emotional crisis all literature seems suddenly irrelevant, empty, even disgusting. Yet it was through literature, through Wordsworth, that Mill came out of this appalling, apparently final mood of self-torturing despair. Wordsworth's poems, he said, "seemed to be the very culture of the feelings which I was in quest of", "the medicine for my state of mind".

Surely this was no intensification of what was peculiar to Mill's personality, but the opposite. The conscious effect, whatever may have been lying latent as a capacity, was one of overwhelming novelty, something like a revelation. And it is with the conscious reader that we and Mr Jackson must be concerned.

You will note that Mr Jackson's cautious, qualifying phrases, such as "rarely if ever", "*primary* effect", "often", "generally", and so on, leave him a loophole for exceptions. He is so eclectic and relativist that he is rather slippery. Of course he admits that in any deep experience of reading, or indeed of living, there is an element of novelty and an element of familiarity. But he has deliberately chosen in this essay to give all the emphasis to the familiarity. In this he fairly records the practice of many readers much of the time. "How like me!" people say; "I've felt exactly like that if only I could have expressed it." But then, the mere reading has not been expression enough, and attempts are made to express it in life. That was Madame Bovary's trouble; and many readers, better educated and better qualified than she, foster a blindness in their understanding through which they fail to recognise the *differences* between the attitudes, sensibility and characters of literature and their own. They fasten on some one marked apparent similarity, and are blind to all the differences of cause and external circumstances. Mr Jackson is fully aware of the follies and muddles in living caused by reading of this kind. Such readers are not "fit readers" in his sense. Fit readers, he says, must always

243

be watchful, alert, critical of the processes of their own minds. Yet still he leaves them with nothing but the fatalistic prospect of expressing and developing what is peculiar to their own personalities.

It is an astonishing feature of his book, which one wakes up to only at the end, that he makes no distinction whatever between the different kinds of literature: novels, lyrics, epics, odes, imaginative essays, drama—the writers of all these things are brought up into the witness-box to say their selected pieces, quite irrespective of the different forms in which they have expressed themselves. I found myself wondering why so many poets have said that all poetry is striving towards the condition of drama, why so many have felt the need to try to write poetic plays, even though they may have failed. One reason, at least, is that in dramatic form the subjective, egotistical element in creation is most under control. And perhaps a good way to describe the fit reader is to say he is striving towards the condition of the spectator of a great tragedy finely acted on the stage. Aristotle does not occur among Mr Jackson's witnesses; yet the famous sentence in the *Poetics* about purging the emotions, enigmatical and exasperating as it is, is probing round the nerve of truth.

But I see Mr Jackson coming with another commonplace book in his hand with Aristotle's sentence in it, and all that the scholars and commentators have said about it, and Sidney and Shelley and all the rest: so I'd better stop, hoping we can have his catena of evidence for something else another time.

A FAMOUS LITERARY PERIODICAL*

THERE are two special reasons for my talking about the famous *London Magazine* which ran from 1820 to 1829—the one to which Charles Lamb contributed as "Elia" and in which de Quincey published the first version of *The Confessions of an Opium Eater*, these two contributing along with many others, like Hazlitt, Clare, and Darley, whose work has survived. For one thing, there has just been published a book about it, the first of a new series of monographs on English literature, called *Anglistica*, produced in Denmark. This book, called *The London Magazine*, is by an American writer, Miss Josephine Bauer. If readers can put up with the handiwork of a malevolent imp who got among the type after the final corrections from proof, and before printing, and scattered more of Miss Bauer's standard English and proper names than of her campus style, then they will find much of interest in it. For another thing, the title has been revived by Mr John Lehmann for the new literary monthly which he began to edit earlier this year; and this suggests a number of comparisons between his *London Magazine* and that of a hundred and thirty years ago: it suggests a comparison between the modern idea of what a literary magazine is, and the idea of a magazine which then prevailed.

In choosing his title Mr Lehmann was a conscious revivalist. There had been about half a dozen different *London Magazines* running at different times in the eighteenth century, with slight variations of title and sub-title. Even in the eighteen-twenties there was a second periodical of the same name, which was ultimately bought up by Taylor and Hessey, the proprietors of the *London* we remember. Then there was *Sharpe's London Magazine* in the eighteen-forties. The title had been used so often that in the second part of the last century there was a fashion for calling magazines not

* B.B.C. Third Programme, 2 July 1954. Printed in the *Listener*, 15 July.

after London as a whole but after different parts of it; the *Cornhill*, *St Paul's*, *Belgravia*, and the *Strand* are just a few examples. Most of these kept some positive reminder of London on their cover or title-page, like the street scene on the cover of the old *Strand*, which fitted so well with the Holmes world of pea-soupers and hansom cabs, opium-dens and the city hideout of the Man with the Twisted Lip. The famous *London* had a green cover with a view of St Paul's looking up-river, with boats in the foreground and London Bridge running across the middle. Mr Lehmann has followed this tradition, too, in a modest way, by having a small vignette on his title-page, of a man leaning against a bookstall in a street, reading a book, with an unmistakably London church-spire in the background. The motives for all this are fairly clear, in a small country with a swollen capital: it all suggests that the magazine comes from the centre of things; that it is in the swim and in the know. There was another nineteenth-century magazine called the *Metropolitan*.

Metropolitan motives of this kind certainly underlay the choice of title for the new magazine which first came out under John Scott's editorship in January 1820. The prospectus said that one of its main objects was:

> to convey the very "image, form, and pressure" of that "*mighty heart*" whose vast pulsations circulate life, strength, and spirits, throughout this great Empire.

But there was another motive, too; the prospectus also made clear that the *London* was started deliberately as the rival of periodicals published in "secondary towns of the Kingdom". In 1820 this meant, in plain words, that it was going to compete with the *Edinburgh Review* and, above all, with *Blackwood's Edinburgh Magazine*. As it turned out, the relationship with *Blackwood's* was something far more positive than mere rivalry and competition; the example of the *London* was to discredit and supersede the whole *Blackwood's* method of literary criticism. There is no need to tell here again the story of how this led to the most melodramatic quarrel in our literary history; it came to a head in a duel in which John Scott, the editor of the *London*, lost his life. Scott can seriously be looked on as a martyr to honest book-reviewing. In this respect the power and example of the *London* were carried on into the Victorian age as Charles Wentworth Dilke became literary editor of the *Athenaeum* when the *London* expired.

This war of periodicals is something quite different from anything that has happened, or could happen, in our own time. The raging of *Scrutiny*—now, sadly, to be published no more—against academicism, against London literary cliques, either openly or by implication against *Horizon* or *The Times Literary Supplement*—was often nearly as violent as *Blackwood's* in the early days; but it was violent in such a different tone of voice, so superior, so aloof, so academic in its own way, that the challenge was never taken up; the war was always one-sided. I think this was partly because people tended to discount the challenging tone for the sake of the interesting and important criticism that was often going on beneath it. But the major and significant difference was that the attacks were cultural and literary and never directly political or personal. It is notable, too, even in our weekly papers nowadays, how the literary half seems to work independently of the political half, the middles being shared; on some papers the editorial staff even divides into two practically self-contained groups, the right hand scarcely knowing what the left hand does. Mr Lehmann's new *London Magazine* is quite startlingly unpolitical, unless you take the view that its lack of politics is itself a political symptom. There are very few journalists writing now—indeed I cannot think of a single one—who would undertake to write the major articles on contemporary politics and those on contemporary literature in a single periodical of any standing. There are some writers who write now and then in both fields —Sir Harold Nicolson and Mr G. M. Young come to mind—but I doubt whether either of them would regularly, as a matter of routine, attempt to tackle major questions and make general surveys in both literature and politics, month after month, as John Scott did in the *London*.

The established way of seeing the history of literary periodicals in England in the last century is to see a progressive improvement in the honesty and independence of book-reviews and literary articles,

247

on three grounds: the decrease of bias caused by direct party-political allegiance; the decrease of puffery caused by the fact that book publishers were frequently also the publishers of a periodical, which they used to boost their own wares, the outstanding instance of this being Colburn's *New Monthly*; and, thirdly, the decrease of personal abuse of authors as individuals, separately from the book immediately under review. And two of the heroes of this progressive improvement are taken to be, as I have already said, John Scott himself and Keats's early friend, Charles Wentworth Dilke. This way of seeing the matter has a great deal of truth in it, but there are many complicating factors.

In the first place, a magazine at the beginning of the last century did set out and claim to be a survey of "manners" in the broadest sense; it did claim to influence style of life and action. In a time of extreme political stress, such as that which followed the Napoleonic Wars, it was impossible to isolate political from social, moral, and literary questions. The famous *Blackwood's* attacks on the Cockney School, which were the chief cause of Scott's increasingly violent protests in the *London*, were neither purely political, nor purely social, nor purely literary. Admittedly Leigh Hunt's radicalism and the political policy of the *Examiner* were the overt points of attack from a Tory magazine; but accompanying it was a social attack on Hunt's manners. "Cockney" was perhaps not the best word; the thing being attacked was the ethos of small, middle-class London suburbia with claims to culture; sentimentality, gush, a talent for vulgar bathos. All these things were unmistakably evident in Hunt's poems—most notably in *The Story of Rimini*, which so vulgarised Dante that even Hunt himself in later life came to regret it: they all made their mark on Keats's early poems, too.

To a *Blackwood's* writer Hunt was in every way a man who ought not to prevail, and should not be allowed to infect others. His kind of political radicalism was regarded as an organised attempt to spread his kind of manners and his kind of life. When a major political question was whether the power of an aristocracy should be perpetuated or modified, questions about manners and "the tone of society" were political questions; and politics became correspondingly personal. The affair of Queen Caroline was the extreme example of a general situation. The epic of the period was not *Hyperion* but *Don Juan*.

The concern with personalities and personal styles of life affected minutely the styles of literary journalism. It is a curious fact that although nearly all periodical writing was either anonymous or pseudonymous, it was yet exceedingly intimate. The pseudonymous people were given fictitious biographies, and wrote about each other as if they really existed. Each periodical tried to give the impression that it was almost a family product. The *Blackwood's* group had their Tent and their horseplay and their whiskey; they played up the unfortunate James Hogg as a cross between genius and buffoon. The result aimed at was that reader and writer should seem to be on extremely close intimate terms; the reader was to be sucked into the life of the paper and made a friend; the Tent was the household to which the reader was asked. The main writers were, in fact, a close group of this kind, and they made up much of the paper in conversation. The interesting thing is that the "Londoners", in their rather different idiom, did the same as the contributors to *Blackwood's Magazine*. Lamb and Wainewright took on fictitious personalities as Elia and Janus Weathercock, and they wrote about each other as if they really existed under those names.

Under the management of Taylor and Hessey, after Scott's death, the contributors to the *London* met frequently at dinner-parties and twitted each other with the same kind of jokes as they used in their essays. Lamb's peculiar style is that of a man of genius struggling with an unpropitious temporary mode. I do not mean that Lamb was conscious of this, or that he was straining to write in a way uncongenial to him; but it is a pity that it was so congenial, and a disaster that for about a century it was held up to schoolchildren as a model of what a typical English "essay" should be. For this mode—Lamb being the one man of genius who wrote in it and Hazlitt a possible second—was the product of a particular phase of literary journalism in which the intimacy of personalities was a primary aim.

Blackwood's and the *London* had that in common, though *Black-wood's* in its early days was more boisterous and abusive. The *London* aimed to set a gentler style of personal manners against the boozy buffoonery of Edinburgh, but still to insinuate its personalities into the reader's range of acquaintance. The feature in the *London* called "The Lion's Head" was a jocular and partly invented kind of "Answers to Correspondents;" after Scott's death it was written for a time by Tom Hood, as a very young man. It seems to be trying to woo readers facetiously into friendship, so that they shall take more kindly to the heavier parts of the magazine which are to follow.

For neither the *London* nor *Blackwood's* was wholly written in the intimate, friendly mode; the political articles were generally written in a quite different tone, even though much political material might be worked into the talk in the Tent. The appeal of both was to a moderately educated middle class, and the aim was to provide something in each number for all the interests of such a class. The *London* prospectus said:

> The *spirit* of things generally, and, above all, of the present time, it will be our business, or at least our endeavour, to catch, condense, and delineate.

Even though it repudiated the aim of passing on secondhand news and rivalling newspapers and the *Annual Register*, it did contain commercial reports, and a monthly register, with colonial intelligence, foreign news and domestic news; and births, marriages, deaths and bankruptcies were later added. It claimed to do a little of everything, to influence people on all sides of their personalities, in manners, morals, politics, and business. But the typical mode was the intimacy and the claim to affection. This had its eighteenth-century precedents in Addison and Sterne (Sterne was a favourite writer of both John Scott and Wainewright). The change in journalism which becomes marked in the eighteen-forties, when Tom Hood is dead and Dickens has given up *Bentley's Miscellany*, is a change not so much to greater honesty as to greater impersonality, a greater distance between reader and writer. There is no mat with "Welcome" on it at the door; you are not asked in; you are not asked to make friends; and, indeed, how could one make friends all at once with the variety of diverse characters a modern literary magazine presents? Mr Lehmann would no more expect to hold regular dinner-parties for his contributors at his expense than he would expect to be killed in a duel by Dr Leavis or Mr Bateson.

AN UNPOSTED LETTER TO
MR G. M. YOUNG

CALCUTTA
5th November 1937

Dear Mr Young,

Your book of essays *Daylight and Champaign* has just been sent to me that I might broadcast a review of it here; but I am going to write you a letter instead and shall broadcast that. It would be artificial to apologise for the addition of formal greetings and a change of pronouns: but I have felt grateful to you so often in the last few years that I was warming up to writing-point in any case.

I re-read the *Portrait of an Age* recently, and decided that the only living writer of history in English fit to hold a candle to you is F. A. Simpson. I must read Last's chapter in Volume XI of the *Cambridge Ancient History*, that you praise so much. His were the only history lectures, A. or M., I went to that had any style. He over-acted slightly, but the acting wasn't, like Tod's for instance, to cover up commonplace. What most depresses me about these composite histories is that if you open a volume at random it's practically impossible to guess the author of the chapter from the way it's written. In the Roman Britain volume of the new *Oxford History of England* even Collingwood writes just like Myres; yet in Philosophy he is one of the few people in Oxford who has got a style of his own. The fault can't be inherent in the committee method of writing history, because the two volumes of *Early Victorian England* are entirely free from it. I suppose it is partly caused by the amount of teaching most scholars now have to do. Few of the people who can afford not to teach are Buckles.

Here the Irish view of history prevails: that way Gandhi lies too. But local evidence doesn't bear out your judgment that the English are immovably incurious about their own past. The people who will retire to become local archaeologists in Devonshire are already exercising their wits on problems. The leading English paper runs a daily column based on letters from readers: they are called the "Tentites". About half the matter put up on the tent blackboard is historical. Many of the problems are rather Tiberian, but not long ago the Tentites overlapped with Collingwood for several days, discussing the origin of the name "Britanni" with quite a large display of secondary authorities. I agree that the inquisitiveness is usually based on the assumption that "everything before last week was a win for our side", and that it stops short at any inconvenient discoveries. When I suggested to an Englishman the other day that perhaps the evidence for the Black Hole story he learnt at school needed looking into, his attitude was: "So they're trying to make out *that* never happened now, are they?" But I think the *emotional pull* of the past on an Englishman is very strong, partly because of his sense of place (which you specially notice in Gibbon) —"the old world was to him a crowded map"; and partly because of the intense visual attraction that Belloc stressed in his essay. Both are perhaps strengthened by living abroad.

Daylight and Champaign has entertained me a great deal—at least much of it has; but the rest has made me feel ashamed because I haven't seen the point. You say that "the failure of the common stock of reference and allusion" is a main disadvantage in the present state of culture; and charge my generation (justly up to a point, I think) with being ill-informed. It is a sign of the times that your index-maker should confuse Dr Arnold with Matthew. Perhaps you are right to praise an "excellent economy of notes, chronology and index", for my own liking for fullness and accuracy in these things is due to a bad memory. I think that is common to many people of my age, and we often do not see allusions because we have come to rely on books for reference. But was there ever a time when most of such references and allusions as your own could have been understood by more than a few, or could all have been understood at sight by anybody? When I do see the point of one of your jokes the pleasure is partly spoilt by an accretion of vanity. You force vanity on your readers to compensate for their shame. Nobody could dispute your wit, but you are sometimes more eccentric than you would like to appear in choosing the content of it. Once or twice in this book you made me feel very uncomfortable by reminding me of Saintsbury. Old Books, Old Wine and Old Logs are excellent things but—unless there's some point I have missed—they make a bad title for a dialogue containing bits of Catullus and Shakespeare. Your reference to Saintsbury on p. 152 makes me more uncomfortable still. I don't think people of my age quite the ignorant prigs you would make us seem, but we would rather be ill-informed than enjoy "knowing" facetiousness.

We don't generally know Latin and Greek, but many of us have improved our English by studying them. Our minds were distracted at school: we had lectures on "Civics" and sermons on "Service"; they tried to make us soldiers or boy-scouts. So we hadn't much chance of becoming scholars. But the old routine of construing and doing proses went on, even though we were perversely encouraged to fret under it: it did teach us to look at words, and hear them, and be inquisitive about them. Arnold failed to liberalise the Classics, so all our themes on interesting subjects were written in English: it was in these that the value of our classical work came out. I agree that the prose of Stephen Spender's *Forward from Liberalism* is shocking; perhaps it is because he wasn't on the Classical Side. But there are bursts of poet's prose in his critical essays and occasionally in his stories. I'm glad you like his verse.

Much of your attack on *Forward from Liberalism* is justified, but I want to argue with you about the ending of it. The political question is, as you say, whether economic security is compatible with private ownership. "But the moment we look at the conception of private property", you go on, "we see that, in its economic and juristic bearings, it is a shifting conception." And later: "The attitudes to property are so various, the whole human tradition is so much mixed up with property, individual, corporate, domestic, tribal, sacred and what not." I think that if Stephen Spender did "write a poem on the feelings of a taxi-man contemplating his own garage and his own sweet peas", the content of it would perhaps be something like this: "I'm very doubtful, as things are going now, whether

I shall be able to maintain this garage and my taxi for another year. These flowers will soon fade; next spring I shall probably not be able to afford seeds. But their beauty, as it is just now, suggests a state of life in which my pleasure in the enjoyment of it could be assured." There would be no particular effort, and he would learn nothing. For my generation—and this is one of the main barriers between us and you—the conception of private property is *so* shifting as almost to escape us. It is no stimulus to "imaginative thinking", and cannot artificially be made to stimulate anything but bad verse. I'm particularly conscious of this because I grew up with an exaggerated respect for freehold, and I once quarrelled with a friend about the ownership of a box of matches. But as I get older property touches my emotions less. Other people of my age are hardly touched by it at all. Even tribal property like the Crown Jewels or sacred property like Westminster Abbey doesn't move us much. I found your *Epilogue* on the Coronation rather beside the mark. If that epitomised the English tradition, I thought, there must be something wrong.

You may say: "But has the conception of private property escaped the taxi-man?" I can only counter with: "Could the taxi-man write the poem?"

This does mean a modification of the human tradition—at least the tradition of the last three or four hundred years. Think of the metaphors based on property, for one thing. What do we mean by "possessing" a woman? How many of the metaphors of friendship are based on book-keeping? of duty on legal contract? The Marxists don't seem to have realised yet that in their literature of the future they would have to "liquidate" such metaphors as these.

You, if anybody, have a right to mock at false or pointless "scholarship". But you sometimes force me onto the opposite side against my will and your intention. You jeer at the "dissertation on the Sources of Macaulay's Essay on Milton with a paragraph on the origin of Fee-Fo-Fum"; but you make me want to see it. You say nothing is more exasperating than to be told that it is all in the *Theaetetus*; but if it is all there I like to know how. Your own notebooks, surely, contain a lot of "curious" stuff—odd references, derivations, infections or influences, plagiarisms, etc., besides the French fragments you mention—which you have never worked up into "history"; in fact there are quite a lot of undigested gobbets in the *Portrait of an Age* itself. Our quarrels with the thesis-writers, influence-mongers and the rest are (1) that the material never has been and was never meant to be worked up into anything else; (2) that they deal in literature without understanding language. As far as I'm concerned the first of these is a doctrinaire quarrel rather than a practical one. They dig up things I might not have the skill or the energy or the time to find for myself. Hardly any information is quite irrelevant, even though it may not be narrowly relevant where it is found. One of the things that make your own writing so good is that you see relevance over such a wide field and apparently let so little information go to waste. We shall see how much only when somebody writes a thesis on *The Note-Books of G. M. Young*. I shall order a copy in advance. But the snag is that even a footnote packed with relevant information can make one feel sick by its style. I agree with nearly everything you say in your review of Stephen Potter's *The Muse in Chains*; but there's one very important thing you leave out. Surely in Oxford and Cambridge, at least, it's mainly the rabbits who read English; it's still thought of as a soft option. I found that in general the only able people who took the English School were either those with a flair for philology who pounced on "Lang" and showed the most eccentric taste when it came to "Lit", or else those who had taken some other School first. Most of the contributors to Richards's *Practical Criticism* weren't "mature students" of anything; but I think the method would produce unexpected results even from people who were.

All this is very much to the point here in Calcutta. The consequences of Macaulay's *Minute on Education*—or rather of the policy he supported—are indeed "not yet exhausted". People here are very grateful to you for publishing a fuller text of it in the World's Classics edition of the *Speeches*. But what has happened to the full text? I wish you gave more footnotes. Macaulay didn't realise that there's a world of difference between Sanscrit and Arabic as taught in their own cultural contexts and as supplied in a government institution; even now a serious student of Sanscrit may choose to go to a traditional pundit rather than to a modern-style professor. Macaulay underrated linguistic work: he himself didn't believe in the cosmology of the *Timaeus* because he knew Greek. Here it is underrated still: there isn't the same unremitting and automatic two-way translating that we went through. The intervention of English has prevented Sanscrit or Arabic and Persian from being what Greek and Latin were to us. English now has to be learnt simultaneously as a Modern Foreign Language, as a Classical Language, and as a normal means of communication. It is an appalling strain on the language and on the pupils, and often means despair. Again and again I've been asked: "Sir, can you tell me a good book for improving my English?"

Macaulay has sometimes not been given credit for seeing that one of the main results of English would be the growth of the vernaculars, but he couldn't have foreseen that it would be so great and so fast as it has been. It seems to me—with very little more than secondhand knowledge—that the first phase of English influence, on Bengali for instance, is working itself out. It meant an enormous widening in the range of subjects and of literary forms, a great increase in vocabulary and in flexibility of syntax: but the resulting language and literature were rather thin, diffuse and vague. The present return of many writers to the classical Indian languages is not merely a nationalistic gesture: they want the precision and body and beauty of sound which translated or transliterated English has failed to give. Technical terms are giving a lot of trouble, as Macaulay saw they would, but then they are mostly ugly in any language. English has never quite assimilated its Greek derivatives as it has its Latin ones. A friend of mine was told in hospital the other day that he had "Pyoitis", and he naturally didn't feel any better. Reduce it to a Latin form and you know where you are.

Yours sincerely,

THE PRESENT ART OF BIOGRAPHY*

Go into any decent secondhand bookshop in a provincial town—
the shop just round the corner from the Cathedral Close, or the odd
little place in St Mary's Passage, where chaotic dusty stacks conceal
the owner's learning. Just look round, especially on the upper
floors. You will find, even now, how right Lytton Strachey was in
one thing. I say "even now" because the war has told. Many of
the old familiars have gone. Hallam's *Middle Ages* now almost
needs a search: Walsh's *Secret History of the Oxford Movement* is
rare compared with the orange volumes of the Left Book Club;
even *Ordeal by Battle* has gone up, say, from twopence to sixpence.
But if you fail to find a cheap copy of Hallam Tennyson's *Memoir*
of his father, it can only be that some local reader has been wondering about the revival of interest in the Victorians. Lytton Strachey
was in one thing certainly right, negatively right:

> Those two fat volumes, with which it is our custom to commemorate
> the dead—who does not know them, with their ill-digested masses of
> material, their slipshod style, their tone of tedious panegyric, their
> lamentable lack of selection, of detachment, of design? They are as
> familiar as the *cortège* of the undertaker, and wear the same air of slow,
> funereal barbarism. One is tempted to suppose, of some of them,
> that they were composed by that functionary, as the final item of his
> job.

Hallam Tennyson's *Memoir* is an obvious example: but there are
countless others—the *Life* of Bishop Samuel Wilberforce by his
son; the *Memorials* of Bishop Hampden by his daughter; the quite
extraordinary *Life* of Professor Owen, the zoologist, by *his* son;
Cross's *Life* of George Eliot, whose ultimate widower he was. The
list could be infinite.

* B.B.C. Third Programme, 13 July 1948.

258

Strachey was plainly right in his Preface to *Eminent Victorians* to say that in such biographies there is no "art". Many of them were rather social symptoms than works of literature, offshoots of an abnormal interest in personalities, not in their subtle and delicate differences or in their intellectual qualities, but in their public size, their outward bearing as Figures, and in their relations with other sizeable Figures. Such books are in fact elaborate obituaries, not biographies, a verbal extension of the visible memorial in church or graveyard.

Most of these books were written in a hurry, very soon after their subjects died, when their names still made news. They were a sort of news, and fitted on to the current public legends about the great. They were cartoons, not portraits; and they were often written by near relations. But they do not at all represent the whole nineteenth-century tradition and method of biography, nor were the conditions of their writing the conditions proper to biography in any age.

The positive qualities which Strachey demanded of a biography, in his Preface, were selection, detachment, design, and "a becoming brevity". Three of these four qualities—selection, design, and a becoming brevity—were plainly present, for example, in Macaulay's essays on Bacon and Milton: it was through such essays as these that a healthy tradition was running, rather than through the mass of miscellaneous obituary volumes that Strachey was attacking. The same three qualities and some detachment too can be seen in Carlyle's *Life of John Sterling*, the most entirely readable work he ever did: it has exactly the excellences which make a book both biographically and historically alive: it gives a man in his setting. In the later part of the century Strachey's four qualities were almost the formula for a standard convention. Several famous series of biographies were started which by their very nature forced the exercise of these qualities upon their authors—the *English Men of Letters*, the *English Men of Action*, the *Eminent Women* series. The compulsory limitation of size forced upon the authors some attention to selection and design. Mark Pattison's *Milton* and J. A. Symonds's *Shelley* are two very good examples of the gain from working within

259

prescribed limits. The books of course varied enormously, but the standard aimed at was high, both in scholarship and in planning. No one man did more to keep these two aims of biography in mind than Leslie Stephen; and it is chiefly to him also that we owe the *Dictionary of National Biography*, where many of the longer articles are in fact biographical essays which might well stand publication by themselves.

It begins to appear then that the four positive qualities which Strachey demanded—selection, detachment, design, and brevity— were an inadequate manifesto of the revolution he sought to bring about. The clue to this revolution lies, I think, in the use of the word "art"; but I do not think Strachey himself anywhere fully explained his use of it; and we must therefore look elsewhere for a statement of what the "art of biography" has, in the light of Strachey's work, been thought to consist in.

In 1936 Lord David Cecil edited for Nelson's an anthology of extracts from modern biographies, and contributed an Introduction to it. The first sentence of his essay was: "Biography is not an important form of literary art." He then went on to make clear that the kind of biography with which he was concerned, which he con- sidered typical of what was then the modern period—and it was pre- eminently the post-Strachey period—was a work of art and not a work of history. He described a kind of biography which is primarily "literature", which is "an expression of the artist's crea- tive powers", a matter of individual vision, "as much an expression of a personality as *David Copperfield*". These last phrases are in fact applied by Lord David to Strachey's *Queen Victoria*, and they carry the whole conception of biography some distance away from Strachey's own professed principles. Strachey did, it is true, say that the biographer should "maintain his own freedom of spirit", but he did so with his eye on the hampered obituaries written by children and widows of the newly dead; his spirit should be free from an oppressive sense of respectable duty; he said also that the biographer should be *detached*: and it is the lack of *detachment* which is so apparent in the kind of artistic biography that is to be an expression of the personality, not of the subject, but of the author. It is just here that Strachey's practice in his less successful essays has led so many of his imitators out into the desert. His aloof manipulation of his persons; the selection of incidents and remarks which contrived to present them in slightly ludicrous situations; the ironical presentation of what was originally intended to be solemn, and the correlative emphasis on the deep significance of what was apparently trivial; the pervasive mockery—things like these have been taken as the essence of his work, whereas they were rather a veneer which he added after the solid building had been done, and in many essays never applied at all.

I think the era of mere de-bunking, of making the great seem small, is now safely over; we have outgrown the pleasures of muck-raking and the gleeful revelation of slightly smelly secrets. But the real danger, weakness and essential badness of the de-bunking phase lay not in the revelation, but in the tone and style and purpose of the revelation. It was done with a patronising air towards the subject and with a rather juvenile delight in catching out the solemn. I believe strongly that whatever can be known about a man, however trivial it may have been, however smelly, or however grand, is proper matter for the biographer, and that to conceal is as great a crime as to come forward as an uncritical eulogist. But that battle, one hopes, has been already won. The present dangers of "artistic" biography seem to me rather different, and rather hard to generalise about. I can best describe what I mean by calling it for the moment a limitation of vision, or of view.

The kind of limitation I mean is caused partly, I think, by an imperfect apprehension of the findings and gropings of psychology. It would explain something of what I mean, to say that the search for the ego has led to the neglect of the superego; that private life has tended to outweigh social life; that personal relations have come to be given more consideration than the wider social context; and that emotional considerations are more prominent than intellectual. I can illustrate what I mean by two recent examples. The first is Mr Gerald Bullett's short life of George Eliot that appeared about a year ago. There are in it traces of the post-Strachey mood of aloofness and patronage, a tendency to pity the subject and to keep saying "Poor Marian!" But, besides this, the book quite fails to convey the full importance of the fact that in several subjects George Eliot was one of the most learned women and in general was one of the most truly intellectual women who has ever lived. In Mr Bullett's book it was said that she had a great intellect, and short accounts of her use of it were introduced; but her intellectual achievements were chiefly mentioned in support of the theory that they interfered with her artistic creativeness. I happen to disagree with the theory; but the immediate point at issue is that a reader not acquainted with George Eliot's life or with her work outside the novels would never have been able through Mr Bullett's book to enter into the daily contents of her mind. All the emphasis was on the emotional needs of her personality and on the personal relations she established with her father, her brother, with Chapman and G. H. Lewes, and with some of her women friends. Her genuine learning in theology, in some kinds of philosophy and science, was not properly discussed or related to her moral and emotional life. Nor was there an adequate treatment of her historical importance either as a channel of spreading undogmatic views about religion or as a very brave pioneer in what is called the emancipation of women. Now Mr Bullett might argue that he was being artistically selective and that such subjects as these did not come within his purposes. To which my answer is that the book is then not to be judged as a biography at all; yet it passes as a biography, and is read by countless people as if it were a biography, and is taken by them as an example of what biography is.

The second example is in some ways rather similar. It is Lord David Cecil's own essay in *Two Quiet Lives* on the poet Thomas Gray; here Gray's interests in many subjects—in botany, architecture, heraldry, Anglo-Saxon, Provençal songs, Icelandic, to name just a few—are duly and properly mentioned, and at various stages they are related to the development of his character and the design of his life; but still one comes with a gasp of something like astonishment upon the often-quoted remark that Gray was one of the most learned men in Europe. There is no attempt to justify it, to make comparisons, to build up the body of this learning so that a reader might begin to appreciate it. His learning becomes a sort of figured backcloth behind which the essay hardly ever penetrates. Nothing is said of Gray's place in the development of the studies that he followed; they are rather used as an interesting channel of communication between him and his friends. This has the sad effect of making Gray appear altogether a smaller personality than he really was. This is the art of selection taken up with a deliberate purpose, to make a "quiet life".

The Prefatory Note to this book does not claim that its two essays are written to express the writer's personality; rather, it sets out more impersonal purposes than Lord David described in his anthology. Yet the style of the essay on Gray suggests that the conception of biography as an "art" was not far from his mind. For it is a very self-conscious, artificial style, which, by its vocabulary, its syntax and the ordering of its paragraphs, demands attention to itself. It is not a personal style; but it is a style typical of its age; it may not consciously derive from Strachey, but it belongs without question to the post-Strachey period. The essay begins with an obvious post-Strachey sentence:

> There is no doubt England's ancient seats of learning present an extremely poetical spectacle.

How much of Strachey is there! The two resounding clichés—"seats of learning" and "present a spectacle"—are used in order to be rescued from the flat commonness they would have in a penny newspaper by the introduction "There is no doubt . . ." Of course these are clichés, the sentence says, but I use them with a just-to-be-called ironic smile, knowing quite well what I'm about. But the word "poetical" makes one stop, and wonder: quite how far does this ironic business go? The irony must continue; nobody would write such a cacophonous phrase as "poetical spectacle" without some irony, some smile. But what weight and purpose is "poetical" meant to carry? We must look at the next sentence:

> The belfrys of Oxford, the pinnacled vistas of Cambridge, the groves and pensive cloisters of Eton and Winchester, made spiritual by the veil of dewy mist that lingers perpetually over the damp river valleys in

which their pious founders have seen fit to place them, induce irresistibly
in the visitor a mood of exalted, romantic reverie.

The ironic clichés, "pious founders" and "seen fit", perpetuate the
opening attitude. But are we to think seriously that the "poetical"
is equated with "a mood of exalted, romantic reverie"? Lord David
knows, as we do, that there is much more to poetry than that. But
as the paragraph proceeds, with "aesthetic sensibility" and "artistic
temperament", the reader is carried along by a sliding process of
suggestion into almost accepting, without irony, dewy mists and
reveries as constant normal conditions of poetic creation. The
obvious truth that underlies this paragraph (and much that follows
it) is that, in one aspect, Gray's peculiar poetic character *was* concerned with dewy mists and reveries; that just this helped to distinguish him from other poets, and poets of other times. The biographer's task is here to be particular, to distinguish, to relate, to
clarify. But this glide from ironic smiling at the word "poetical"
(where the smile plays round the word's dual application to poets and
to spectacles), through mists and reveries, to generalisations about
the "artistic temperament", obscures the very truth from which we
must suppose the whole train of thought to have begun. Biography
is being strangled by art; and we have to unwind the silken scarf
from its throat.

The style obscures the thought; and besides, there is softness and
weakness in this prose that make a reader long for "the naked thew
and sinew of the English language". A marked pervasive man-
nerism is the love of adjectives, adverbs and abstract nouns ending
in the delicate letter "y". We have met "extremely", "dewy",
"perpetually", and "irresistibly" in the first two steps. It is all in
keeping that Gray, Walpole, West, and Ashton should be called
"exquisitely civilised"; but the same predilection has overshot the
proper bounds of its keeping when Lord David writes:

> He was not *sufficiently* impersonal to be *completely* satisfied by intel-
> lectual *activity*.

or:

> *Unluckily*, too, he was the type of character who minds *poverty
> particularly acutely*. It intensified his nervous *anxiety* about the future.

264

The italics, of course, are not his: but why should he not say that Gray, more than most men, disliked being poor? There are countless other examples, almost as startling, of this disease. The fashion for adjectives in the soft final "y" that Coleridge slew in one of his Nehemiah Higginbottam sonnets owed much to Gray's own poems: a single stanza of *The Bard* produces stormy, craggy, dreary, ghastly, ruddy, grisly, and bloody. Excessive use of such normal forms preceded the craze for oddities like "dampy" and "paly", a craze in which Charles Lloyd distinguished himself. Lord David, on the whole, keeps to the normal forms in all three parts of speech; but his excessive use of them produces a light, thin, cobweb-like effect, of which Gray himself was not guilty in his prose. Of course it is not expected that even this kind of biography should be so written as to imitate or reflect the style of the man whose life is being treated; but a marked and mannered style infects the whole treatment and sets up in the reader, unless he is on his guard, an attitude to the subject consonant with it. And the guarded reader has to look for Gray through the cobwebs.

For Gray, as revealed in his letters, is a far more robust, far less effete and exquisite person than this essay suggests; and it is exactly in the details of his writing, in his words and rhythms, that we find him so. In the famous descriptive passages, such as the letter about Netley Abbey of 1764 and the Journal and Journal-letters to Wharton about the Lake District in 1769–70, he does not lapse into "graceful preciosity" even when sweetness and softness are the theme:

> From hence I got to the *Parsonage* a little before Sunset, & saw in my glass a picture, that if I could transmitt to you, & fix it in all the softness of its living colours, would fairly sell for a thousand pounds. this is the sweetest scene I can yet discover in point of pastoral beauty. the rest are in a sublimer style.

The movement is firm; and all is saved by that joke about the price. But what went just before shows the vigour of writing produced by "the sublimer style":

> While I was here, a little shower fell, red clouds came marching up the

hills from the east, & part of a bright rainbow seem'd to rise along the side of Castle-hill.

It is precise and energetic, just as Lord David's prose is not.

Nervousness may be tense and alert, a vice of great intelligence and acute observing; or it may be dreamy and inexact, a vice of honest rumination. In Gray the intelligence, the powers of observing and the love of things seen in detail predominate: in this essay the other kind of nervousness has the field. The mixture of wit, fun and accurate observation shown, for instance (with lists and dates of the flowers' blowing), in the letter to Wharton of 21 July 1759 is not fully described or analysed at all; and the quotations made from Gray's letters do not illustrate it.

For this problem of biographical "selection", which Strachey saw to be so important, is not confined to the ordering of an unwieldy mass of documents and evidence; it involves also the fair allotment of attention and sympathy; it involves the patience of the ear to every voice in which the character speaks; it involves the preservation of these voices, with a fair proportion given to each. But, where the biographer has a mannered or highly personal style of his own, a new kind of unconscious and illegitimate selection occurs, by which some of these voices are muffled and others amplified; and even in descriptive passages an alien rhythm and an alien style of vision may distort the mood and lineaments which the original documents reveal.

One can see only too clearly why these things happen: it is because the writing of biography is so difficult and so exacting. The writing of the first full biography of a dead man is allied more to the struggle of living than to the struggle of artistic creation. Too much is lost if there is great emphasis on brevity and formal design. It is not merely that detail has to be left out and the passage of time compressed, but the very quality of the life, the quality of the consciousness and action, has to be simplified and emptied of some of its richness and vitality. When a life is fully documented, and the biographer's mind plays over the sources from which he has to draw, he can see and sense and almost re-experience something of the complexity of the life with which he has to deal. One can often get to know a dead man more completely and intimately than one can know a living person in the flesh. If the evidence is good he appears in it in all his bearings to the outward world; whereas a living man is known only in his bearing towards us and in the talk and attitude of common friends. And beyond the public bearing there may be untold intimacies of private life committed to diaries which might never have reached the stage of talk, or never in talk have been spoken to one man, or spoken in such a way that their full cumulative impression could be felt. The impact of the dead upon biographers should be more compact, continuous and complete than the impact of a living friend.

That is why a perfect biography is impossible, and why biography should not properly be spoken of as an art. An artist creates his own limits without the violation of anything except his own larger designs. A biographer has to adapt and adjust limitations under the stress of a great many different external influences. The last thing a biographer should express is himself; he cannot, of course, be wholly detached; but every sentence he writes should be an exercise in detachment, designed exactly to bring forward something other than himself. The familiarity with this "something other" must be total. And, among other things, it must be social. A biography should be, if not a *Life and Times*, at least a *Life and Setting* or a *Life and Circumstances*. It is just this focus on the whole context that can provide the discipline necessary in the struggle for detachment.

In many ways all this means a return to Strachey's principles and practice at their best. In the Preface I have already quoted, he describes the business of the biographer as being to "lay bare the facts of the case, as he understands them". The wide, deep and imaginative understanding of fact is as much the basis of good biography as it is of good history. It is this that is most obviously missing in the current "artistic" convention; there is a lack of solidity and a lack of range; personalities move in a dim, artificial light in surroundings like a stage set. In some cases this lack of solidity is plainly caused by the fact that the writers do not know their subject well enough; they have studied a few main sources, but have not spread outwards into all the surrounding evidence of other personalities and the detail of the time. This is a fault that Strachey himself was not guilty of, unless perhaps in *Elizabeth and Essex*. In his Victorian studies there is plainly an enormous amount of knowledge in reserve; and the virtue of his detailed knowledge and of his sense of the importance of detail is greatest in the essay on Florence Nightingale. One feels that his very finger-tips were sensitive to the practical tasks which Florence Nightingale had to do, and his nose to all the smells of Scutari; and yet the design and proportion and becoming brevity are kept.

Exactly there lies the great dilemma for a biographer at the present time. Our present practice illustrates the choice at two extremes. On the one side are the artistic biographical essays of which I have been speaking. On the other are academic volumes full of fact and detail, informed about all the circumstances and the physical setting of life, learned on the interaction of events and the adjacent history, but which yet fail. And they fail, too, I think, for the same kind of reason—they also are too thoroughly impregnated with the personality of their authors; but it is a personality of a different kind—the scholar's personality, obsessed with the evaluation of evidence, with cruces, with doubts, with anxiety to fill in gaps and to prove points: and the style in which such a personality expresses itself is usually a heavy, hesitant, circumlocutionary style: the multiform vitality of the life, the startling inter-relevance of detail is lost in a series of problems, and the work becomes not a biography, but an invaluable reference-book.

I think the scholar's degree of knowledge is essential if a great biography is to be written now; but even so the writer has to make the frightful effort in every sentence to be detached, detached above all from the fascination of the methods by which his knowledge was acquired and his opinion formed; he has to treat his evidence so scrupulously and so fully that it ceases to be evidence and becomes a re-statement (one can never say a re-creation), however faint and imperfect, of what was once not a story but a man.

PART FIVE

HOME AND AWAY

THE NATIONAL GRID ON MAPS*

JUST over a year ago I broadcast a talk about maps, in which I said how useful I thought the national grid will be in civilian life, how it will add to the efficiency and pleasure of living. The national grid—the reference system with which millions of people became familiar during the war, in the services and Home Guard and civil defence—is now printed on all the sheets of the Ordnance Survey "New Popular" one-inch, and "Fourth Edition" quarter-inch maps. In the covers of each folded sheet is a description of how to use the grid; and you can now buy these sheets in most stationers' shops. Numbered lines are printed over the map, so that you can give an exact reference to any point straight and quickly in figures without any description in words with the names of places. It is very accurate, and its use saves a lot of long writing, talking, and tracing, much reading and hunting and asking and cursing.

I was amazed that in correspondence in the *Listener* after my talk one writer said indignantly that the grid would be practically no use in civilian life; that it was a mere fad, that it spoilt the maps and even spoilt his pleasure in the country. So I accepted a sort of challenge to collect some evidence of how the grid is already used by civilians for their work and pleasure, and how people wish it might be used. This talk is the result. I cannot thank by name all who have helped by sending evidence and suggestions; but I do owe a special debt to the Director-General of the Ordnance Survey and his staff for passing on many interesting facts.

The grid is already used by local authorities in various branches of the business of local government. The head of the maps-and-plans section of a borough engineer's department says he uses the grid in all kinds of ways, and wishes "this system had been introduced years ago". The clerk to a rural district council says the grid saves him much long letter-writing, and he adds: "It would

* B.B.C. Home Service, 20 Oct 1948. Printed in the *Listener*, 28 Oct.

appear that the correct answer is for all maps, of any publication, to be gridded on the national scheme and for the immediate teaching in all schools, universities, etc., of the use of the grid and its standard adoption."

Map-references are used as a basis of large-scale local surveys of various kinds, and for keeping statistics and records. They are used by education authorities and housing authorities for reference to the sites of schools and houses. The Ministry of Health already accepts map-references as an adequate description of a site. The grid has for some time past been used for recording collecting-points for road transport, and by contractors for dumping material for road repairs. Scientific associations use it for annotating the results of study in the field, and also for giving the exact place of rendezvous for meetings in the countryside. A big taxi-firm using wireless communication gives directions by grid-reference to its cars on the road. The grid is valuable for the quick calculation of distance, and I have heard from one borough that it is specially useful in giving distances to the ambulance service. A man in charge over an enormous area of the maintenance of specialised machinery made by his firm needs references to keep his location-lists and also for sending out his engineers; but he and others ask for gridded half-inch maps. The Ordnance Survey have already begun work on a new half-inch series, with the grid.

The most obvious job for which I thought the grid might be useful was the policeman's; so I wrote a circular letter to the chief constables of nine counties in different parts of England. One had "no observations to offer". One was opposed to the use of the grid for the odd reason that it would waste time; he and another said it was unnecessary because their men knew their ground so well. But a grid-reference, however well you know the ground, saves time by avoiding verbal descriptions in talk and writing; and it is obvious that the higher a report goes in a police force the less detailed the local knowledge becomes. And the police of the other six counties do in fact use the grid for numerous purposes. One chief constable said that all ranks in his force are now trained to use it; he and others were truly enthusiastic.

The police find the grid most useful in dealing with road accidents—both for locating exactly the site of an accident and also for plotting all accidents in their areas. Other things police use the grid for are locating crimes; searching for escaped prisoners; searching for aeroplane crashes; plotting proposed bus-routes; recording the dimensions of bridges; recording exactly what stretches of road are closed by snow, flood, repairs, etc.; defining areas where wireless reception or transmission is bad. The police use map-references in wireless communication with their own patrol-cars, and in dealings with the armed services. One non-policeman told me of the terrible trials he suffered as a senior flying-control officer in the R.A.F. from policemen who could not give map-references for crashed aircraft; but plainly things are now much better in some counties.

A specially interesting question in my correspondence with the police was the use of map-references in emergency telephone calls. Several chief constables said they would be extremely useful, but that they did not see a hope of training people to do it. But I do not think any training is necessary before making a start. If every telephone had its map-reference attached when it was installed, anybody receiving an emergency call could ask for this to be given if he needed it to help him find the place. Of course the reference of the telephone might not be that of the trouble; but in difficult cases the caller could wait at the telephone to be picked up as a guide to the exact spot. Also the map-reference of every house could be supplied by the local authority. These references, once given, would also be very valuable to the Post Office telephone department and the local authority in keeping their records.

As things are, the "address" of a house is designed for the convenience of the Post Office for letter-delivery; in a country district the last name in it is that of the post town, which may be miles from the town or village nearest to the house. I know well from experience, and my correspondents bear me out, that the "address for visitors" is often quite different, and hours are wasted writing out instructions how to get there. This address for visitors can, and now sometimes does, include the map-reference; and anyone who can read it needs not a single word to tell him the way. Such references should also be given in all advertisements of houses and businesses for sale and to let, and on all "orders to view". One man tells me how he went to inspect a farm by car; he covered 130 miles in four hours and then spent another half-hour hunting for the place in an area two miles square. Everyone knows how you always seem to ask the way from a half-wit or a stranger.

The value of the national grid for journeys of pleasure and general interest has already been widely discovered. The Youth Hostels Association, which is so popular with walkers and cyclists, has for the first time this year published in the *Y.H.A. Handbook* the six-figure map-reference of every one of its hostels all over the country. I know this was a felt want, because of the difficulty of many of the verbal directions. And the new-year edition of the Y.H.A. periodical the *Rucksack* contained a short article called "Grid References for Beginners". Other similar clubs will find the system just as useful as the Y.H.A. I must also mention a recent book called *The Mountains of Snowdonia* by Messrs Lister and Carr: this gives 370 grid-references to features in the Snowdon area which walkers and climbers would want to identify exactly on their maps. This principle can extend to all topographical works and guide-books in time. The actual maps and plans in guide-books, whatever the scale, can have the national grid on them, copied from Ordnance Survey maps, if the publisher applies to the Director-General and pays a small royalty charge. Topographical photographs can also be more readily placed by this means. A firm of lantern-slide makers is already preparing a series of slides of the Scottish counties, and the reference of the point from which each photograph was taken will appear in the catalogue; and an article in the *Amateur Photographer* for May 12 this year describes the recording by means of the grid of each photograph taken on a holiday. For holidays too, how very much easier everything would be if all advertisements for hotels, guest-houses and lodgings told us exactly by reference where they were; if a good tradition were set up, the absence of the tell-tale figures might make one suspicious of the boasted sea-view, or the broad acres of park.

I hope I have said enough to convince anybody that the grid is already of great use in civilian work and is also an aid to interest and pleasure: but I still have to meet two kinds of objections. The first is that the thing is too difficult. My own army experience was that almost any man could learn to use it quickly without trouble if taught by a sensible method and given the right kind of practice; and children can understand it by the age of ten or eleven. The real point is getting the map habit and the map love in the first place. I am sure much more can be done in schools even at early ages, and that not enough use is made of local one-inch maps in the beginnings of geography; they can provide fascinating exercises and games if only enough copies are available, and the grid can be brought into these very soon. It has already found its way into the education system this year; for the first time its use was compulsory in the geography examination for the Cambridge School and Higher Certificates. Linked up with home and bus-routes and railways and rivers the grid can seem less solemn and advanced. I do not see why the love of maps should not grow till a household would no more be without the local one-inch sheet than without a daily paper. Why should not the map-reference be displayed on every signpost?

The other objection is emotional; a writer to the *Listener* said the use of the grid was a fad of people who "attempt to force the world and its richness into the pigeon-holes of their neat and arid conceits". But mountains are not less beautiful because a map records their height. A sailor does not lose all delight in water and light and sky because he regularly writes his position in figures in a log. A train journey does not become less rich in visual pleasure because its intended timing has been recorded in a column of figures in a timetable. A beautiful object does not give less pleasure because its price was calculated in simple arithmetic. The Bible is not less holy because its numerical reference system has given us the very phrase "chapter and verse". Nobody supposes that an Englishman of the future, asked where he lives, will answer: "Point 574821." Rather, the knowledge that he can use this quick reference when he needs it, to help his friends, to help save life or goods, to avoid the unnecessary toil of tracing or describing or hunting—this knowledge, if he is wise, will in fact give him more, not less, freedom for pleasure in the things of his country that he loves.

NEW LANARK*

EARLY in the war I was stationed for a short time at Lanark, in the new barracks out by the racecourse. There were few troops about and we were popular—made at home in the pubs and tea-shops, and invited out. The food was good and the countryside was good; only the bitter winds that blew across the square and whistled into the training huts sharpened the value we put on warmth in quarters and in the people's welcome.

There are many things to remember from that time—the Clydesdale horses, the colour of the ploughland at the end of winter, when spring was almost in the air; snow on Tinto; the desolation of mining villages like Douglaswater; week-ends in Edinburgh; an adjutant's parade when we were made to double and re-double in our packs on the icy ground. But one evening will stay sharp in my mind when all the rest is half-forgotten and confused.

Between the racecourse and the town of Lanark a road sets off at right-angles, towards the Clyde, lined with an avenue of magnificent old trees. Back in barracks I found from the map that this must be the way down to New Lanark, where possibly I might still see something that had to do with Robert Owen, and the firm of Dale and Owen, the village known in every capital from London to St Petersburg, and the most famous factory in the world. I had no idea whether anything to do with Owen still survived, had spoken to nobody about him beforehand, and indeed remembered very little of what I had ever read about the details of his life there. I set off after duty on a private expedition of discovery, with no great belief that anything would come of it.

When I had just turned into the avenue, there happened to be a solitary boy idling in the next field and, to make sure of the road, I asked him if this was the way down to New Lanark, adding, by

* Not published before.

277

some freak, as if to explain myself, "Robert Owen's place". The
boy was about twelve or thirteen and, perhaps not being used to a
southern voice, waited a few seconds before he answered. Then
he said:

"Robert Lewin? Never heard o' him."

"No; not Robert *Lewin*, Robert *Owen*."

"Oh! he's dead."

The sweetness of his lowland accent, his quickness once he
understood, and the silence under the trees made this astonishing
answer indescribably moving. Owen had died in 1858, and the
first child I met spoke sorrowfully as if he had been buried yesterday. What equal fame could be met with in the world? What a
way to learn I was on the right road!

Just over the crest, where the track began to drop towards the
river, the straight avenue came to an end; in place of the evenly-
spaced trees, groups of trees and bushes grew on either side, screen-
ing at each turn what lay ahead; so it was clear that the whole had
been planned and planted as a formal approach. As the road grew
steeper there was a seat at each sharp bend, protected from the
wind: yet even when the river was in hearing there was nothing
to be seen. After a time there was a choice of ways; the road went
off to the right on higher ground, towards a group of new houses
showing between the trees: I took a footpath more sharply down
to the left. In all this time I had not met another soul or heard a
sound of people: the place seemed dead and even the voice of the
boy perhaps was an echo from the dead.

Then quite suddenly, round the last bend, there was the Mill!
—a great factory, like a fortress, built in thick grey stone. To the
left were open fields, with cattle grazing up to the walls: beyond
was the river, a fast, rocky, hill-country stream with trees on the
steep further bank growing right down to the water: to the right
were newer factory buildings and the houses of work-people strag-
gling up the valley-side: in the foreground a tall block of tenements
in the same grey stone. Over the whole group of buildings stood a
smokeless chimney and a clock.

I went down into a kind of yard between the tenements and

278

the mill: the huge gates were locked, windows shut; there was still not a person to be seen. But as I was standing there, thinking that all this must be nearly stone for stone as Owen built it at the beginning of the last century, wondering at its solidness, contrasting the houses with the jerry-built brick that had disgraced the later industrial landscape, I realised there was a lonely man in shirt-sleeves leaning out of a window in the tenements behind me.

I was there alone incongruously in battle-dress and shouted good-evening to him and asked him about Owen; and he began to tell me about Owen. The factory stood there as he built it; these tenements were as he had built them, lived in for over a hundred and thirty years; the building over there was the meeting-place of the Institution Owen had founded; the mill had grown and there had been additions; the things that Owen introduced had not survived; the firm of Dale and Owen had expired years ago and the mill now belonged to a Glasgow firm owning many others, and the old personal interest in the place and people was dead. He told me, too, that this firm had taken over many of Robert Owen's books and papers and had burnt them.

I do not know the name of the firm or of the man who told me this; I do not know whether what he told me is true or false: I am giving nothing but the history of an evening. I was filled with wonder and sadness (for this was a historic place): with wonder that the two human beings I had met, a boy of twelve and a chance cotton-mill worker in his shirt-sleeves, should have conveyed so simply and so clearly this vivid impression of a great and valued memory; with sadness that what Owen had done seemed to survive as little more than a memory. His great ideal of an industrial village in a rural setting, linked to rural life, had been achieved; the evidence of it was under my eyes, stone by stone and field by field, the avenue and pathway leading to it. But the spirit that inspired it, the ideal of human relations, the "New View of Society", the system of education and of corporate social life that lay behind it, were all gone. I went back to get ready for the morning's parade on the windswept square, thinking: "Oh! he's dead! he's dead!"

279

BARNARD CASTLE*

BARNEY is now known and nicknamed to thousands of people who had hardly heard of it before the war; for then Barnard Castle won a new place in history. But its local name had been Barney as long as anyone could remember. A poetess of the town, too, recognises the nickname's emotive power, and has no doubt it will go to her readers' hearts:

> Hullo! Barney calling! all you folk in town,
> All you busy workmen, throw your hammers down!
> All you tired housewives, kiddies home from school,
> Barney moors are breezy, Barney woods are cool!
>
> You in shop and office, men from noisy docks,
> Barney fields are smiling in their summer smocks,
> All the flowers are calling, all the rustling trees
> Singing, "Come to Barney, by the silver Tees!"

For thousands of men now the name Barney means nothing like this at all. It means the thump, crack and whistle of live bullets; the bursting of grenades and mines and gun-cotton; digging slit-trenches in rain and wind on the moors; bren-group, rifle-group, fire-platoon, right or left flanking; greenstuff in the hat and blackened face; mortar-bombs, smoke-screens, covering-fire; crawling in mud, running over water-logged fields; running—running everywhere, with a fierce instructor perhaps running alongside shouting slogans about Blood and Guts. For Barnard Castle was the place of the grandmother of all the Battle Schools; and in the grim time after Dunkirk, and during all the risk of invasion, the new doctrines of infantry tactics and battle inoculation and the complex gospel of toughness spread out from Barney to Commands, Divisions and Units; till the wild fanaticism of those early in-

* B.B.C. Third Programme, 10 Apr 1949.

structors had done its work, and their fierce excesses could be toned down into the hardness and knowledge that saw the infantry across Europe.

The history of the Battle School should some time be written—not just as a technical military affair or part of the history of tactics in the war, but as a study of personalities, of methods and of human behaviour in a time of crisis; for Barnard Castle then became the symbol of something primitive and frightening called up from unexplored depths by the needs of the war. And I find it hard now not to think of the town with all that in mind, not to impute to the landscape of the moors something of that spirit. The young officers who went on those courses must remember it in much that way. Beyond the training, they will remember little but two broad receding streets of grey stone houses seen over the tail-board of a closed truck, the sudden race of gear-changing before the sickening bend on the bridge approach; stone walls rushing by on the Yorkshire side of the river, and tall, ivy-clad trees. When they were dead to the world with tiredness, heavy in hand and foot, conscious of being now officially tough, was hardly a time for history or literary reminiscences or pondering on architecture.

The town is in Teesdale on the Durham bank of the river. The oldest part of it is clustered on a steep slope right down to the water's edge, the buildings packed against each other in a huddle which comes quite suddenly to an end on either side. To the west the buildings end abruptly by the bridge—a fine, high, stone bridge with two vigorously prancing, pointed arches—because the rock on which the castle stands comes down to the river. To the east this old part of the town ends in a sharp straight line; for there was the beginning of the demesne, and the fields downstream are preserved perpetually as an open space. The buildings spread out at the top of the bank and above the level of the demesne.

The town began and grew under feudal patronage, and is still overtopped by the ruins of its castle. This was once the Castle of the Baliols, the family that gave a College to Oxford and a King to Scotland. Now the castle is still a genuine ruin of the old-fashioned kind; no Office of Works has come to tidy it up, plot out the

ground-plan and put up archaeological notices. The ruins even
now play a part in the town's life. You come at them through an
archway under the buildings of the King's Head, past a sort of
small farmyard. Inside the huge surrounding wall, in the Outer
Ward, there is grazing on one side, and on the other a long, private
sunk garden with vegetable plots, and fruit trees trained on the
ancient masonry. There is a cottage still lived in at the farther end,
built up against the ruin of a tower, and you pay threepence at its
wicket-gate to be admitted to the Inner Bailey. There live the
weeds and the wilderness yet. None of the main middle buildings
are standing. You go along with the great wall on your left, past
the remains of another tower, past two windows in the wall that
belonged to the Hall, past the fine Tudor oriel of the Great Chamber looking out over the river, till you come to the one standing part
that you can go in and up. This is a fine round-tower in the angle
of the wall. A crazy wooden door lets you in; and chalked in
scrawling letters on it is a notice saying that visitors may climb up
to the top of the walls if they like, but that it is dangerous.

The lowest chamber of the tower is roofed with a sort of very
flat dome made of small stones set in mortar spirally so that its
centre is only about eighteen inches higher than its springing from
the walls. The walls themselves are ten feet thick, and let into
them are closets and staircases and little rooms. But even more
interesting than the tower's architecture proper are the traces of
various later use and habitation after the castle became a relic and
a ruin; the doors still have quite modern wooden door-frames, and
one of the little rooms has a miniature eighteenth-century or
Regency fireplace with built-in cupboards beside it. I don't know
in detail the history of all these adaptations; but the *Durham
Directory* for 1827 tells a scrap of the story. "This tower", it
says, "is now in a fine state of preservation, having been repaired
some years ago, and fitted up as a shot manufactory."

This same guide comments on the whole castle area like this:

A few years ago the place wore the aspect of a dreary solitude, but it
has since been converted into a pleasing seclusion, where the romantic
admirer of chivalrous times may wander back in imagination to the iron

ages of feudal tyranny, now happily contrasted by peace, freedom and equal laws.

A rather different contrast is likely to strike a modern romantic here. If you look out from the castle windows—from the oriel window or the slits in the round-tower—or if you are the adventurous visitor who climbs to the top of its walls, you have a view of startling interest. You are looking down first into the tops of trees, long spindly trees that have pushed their way up towards the light, every one of them wrapped in ivy, which runs up sometimes into the highest branches. The trees spring from ledges in the rock which falls away, here sloping slightly, there almost vertical in terraces, to the river below. Between the trees you can see the river itself, a fast, shallow northern stream racing over boulders, with eddies and tufts of scum. To the left is the ancient bridge, and away upstream some distance to the right you can see the railway viaduct of the 1860's. But immediately opposite you on the Yorkshire bank at Low Startforth is a huge stone mill. It is one of those early nineteenth-century factories, like Robert Owen's mill at New Lanark beside the Clyde, in which the eighteenth-century sense of proportion and overall design suddenly for a short time took on a new vigour and a new purpose. It is three great blocks of building lying against each other, stepping up and topped by the tall chimney: and this austere plan is broken by range on range of well-proportioned windows.

Looked at from downstream this whole group makes the contrast that a modern romantic eye would spot. A foreground of boulders and the river, on the left Ullathorne's mill; in the centre the great bridge; on the right the medieval fortress topping the ivy-clad trees. Two civilisations stare at each other over a tactical crossing.

Barnard Castle was never a big industrial centre, but it was busy with spinning and the making of shoe-thread in the earlier part of the last century, and in the eighteenth century with handloom wool-weaving. Many of the houses on the lower part of the bank still have the long rows of big upper windows that lit the looms, and all about are traces of the prosperity of that time. There are decorative pediments over the entrances to passages, and a special local feature in the foot-stop—a sort of extended corbel projecting from under the eaves in shaped wood or stone. A fine wooden pair in Bridgegate has at the inner end of each stop a carved head of a helmeted woman, like Minerva or Britannia, to be seen silhouetted against the sky. But all that part of the town, along Bridgegate in the countless, crowded courts, yards and alley-ways that lead off either side of the bank, has now come to a strange state of desolation and decay. Houses have fallen down, and the rubble been scarcely cleared away, but left to grow with weeds and rubbish; empty houses can be seen with fallen ceilings. In the packed, crowded courts there are ruinous outbuildings that used to be pigstyes; and there are the sites of the middens and swampy cesspools that made the town one of the worst centres of cholera in 1848–9. Many of the same houses in these yards are still inhabited, though condemned; and some of the same families have lived there for generations, where the ruins of the eighteenth-century houses literally mingle under the castle walls with the ruins of "the iron ages of feudal tyranny". This is no fanciful expression or metaphor, for in the last cluster above the bridge, just before the rock becomes too steep for building, are a number of houses actually using the outer castle wall as their own back wall, standing like lean-tos on terraces, with paths winding up to them from the street.

This is a fascinating town. At the top of the bank there is an octagonal covered market, with a council-hall above. Nearby is the King's Head, where Dickens stayed when he came to collect copy about the Yorkshire schools for *Nicholas Nickleby*; just over the way on the opposite corner was the site of Master Humphrey's Clockmaker's shop, which gave him the title for his next periodical. If you skirt round Master Humphrey's site on Amen Corner and make along Newgate you pass the church on your right, which stands on the top of the crest, you pass a house with a stone inscription over its door in seventeenth-century lettering which says "O Remember Man is Mortal": the street runs on parallel to the river with the fields of the demesne below you.

When you have passed a little Catholic church on your left, something suddenly starts happening. A huge wall begins, high, very imposing, blocking everything out; you come to a lodge and a vast pair of iron gates; you look through; and there is one of the most startling things you ever saw. It looks like a tremendous Casino, or a French Royal Palace. It is so utterly unexpected, so incredible, that it looks even bigger than it really is; which means that it looks very, very big indeed. For it is in fact a hundred yards long, something like 125 feet high in the centre, and the building alone covers only just less than an acre. This is the Bowes Museum and there is nothing else like it in any town in England.

If you approach on wheels you can go left or right from the gates up one or other arm of a wide, rising, horseshoe drive. The inner edge of the horseshoe is banked with grass, and when I first saw it there were cut long festoon-shaped flower-beds in the grass, now turfed, in austerer taste. If you approach on foot you make more or less straight forward across a parterre past mounded lawns cut with shaped flower-beds. You then dodge right or left to avoid an iron bandstand, and choose your route to one end or other of a long blind arcade which fronts the high terrace on which the Museum stands. You then mount up stone balustered steps in two broad flights to the terrace itself, where you join the converging arms of the horseshoe on a wide area of gravel.

The building, it is hardly necessary to say, is in the French Renaissance style. At each end is a square wing that stands forward like a projecting tower capped by a very steep, high mansard roof with two stories of dormers; the central block projects less far, but is higher and has a curved mansard, also with dormers, so that it makes in effect almost a third tower. A lower mansard runs along the main front between these towers. The next range of windows below are round-headed with fussy, little triangular pediments rather highly raised, then, below, another range, also round-headed but with flat mouldings above, and a ground-floor range square-headed and small. The main entrance rises to a level with the top of the first-floor windows and is closed by huge black doors with iron studs picked out in yellow. You go in through a wicket.

The story of this place is so fantastic that it hardly sounds true.

In the last century there was a certain John Bowes who was for eleven years the illegitimate son of the Earl of Strathmore, but was legitimised by his father marrying on his death-bed. John Bowes inherited the family's English estates; he was a great sportsman and racehorse-owner, for years a Member of Parliament. He was very rich. After 1845 he spent much time in Paris. He there married an ex-actress who was an amateur painter in oils and was known, for some reason I have not fathomed, as the Countess of Montalbo. Her husband and she decided to spend a great part of Bowes's fortune on works of art, furniture and china. When their house was fully, not to say over-furnished they stored the surplus away until they began to form the idea of founding a permanent collection. At first they planned to have a museum at Calais, in France but as near to England as could be. But in the troubled days after 1870 the political future seemed uncertain, and this project was given up. But a French architect drew up plans; and with a boldness that makes one gasp they decided in the end to use these plans for a museum at Barnard Castle, near the Bowes family estates. And so here, after many troubles, this portentous building, "modelled on the Tuileries", arose.

The collection inside is one of the most remarkable in any provincial museum in England. No other town the size of Barnard Castle has anything like it. The famous pictures that are often lent and seen elsewhere are the El Greco of St Peter and the Goya portrait of the Spanish poet Valdez. There is also a well-known David of Napoleon taking the oath to the Constitution. There are many very good second-rate pictures of the Italian and Dutch schools; there is an enormous mass of French nineteenth-century painting by the duller artists, and many works by Madame Bowes herself and by her art-master. There is furniture and china of almost every period and country; there are ecclesiastical objects, including reliquaries, altar-pieces and even a whole set of choir-stalls from Switzerland. There are mechanical ornaments, and models and dolls. And there is a very fine collection of tapestries indeed. All this used to be shown in an amazing jumble, untouched, I believe, since the Museum was started. But it was disordered in the war, and the present Curator has taken in hand the task of selecting, sorting and arranging the best things in the way they can best be seen; the place is lightened and simplified. The old jumble had its points, but to have kept it would have been to perpetuate a sort of period mood overlying the true beauty and interest of the things. The festoon flower-beds have gone. But nothing can alter the building.

There it stands, huge and immovable, unperturbed. It is a foreign aristocrat transplanted, with a great deal of *sangfroid* and at least a touch of vulgarity. It looks at Teesdale, and downstream to Egglestone Abbey; it looks at the Yorkshire moors beyond, up towards the village of Bowes. It looks at the grey huddled town under the castle; it glances sideways at the castle itself, with memories of the Baliols and all its royal owners. To them all it says: "I have nothing to do with you. I know I am incongruous. I know I don't fit the landscape or the architecture or the local mood; I know I am a displaced person. But I am big enough, assertive enough, rare enough not to care a damn. Here I am and I mean to stay. The houses in Bridgegate can fall down, the castle can go to ruins and flourish with weeds; camps and battle schools can come and go; novelists can copy-hunt as often as they like, for what they like; tired housewives may 'come to Barney by the silver Tees'. But 'O Remember Man is Mortal'. J'y suis, j'y reste. They may even spoil my parterre and bandstand: but there can only ever be one Bowes Museum, 'modelled on the Tuileries'— and I am it."

BENGAL LIGHTS*

ONE day in 1799 a messenger came up to Calcutta to announce the arrival from home of the East Indiaman *Charlton*, Captain Well-advice, at Diamond Harbour. Sir Henry Russell, third Judge of the Supreme Court, sent round at once to Mr William Hickey to borrow his boat, so that he could go down the Hooghly to meet his wife. Lady Russell had made the long, tedious, risky voyage in safety, bringing with her two nieces—a passage to India, like the later one of Mrs Moore and Miss Quested, fraught with sad and memorable consequences. The elder niece, Miss Mary Lloyd, "was about five-and-twenty, by no means pretty, but a good figure and exceedingly clever, indeed she had a masculine understanding"—so Hickey wrote—"with a high independent spirit". The other niece was "a very charming and lovely girl about seventeen years of age", who "soon had several professed admirers". Among them chiefly were Mr Charles Ricketts and her own first cousin young Henry Russell, whom Hickey thought without doubt to be "the received and favoured lover". Then his *Memoirs* go on: "The poor young lady, however, instead of becoming a bride, was doomed to sink into a premature grave. She was attacked with a most severe bowel complaint, brought on entirely by indulging too much with that mischievous and dangerous fruit, the pineapple, against eating so much of which I had frequently cautioned her, but instead of my remonstrances being attended to they only excited her mirth, and she laughed at me for my grave sermons, as she termed what I said upon the subject. The disease made a most rapid progress, baffling the skill and exertions of the physicians. At the end of a few days this lovely girl fell a martyr to the obstinacy of the malady, leaving poor Henry Russell truly miserable. As for her other lover, Mr Ricketts, he very shortly after her premature death sought comfort

* B.B.C. Third Programme, 27 Feb 1949. Printed in the *Listener*, 10 March.

for himself in the arms of a vulgar, huge, coarse Irish slammerkin, Miss Prendergast." Over the grave in the European cemetery in Calcutta a notable monument was raised among a strange collection of memorial freaks. The news of her death came back to a young man who had known her for just a short time in Swansea, and he wrote:

> Call'd far away,
> By one she dared not disobey,
> To those proud halls, for youth unfit,
> Where princes stand and judges sit.
> Where Ganges rolls his widest wave
> She dropt her blossom in the grave;
> Her noble name she never changed,
> Nor was her nobler heart estranged.

And he also wrote these lines, more widely known and even now widely remembered:

> Ah what avails the sceptred race,
> Ah what the form divine!
> What every virtue, every grace!
> Rose Aylmer, all were thine.

> Rose Aylmer, whom these wakeful eyes
> May weep, but never see,
> A night of memories and sighs
> I consecrate to thee.

A lock of Rose Aylmer's hair was found in Landor's desk after his death, and one wonders how much he heard of young Henry Russell, the pineapples and the laughter.

Hickey's *Memoirs* are in print again; not, unfortunately, a new edition, but a reprint of the old one, still bearing the imprint of Hurst and Blackett, and priced at the rather formidable sum of four guineas the set of four volumes. The dust-cover says that the *Memoirs* are "an inimitable picture of life in London, interesting sidelights on travel in Africa, the West Indies, France, Portugal and

Holland and intimate records of a long residence in East India by a gentleman of fashion in the latter end of the Eighteenth Century".

This in its way is true; but the *Memoirs* are in fact much more than this; they are one of the greatest works of English reminiscences, written with extraordinary vigour and honesty, with no idea of publication, to amuse the author in the tedium of his retirement after leaving India.

For India—indeed just Calcutta—had in the end been Hickey's life: even though he avowed that he had worked and lived there solely to pay off his English debts and make enough money to get hor c again and live in style, even though he had been buoyed up by the common exile's dream, Calcutta had become his life, and without it he was bored and lost. His Calcutta was the Calcutta of the great days of the Nabobs, the place that was called "the city of palaces", the city of the huge houses with pillars and porticos built with the fortunes that were quickly to be made in "that common receptacle of abandoned and undone men".

That was a temporary phase of history, a phase that was beginning to pass even when Joseph Sedley went back to Bengal to boast of his part in the Battle of Waterloo. It was a phase of history that no Englishman can conscientiously be proud of, a period of unscrupulous exploitation and fortune-hunting, with all the worst features of commercial imperialism. Hardly a character in all Hickey's four volumes is moved by any other motive than self-interest and self-aggrandisement. But he gives a picture of an alien life engrafted on India that makes one wonder now, particularly this year, when the syllables "Ind: Imp:" have gone off our coins for good, whether any other kind of civilisation might have grown from these beginnings.

It is often said, and I have often thought myself, that the estrangement of the races in India came about chiefly in the nineteenth century. The adoption of English as the official language, its compulsory use as the medium of higher education, the invention of steamboats, the mutiny, the cutting of the Suez Canal—these things are often pointed to as the contributory causes of the peculiar life of isolation and exile that the English community devised for itself.

But whatever may have been true of other parts of India or in the countryside, even in parts of Bengal, this division of life was a continuous tradition in Calcutta lasting from the days of Hickey and before them. And in reading the *Memoirs* again now, I have been struck by the likenesses, the underlying similarity of attitude, shared by these monstrous Nabobs and the milder, less vigorous, less spectacular British who haunted Park Street and Chowringhee, Ballygunge and Alipore when I lived there for a short time before the war. All the genuine gusto and style and grandeur had gone, except in a remarkable man here and there; but the vulgarity, the go-getting, pale editions of the special vices, often these remained. Hickey had no less than sixty-three servants to look after him; and his friend Bob Pott had also a squadron of private cavalry: but this surprises and shocks me less than that a young man in 1936, within three months of arrival, should have been allowing a servant to dry him and put on his clothes after he had had a bath. Hickey's book is full of stories of men who had been failures in England and who acquired a "handsome independence", or amassed "a prodigious fortune". He is full too of stories of the men whose social status rose by their going to the East, who lived there in a style and with pretensions and with power that they never could have acquired at home.

There was the Governor-General who was a silk-mercer's son, who denied any knowledge of having worked in his father's shop when asked about it at dinner. There was Mr James Agg who acquired "a handsome independence" in the Bengal Corps of Engineers and then went back to become a J.P. and a Deputy Lieutenant of the County at Cheltenham, where his father had been "a common hard-working stone-mason". But the best case of all is perhaps that of the Mr Sherif, who "acquired a handsome competence"—upwards of two lacs of rupees—in the situation of "an assistant extra clerk in the Calcutta treasury". He had treated a woman very badly and, in being cross-questioned about this by a Judge, was asked what he called himself. He said "A gentleman!" And the comment came back: "Oh! a gentleman. What, you wear shoes, I suppose! Every fellow that wears shoes in this

291

country dubs himself a gentleman." One thinks at once of the dinner jackets and cocktails, and of dinner-parties always with tinned asparagus, and of heavy talk in clubs: one thinks both of the social pretensions, and of the malice roused against them. And in these recent days the talk of money itself was not more attractive because it no longer dealt with the justifiable hope of amassing large or handsome fortunes, but ground inexorably on about allowances and leave and pensions. One was almost grateful for the jute-wallahs, for they at least did not pretend that they had gone to India to do the country good.

No more did Hickey and his friends; they knew scarcely anything of it, and cared less. One is barely conscious in his book of Indian life or of any Indian society between servants and Princes. It makes me think that underlying differences of manners, personal life, private and domestic habits, counted then and since for more than is always allowed. He tells the story of an Indian who in the middle of a court-martial "with the utmost composure, belched, making a loud noise in the operation"; when he was rebuked for this insult to the court and asked how he could be "guilty of so indelicate and rude an act", he replied "with great sang-froid and indifference": "To ease my stomach." And Hickey comments that the Judge-Advocate ought to have known quite well that "so far from thinking it a breach of good manners to break wind *upwards*, the natives of India, high and low, consider it a compliment in a guest to do so", and "they have a compliment ready for the belcher signifying, 'Much good may it do you.' " So too with the hawking and spitting which the fastidious British found so distressing—I well remember the head of a large college trying to spit out of the window of his study, and missing, so that a stream of saliva, red with betel-nut, streaked down the wall; but Bengalis find it unpleasant that we should wrap up the produce of our noses and throats in a piece of cloth and put it in a pocket of our clothes.

In my first week I went to the house of a friend whom I had known in England, who had just got married. I said it was a pity he had not managed to find a house with a proper bathroom, totally ignorant that an Indian thinks it dirty and unattractive to wash one-

self in a tub of standing water. Other sanitary arrangements draw
another line. These are intimate things, where differences are
rarely spoken of, and adaptations are very self-conscious and very
slow. Eating with the fingers, sitting on the floor, come into the
same category of highly personal, dividing customs; and all the
long tradition of Calcutta was for the British to keep the western
style.

Over all was the climate; the peculiar damp heat of Calcutta is
unlike that of any other Indian city, and it is without parallel
exhausting. In the hot weather before the days of electric fans
people must have lived in a stream of continuous sweat. String-
pulled punkahs flapped too idly and stirred the steamy air too little,
and in Hickey's day even those were few; he and his friends must
have sweated like hogs. No western science of tropical medicine
existed for their countless ailments, and the local traditional cures
were liable to be ignored or damned as witchcraft. Hickey's book is
full of illness and sudden death. Long wasting fevers reducing large
red-faced men to pallor and thinness; diseased livers; sudden
dysentery and stabbing affections of the bowels; deaths on journeys;
the discovery of people dead in their beds; hasty funerals, the horrid
exploitation of death by undertakers and mercenary chaplains. The
strange memorials in the European cemetery at Calcutta record not
only the romance of Rose Aylmer guzzling pineapples, but the
belly-aches of countless hardened fortune-hunters who did not survive to enjoy the prodigious fortunes or handsome competences they
amassed.

Over the climate, the heat, the damp, the sweat, the pains, the
fevers, the sudden death, hangs the bottle, the consoler, the medicine,
the exile's resource, the cause of wild pleasures, disaster and madness.
And drinking is one more great dividing-line between the eastern and
the western ways of life. Drinking has never been described so
often, so fully, with such gusto as in Hickey's *Memoirs*; each day
leads up to dinner, and each dinner rises with the pace of the passing
of the bottle; officers and clerks and merchants are tumbled insen-
sible out of houses into palankeens; tight boys driving after dinner
knock down pedestrians or end up in potholes; insults in wine lead

293

to law-suits and duels; headaches and sickness delay the business of courts, armies and administration; hangovers even thwart the task of making money.

Here too, in its muted, meaner way, the Calcutta I knew was the counterpart of Hickey's. As the short sweet Bengal twilight came, when the air for a moment cooled and even the heavy sacred bulls could get up from the shady side of the pavement to forage in a dustbin, and all the traffic of rickshaws and cars turned towards the Maidan taking people to their evening walk, the thought came into British heads that it was nearly time for a sundowner. In all the clubs the barmen got busy and a new life seemed to break. One at home in the flat, a few more at the club before dinner, something with dinner too—drink added on to drink, and thoughts were borne away from the heat of the day, and the day's country and the tropical sun. After dinner the drinking could move to one of the equivalents of Hickey's taverns, to the Casanova behind the Grand Hotel, or some shady club near Park Street, or down the Lane, or to Firpo's where there was dancing and pseudo-French furniture under huge glass-dropped chandeliers. Or one might go to the Continental, where a band on a platform at the end played dance music all the evening, in tireless relays with feeble little leg-showing dancers, and the blonde band-leader, Ilsa, a six-foot woman with curled northern locks, took her saxophone and blew on it blasts of whining homesickness and regret till the thing became a trumpet in her hands and she was summoning to song; and the jute-boys from Dundee, soldiers from the fort, and an odd collection of strays from country rectories and London offices and Oxford and Manchester began a yowling chorus while the bare-footed waiters picked their way among the broken glass. In the Casanova the lights dipped for the fan-dance in the cabaret; at Firpo's the chandeliers dimmed and a spotlight broke in colours on the dancers; burra-pegs came quicker, suddenly as in dreams, and swizzle-sticks whirred in the soda-water. There was no India any more; this was no place, no time, not even a city of palaces, no civilisation; it was a whirl of changing lights till one came out into the soupy air beneath an unbelievable tropical moon; and a leper at the door held out a bowl for pice and a tiny boy did cartwheels singing: "John Brown's baby's got a pimple on his arse."

It was a Calcutta that Hickey would have recognised, a Calcutta that Rose Aylmer might have hesitated to laugh at but for the pineapples; a Calcutta Gandhi and his followers loathed. Perhaps those lights are going out now; perhaps even the climate seems to remit its rigours for heads and bowels and livers trained in decades of generations to take it; perhaps now

The Sun has left his blackness and has found a fresher morning,
And the fair Moon rejoices in the clear and cloudless night;
For Empire is no more, and now the Lion and Wolf shall cease.

INDEX